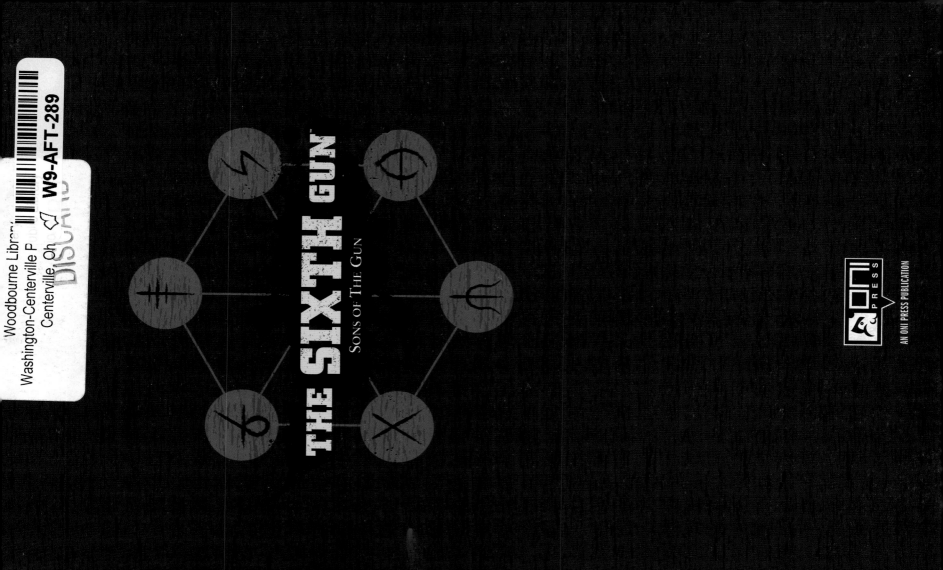

THE SIXTH GUN

SONS OF THE GUN

AN ONI PRESS PUBLICATION

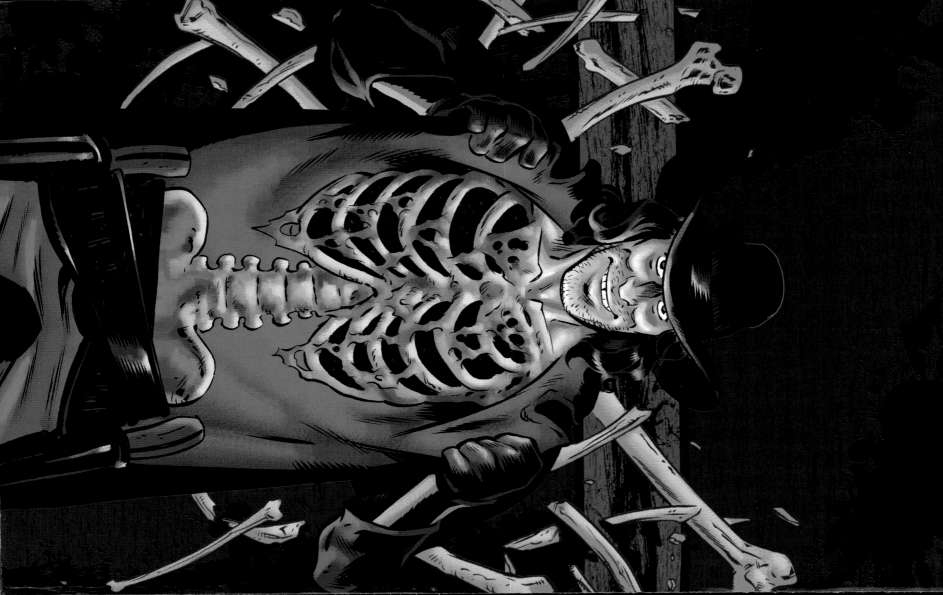

THE SIXTH GUN

SONS OF THE GUN

Written By
CULLEN BUNN & **BRIAN HURTT**

Illustrated By
BRIAN CHURILLA

Chapters 1-3 Lettered By
DOUGLAS E. SHERWOOD

Colored By
BILL CRABTREE

Chapters 4-5 Lettered By
ED BRISSON

Edited By
CHARLIE CHU

Designed By
KEITH WOOD

THE SIXTH GUN™
BY CULLEN BUNN & BRIAN HURTT

PUBLISHED BY ONI PRESS, INC.

JOE NOZEMACK *publisher*
JAMES LUCAS JONES *editor in chief*
KEITH WOOD *art director*
JOHN SCHORK *director of publicity*
CHEYENNE ALLOTT *director of sales*
JILL BEATON *editor*
CHARLIE CHU *editor*
TROY LOOK *digital prepress lead*
JASON STOREY *graphic designer*
ROBIN HERRERA *administrative assistant*

This volume collects issues #1-5 of the Oni Press series
The Sixth Gun: Sons of The Gun.

THE SIXTH GUN: SONS OF THE GUN, DECEMBER 2013. Published by
Oni Press, Inc. 1305 SE Martin Luther King Jr. Blvd. Suite A, Portland,
OR 9714. THE SIXTH GUN is ™ & © 2013 Cullen Bunn & Brian Hurtt.
Oni Press logo and icon are ™ & © 2013 Oni Press, Inc. All rights reserved.
Oni Press logo and icon artwork created by Keith A. Wood. The events,
institutions, and characters presented in this book are fictional. Any
resemblance to actual persons, living or dead, is purely coincidental. No
portion of this publication may be reproduced, by any means, without the
express written permission of the copyright holders.

ONI PRESS, INC.
1305 SE MARTIN LUTHER KING JR. BLVD.
SUITE A
PORTLAND, OR 97214
USA

onipress.com
facebook.com/onipress
twitter.com/onipress
onipress.tumblr.com

cullenbunn.com • @cullenbunn
bribrttl.com • @bribrttl
brianhurtt.com • @brianhurtt
@crabtree_bill

First edition: December 2013

ISBN: 978-1-62010-099-8
eISBN: 978-1-62010-100-1

Library of Congress Control Number: 2013937934

1 0 9 8 7 6 5 4 3 2 1

Printed in China

"Bloodthirsty" Bill Sumter – Possesses the The First Gun, which strikes with the force of a cannon shell.

Will Arcene – Wields the Second Gun, spreading the very flames of Perdition.

"Filthy" Ben Kinney – Possesses the Third Gun, which spreads a flesh-rotting disease.

Silas "Bitter Ridge" Hedgepeth – Holds the Fourth Gun and the ability to call forth the spirits of the men and women he has killed.

Missy Hume – The sadistic widow of General Hume. She possesses the Fifth Gun, which keeps her young... as long as she indulges in murder.

General Oliander Bedford Hume – A sadistic Confederate General who called the Six into our world.

CHAPTER ONE

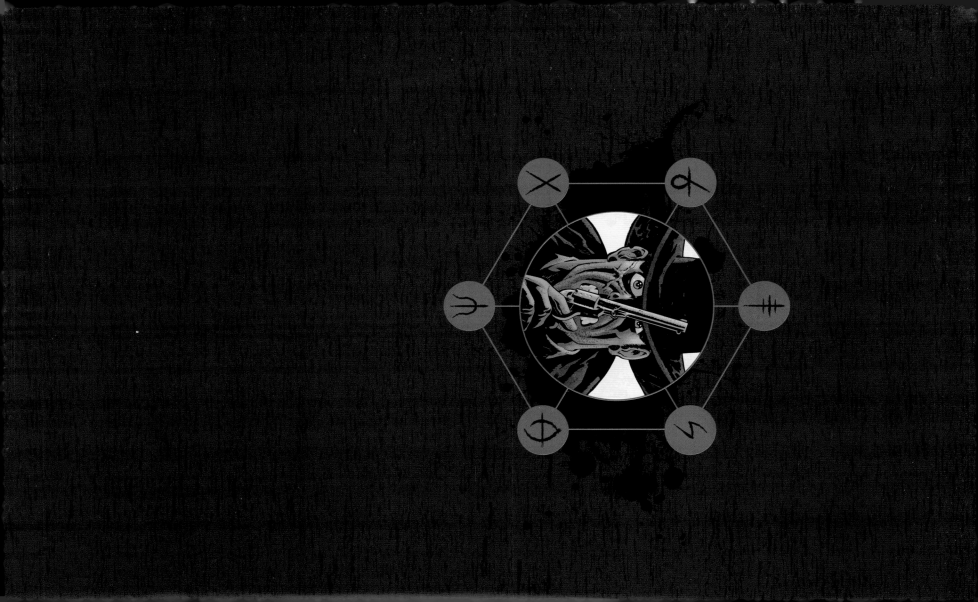

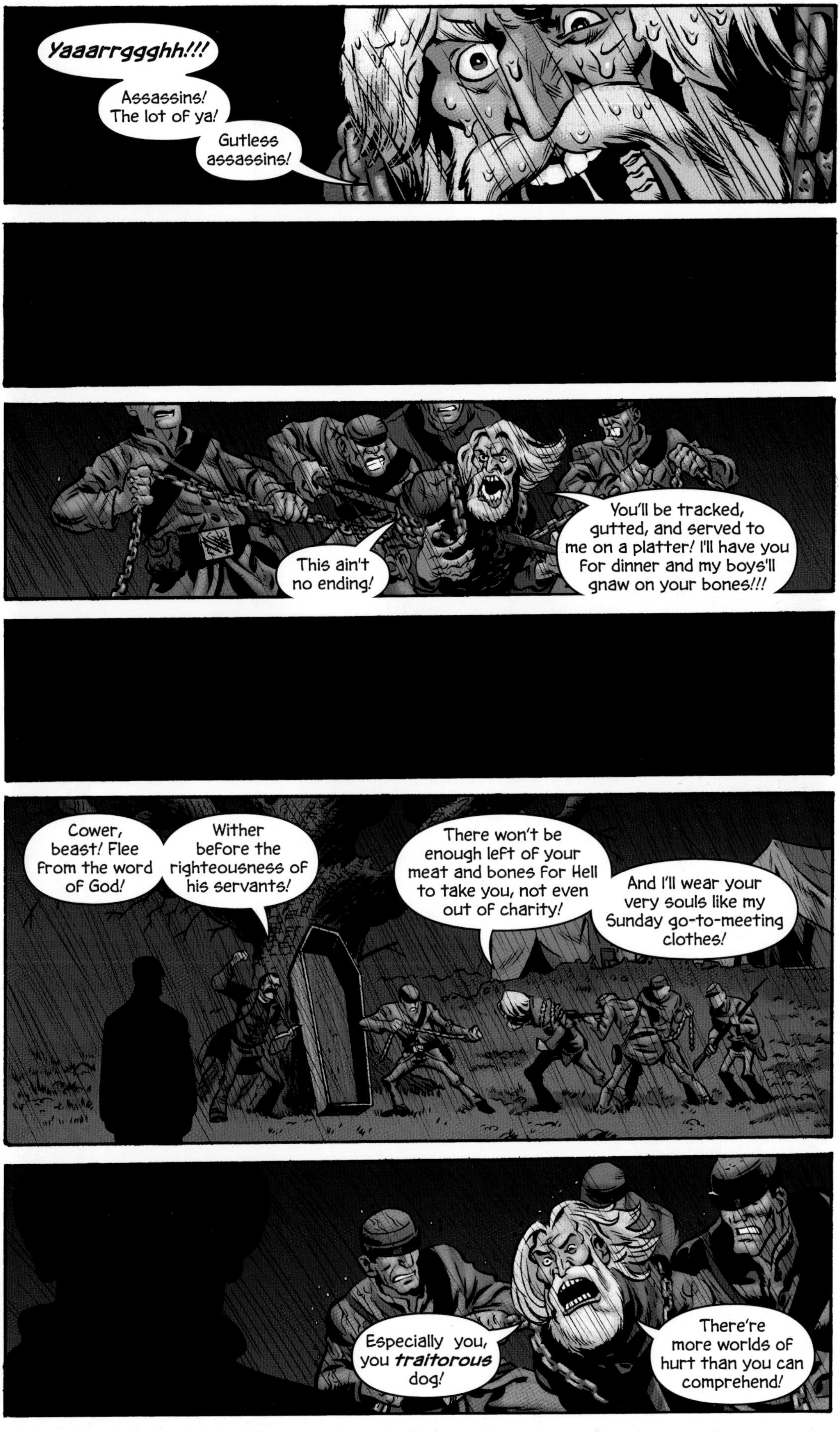
Yaaarrggghh!!!
Assassins! The lot of ya!
Gutless assassins!
You'll be tracked, gutted, and served to me on a platter! I'll have you for dinner and my boys'll gnaw on your bones!!!
This ain't no ending!
Cower, beast! Flee from the word of God!
Wither before the righteousness of his servants!
There won't be enough left of your meat and bones for Hell to take you, not even out of charity!
And I'll wear your very souls like my Sunday go-to-meeting clothes!
There're more worlds of hurt than you can comprehend!
Especially you, you *traitorous* dog!

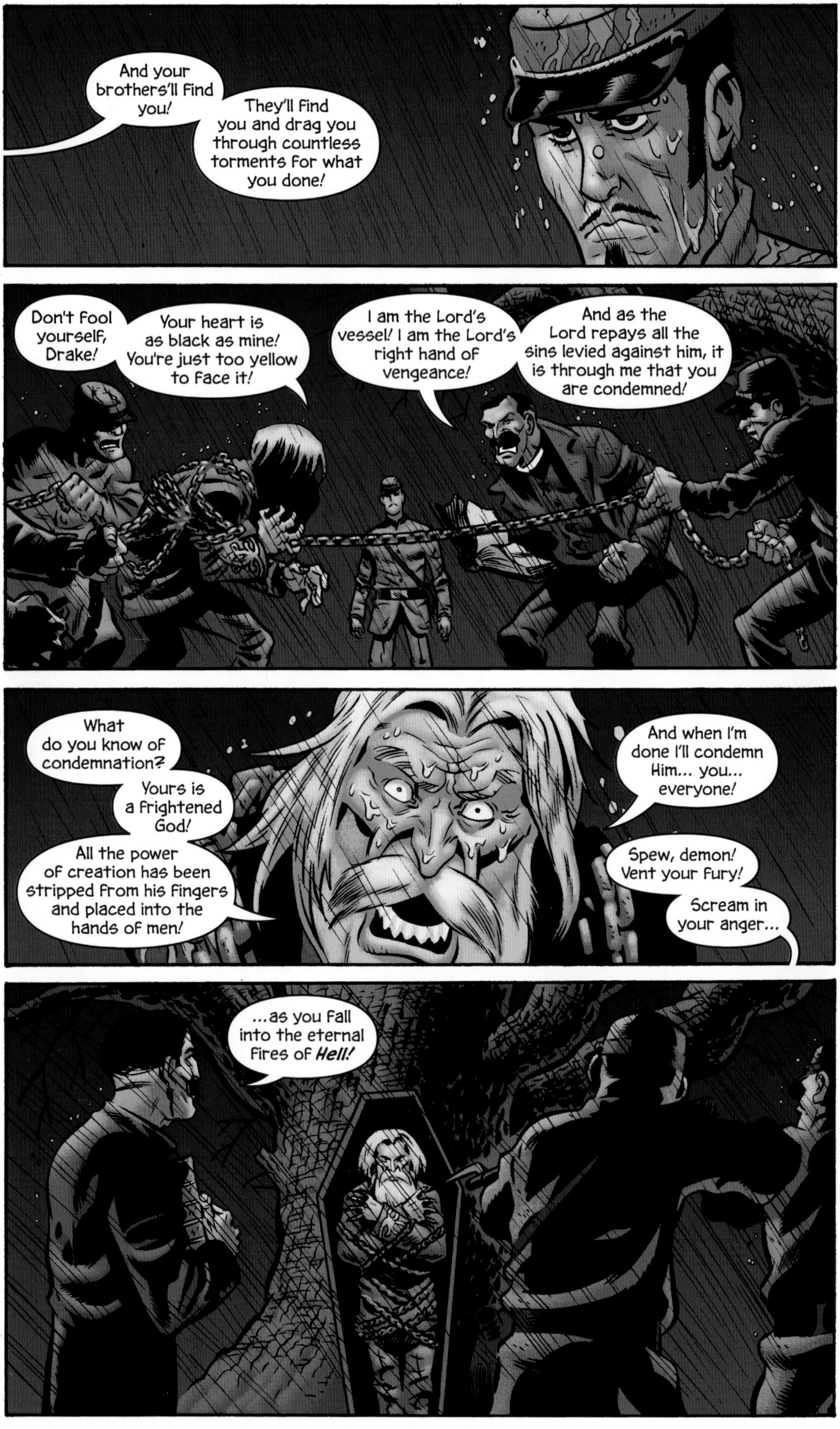
And your brothers'll find you!
They'll find you and drag you through countless torments for what you done!
Don't fool yourself, Drake!
Your heart is as black as mine! You're just too yellow to face it!
I am the Lord's vessel! I am the Lord's right hand of vengeance!
And as the Lord repays all the sins levied against him, it is through me that you are condemned!
What do you know of condemnation?
Yours is a frightened God!
All the power of creation has been stripped from his fingers and placed into the hands of men!
And when I'm done I'll condemn Him... you... everyone!
Spew, demon! Vent your fury!
Scream in your anger...
...as you fall into the eternal fires of *Hell!*

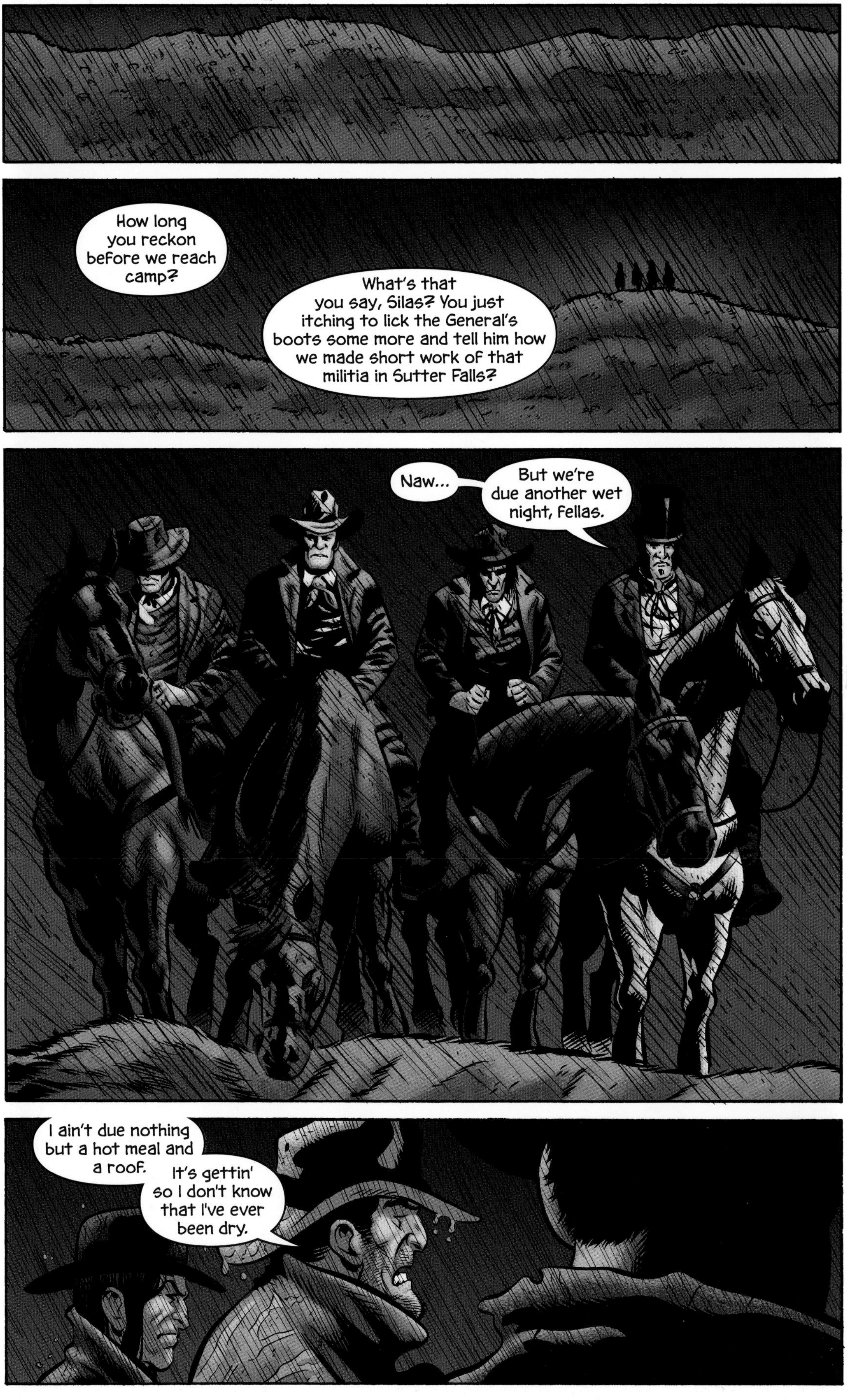
How long you reckon before we reach camp?
What's that you say, Silas? You just itching to lick the General's boots some more and tell him how we made short work of that militia in Sutter Falls?
Naw...
But we're due another wet night, Fellas.
I ain't due nothing but a hot meal and a roof.
It's gettin' so I don't know that I've ever been dry.

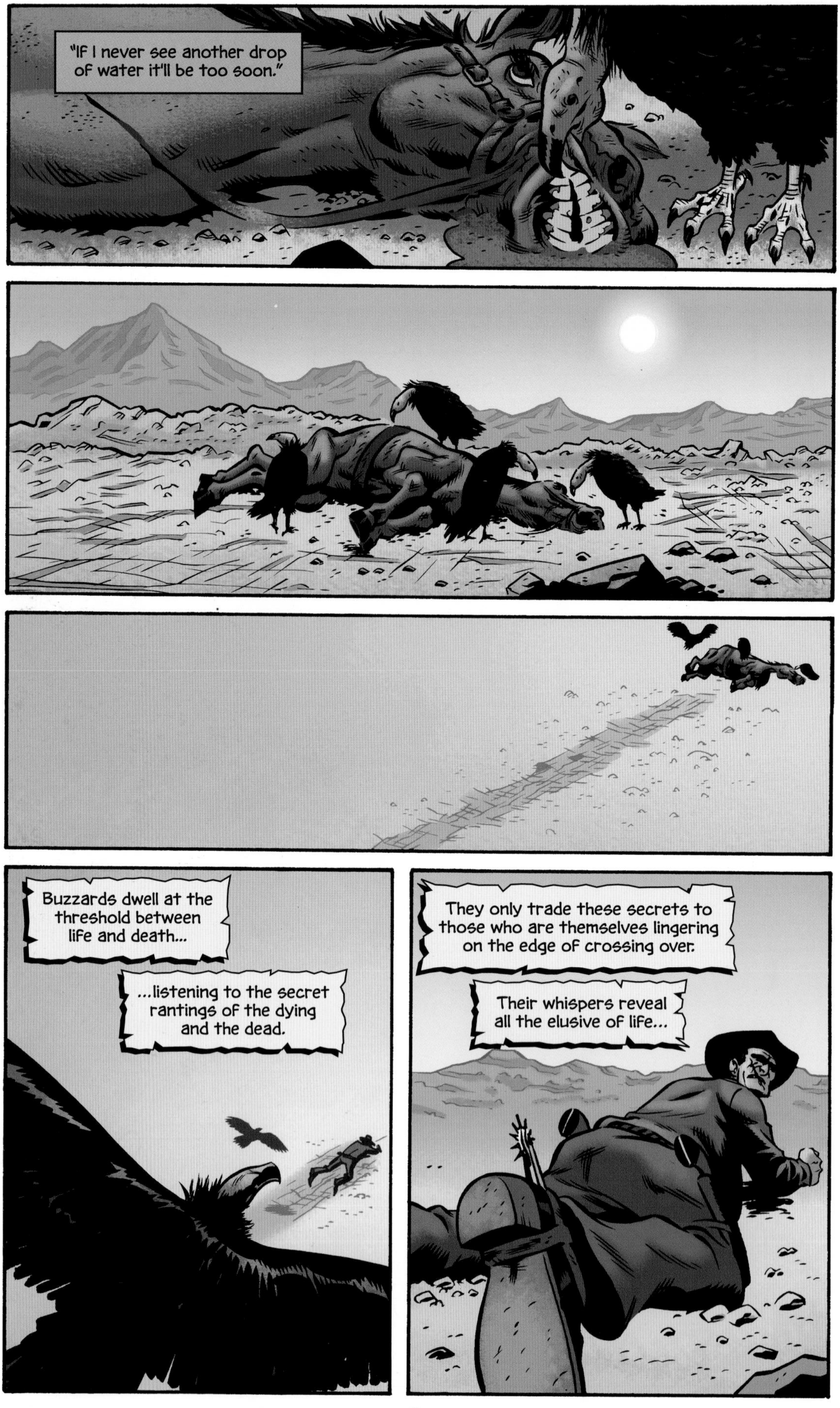
"If I never see another drop of water it'll be too soon."
Buzzards dwell at the threshold between life and death...
...listening to the secret rantings of the dying and the dead.
They only trade these secrets to those who are themselves lingering on the edge of crossing over.
Their whispers reveal all the elusive of life...

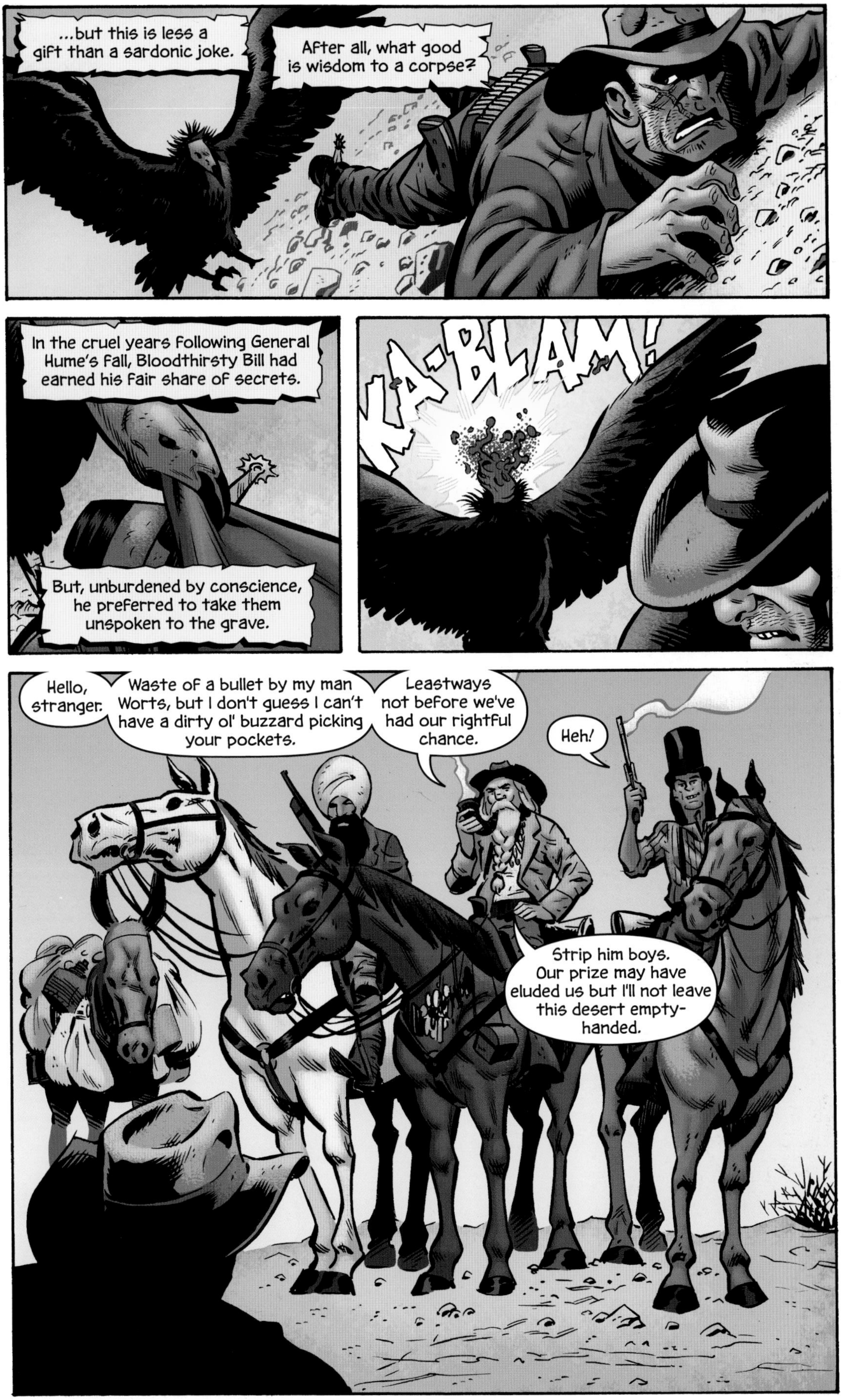
...but this is less a gift than a sardonic joke.
After all, what good is wisdom to a corpse?
In the cruel years following General Hume's Fall, Bloodthirsty Bill had earned his fair share of secrets.
But, unburdened by conscience, he preferred to take them unspoken to the grave.
KA-BLAM!
Hello, stranger.
Waste of a bullet by my man Worts, but I don't guess I can't have a dirty ol' buzzard picking your pockets.
Leastways not before we've had our rightful chance.
Heh!
Strip him boys. Our prize may have eluded us but I'll not leave this desert empty-handed.

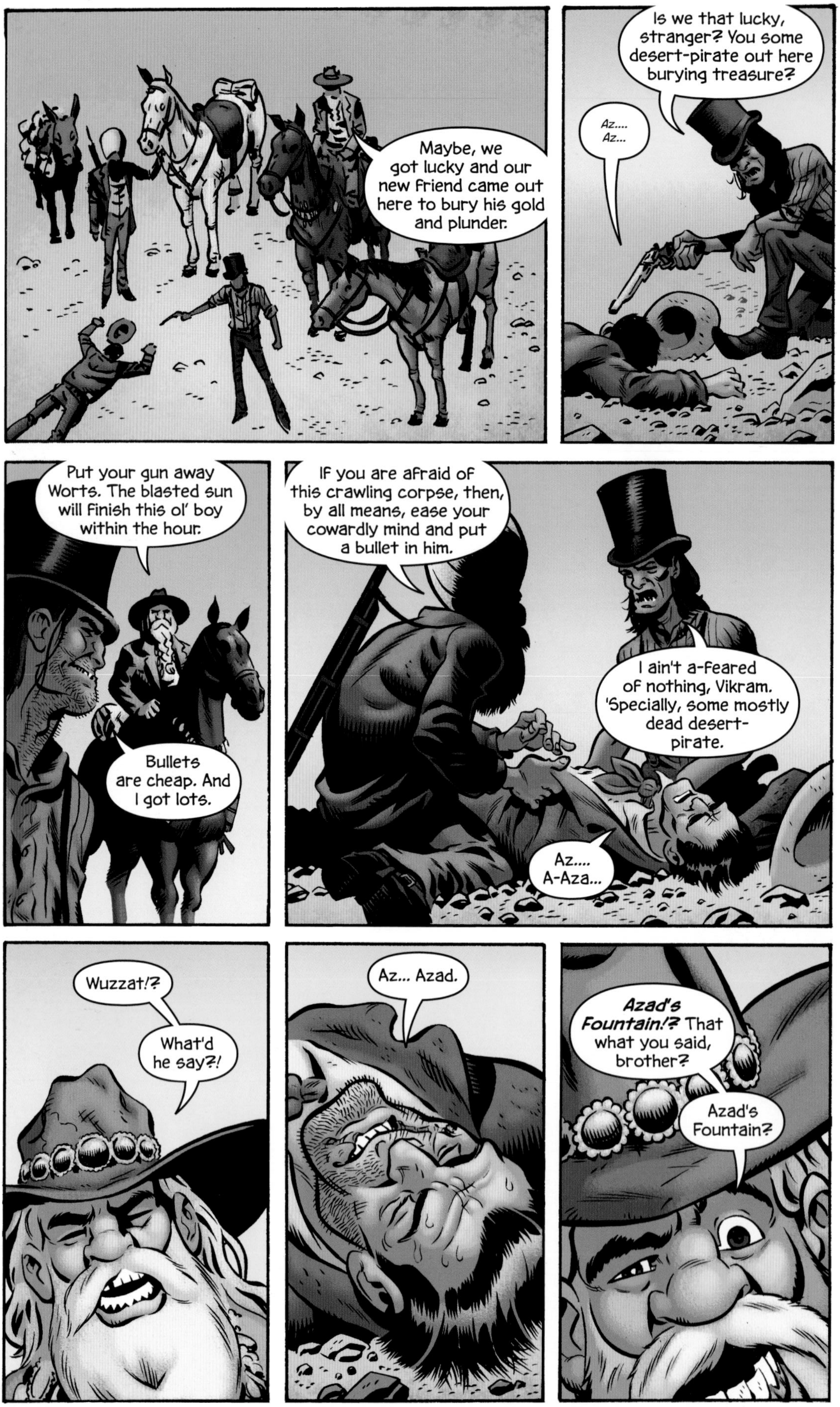

Maybe, we got lucky and our new friend came out here to bury his gold and plunder.
Is we that lucky, stranger? You some desert-pirate out here burying treasure?
Az.... Az...
Put your gun away Worts. The blasted sun will finish this ol' boy within the hour.
Bullets are cheap. And I got lots.
If you are afraid of this crawling corpse, then, by all means, ease your cowardly mind and put a bullet in him.
I ain't a-feared of nothing, Vikram. 'Specially, some mostly dead desert-pirate.
Az.... A-Aza...
Wuzzat!?
What'd he say?!
Az... Azad.
Azad's Fountain!? That what you said, brother?
Azad's Fountain?

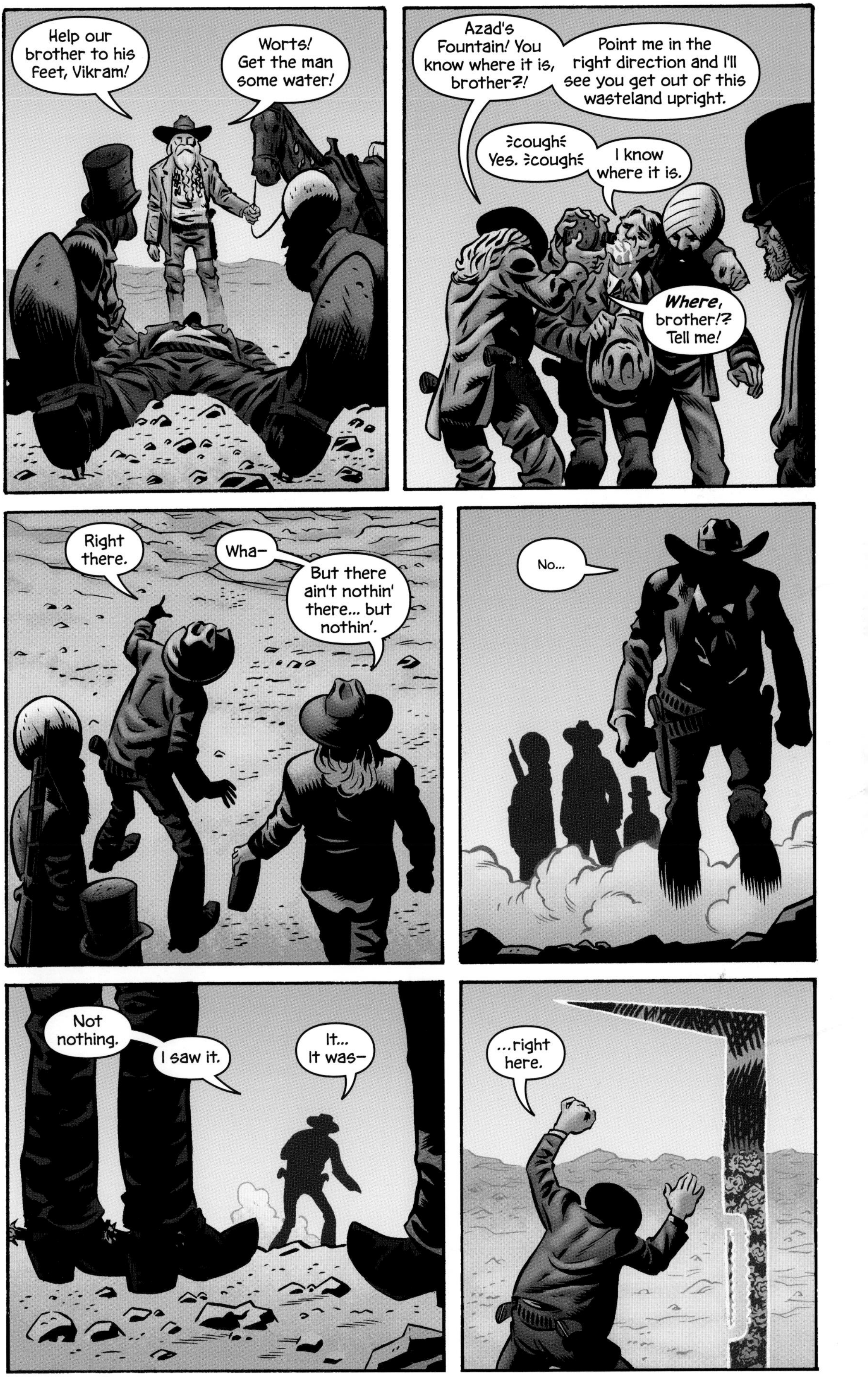
Help our brother to his Feet, Vikram!
Worts! Get the man some water!
Azad's Fountain! You know where it is, brother?!
Point me in the right direction and I'll see you get out of this wasteland upright.
cough Yes. cough
I know where it is.
Where, brother!? Tell me!
Right there.
Wha-
But there ain't nothin' there... but nothin'.
No...
Not nothing.
I saw it.
It... It was-
...right here.

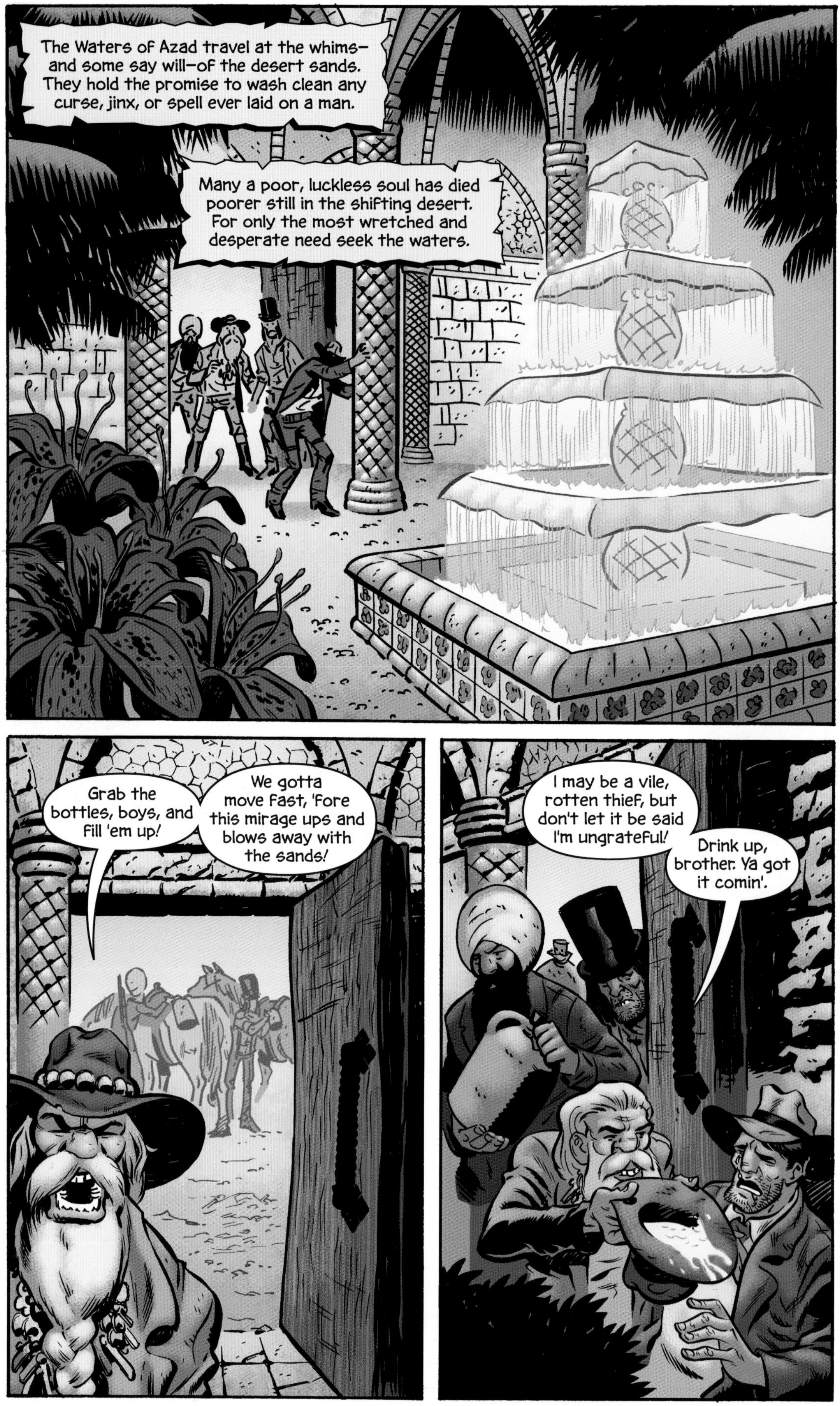
The Waters of Azad travel at the whims–and some say will–of the desert sands. They hold the promise to wash clean any curse, jinx, or spell ever laid on a man.
Many a poor, luckless soul has died poorer still in the shifting desert. For only the most wretched and desperate need seek the waters.
Grab the bottles, boys, and fill 'em up!
We gotta move fast, 'fore this mirage ups and blows away with the sands!
I may be a vile, rotten thief, but don't let it be said I'm ungrateful!
Drink up, brother. Ya got it comin'.

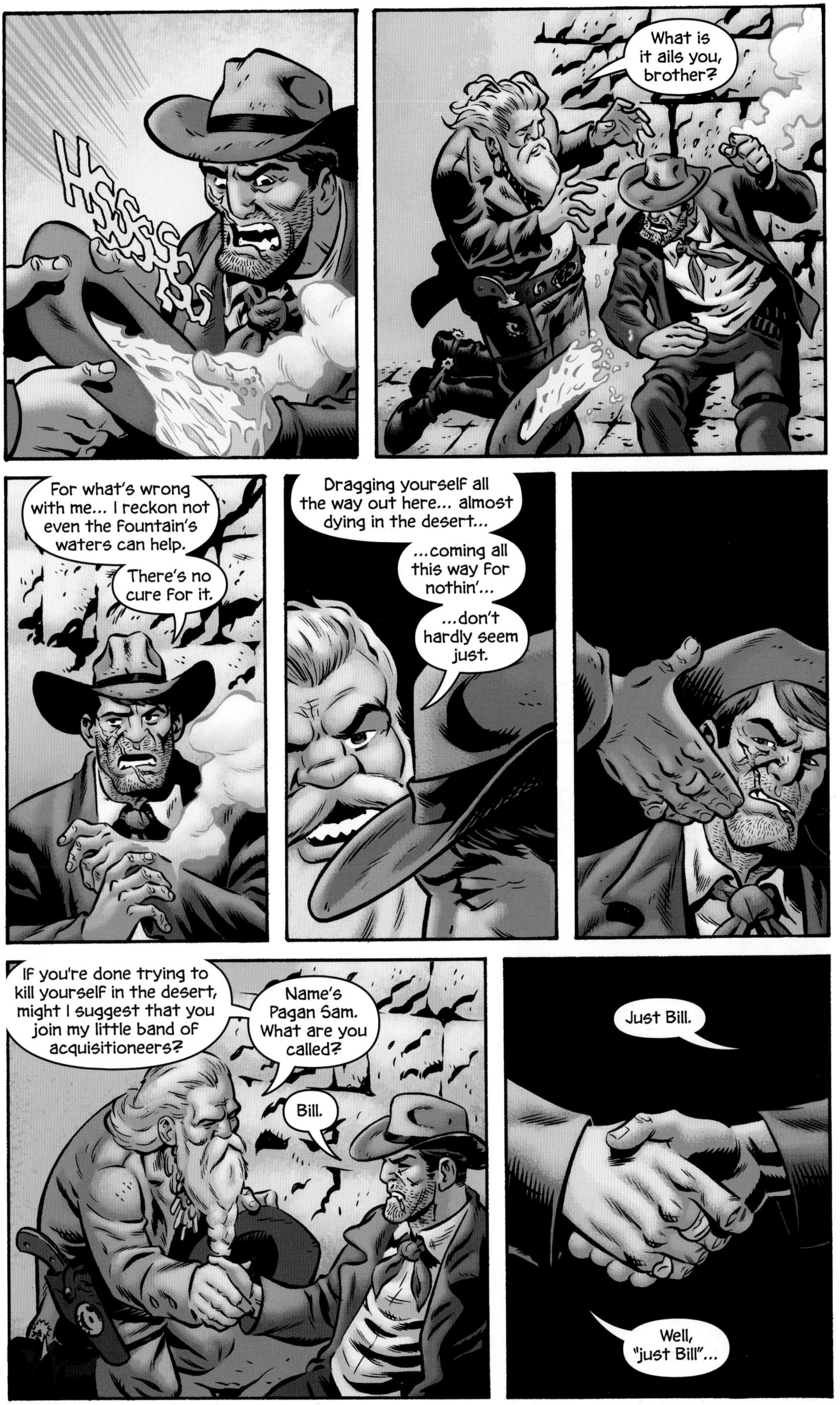
HSSSSSS
What is it ails you, brother?
For what's wrong with me... I reckon not even the Fountain's waters can help.
There's no cure for it.
Dragging yourself all the way out here... almost dying in the desert...
...coming all this way for nothin'...
...don't hardly seem just.
If you're done trying to kill yourself in the desert, might I suggest that you join my little band of acquisitioneers?
Name's Pagan Sam. What are you called?
Bill.
Just Bill.
Well, "just Bill"...

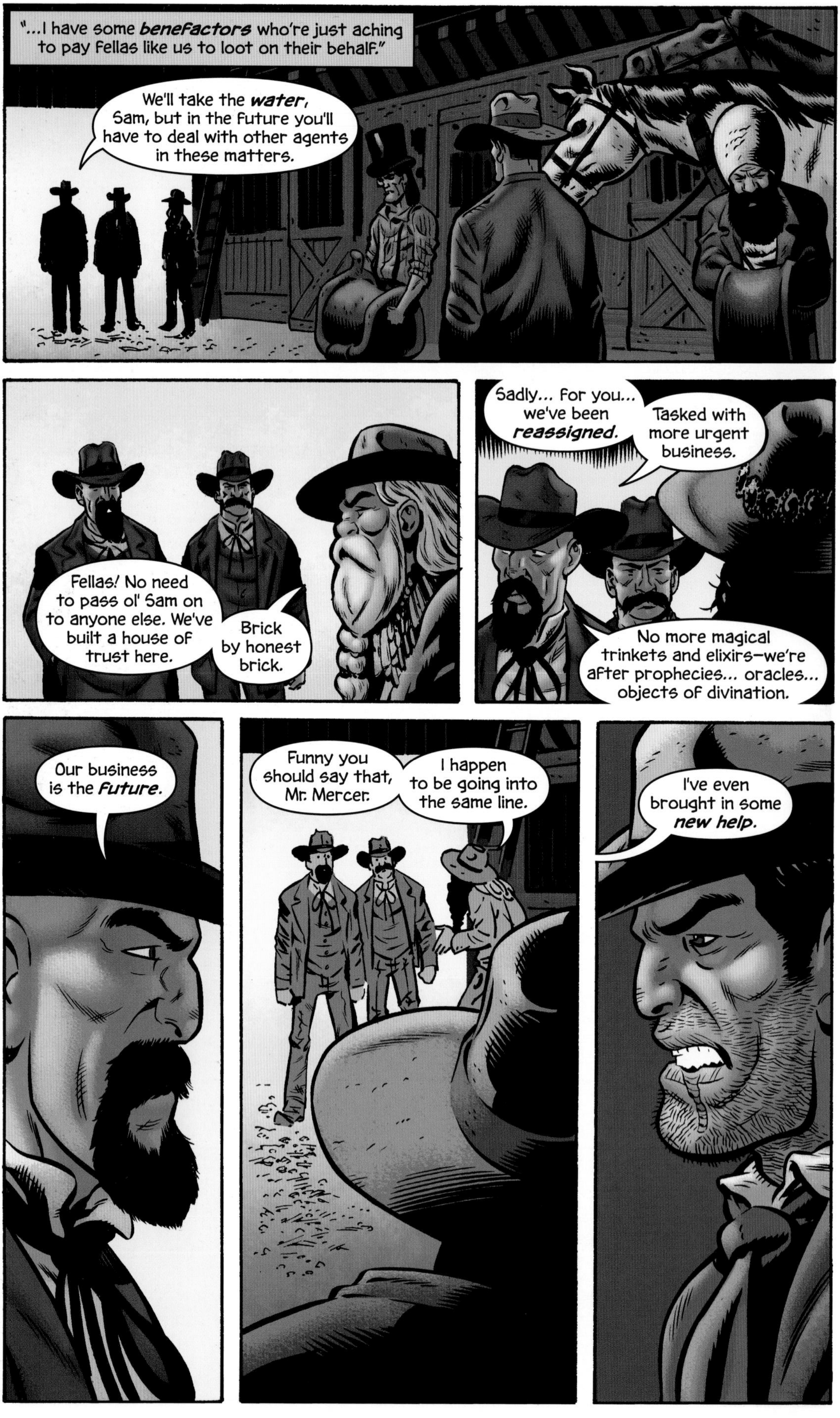
"...I have some *benefactors* who're just aching to pay fellas like us to loot on their behalf."
We'll take the *water*, Sam, but in the future you'll have to deal with other agents in these matters.
Fellas! No need to pass ol' Sam on to anyone else. We've built a house of trust here.
Brick by honest brick.
Sadly... for you... we've been *reassigned*.
Tasked with more urgent business.
No more magical trinkets and elixirs—we're after prophecies... oracles... objects of divination.
Our business is the *future*.
Funny you should say that, Mr. Mercer.
I happen to be going into the same line.
I've even brought in some *new help*.

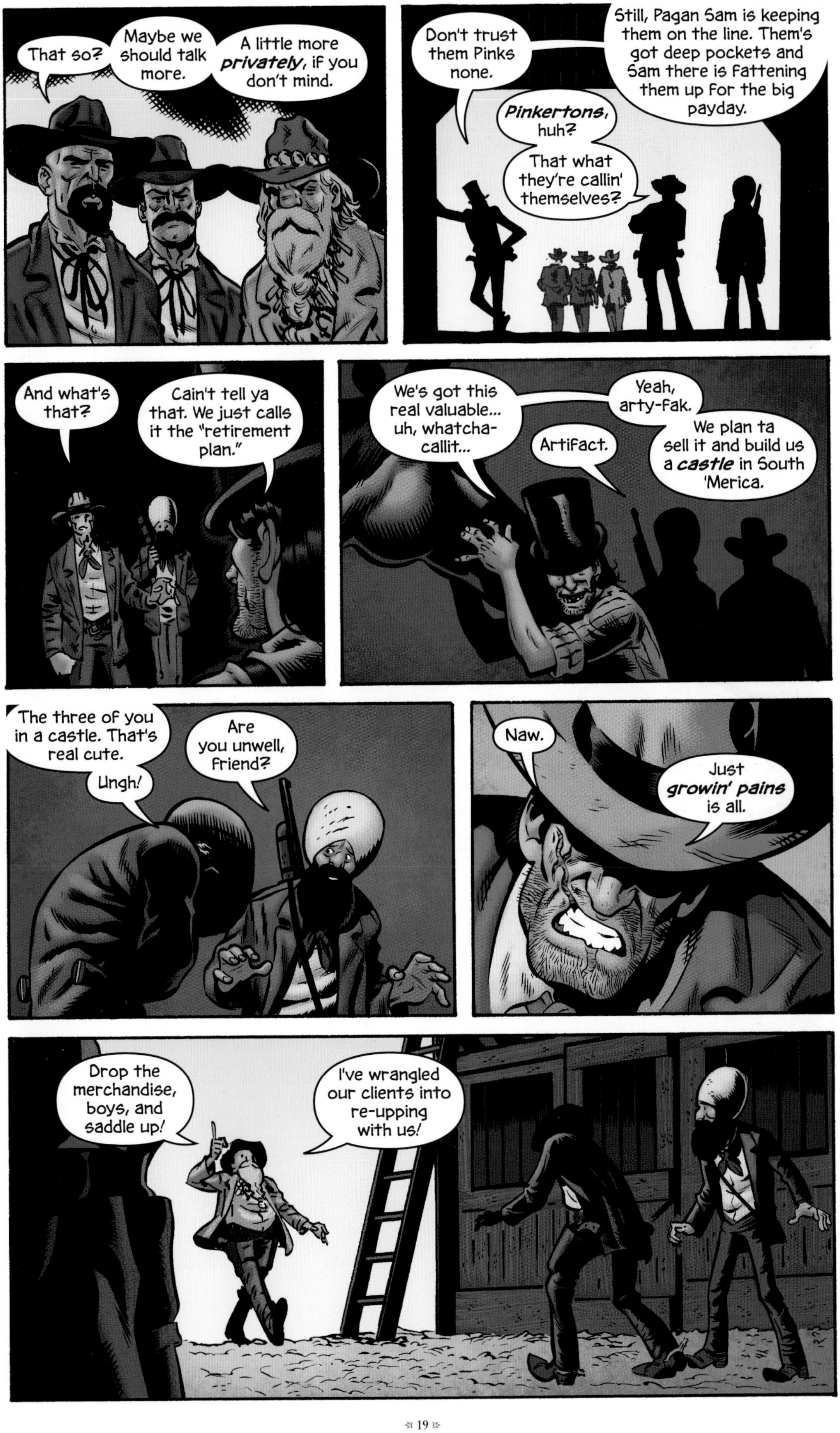
That so?
Maybe we should talk more.
A little more *privately*, if you don't mind.
Still, Pagan Sam is keeping them on the line. Them's got deep pockets and Sam there is fattening them up for the big payday.
Don't trust them Pinks none.
Pinkertons, huh?
That what they're callin' themselves?
And what's that?
Cain't tell ya that. We just calls it the "retirement plan."
We's got this real valuable... uh, whatcha-callit...
Yeah, arty-fak.
Artifact.
We plan ta sell it and build us a *castle* in South 'Merica.
The three of you in a castle. That's real cute.
Ungh!
Are you unwell, friend?
Naw.
Just *growin' pains* is all.
Drop the merchandise, boys, and saddle up!
I've wrangled our clients into re-upping with us!

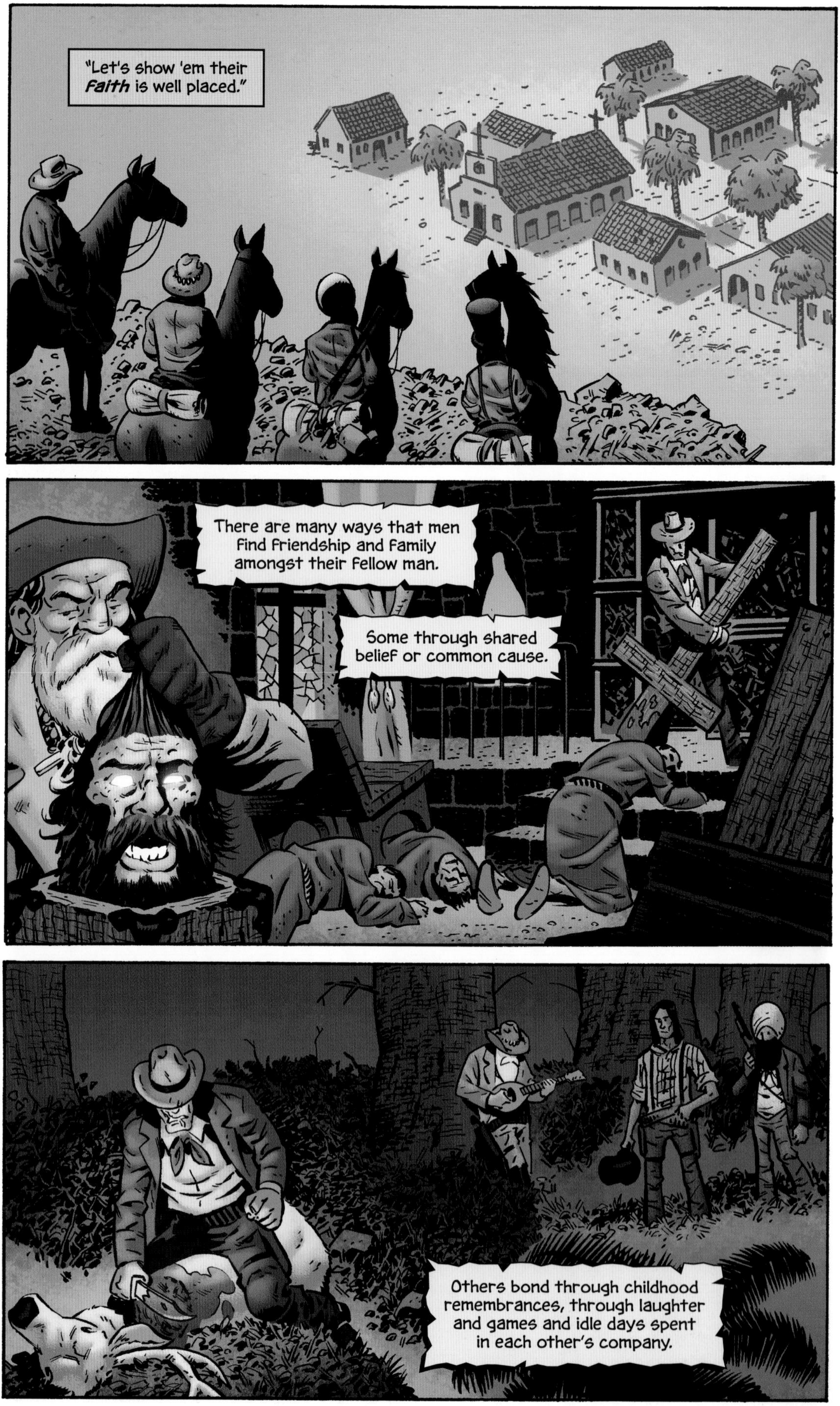
"Let's show 'em their *Faith* is well placed."
There are many ways that men find friendship and family amongst their fellow man.
Some through shared belief or common cause.
Others bond through childhood remembrances, through laughter and games and idle days spent in each other's company.

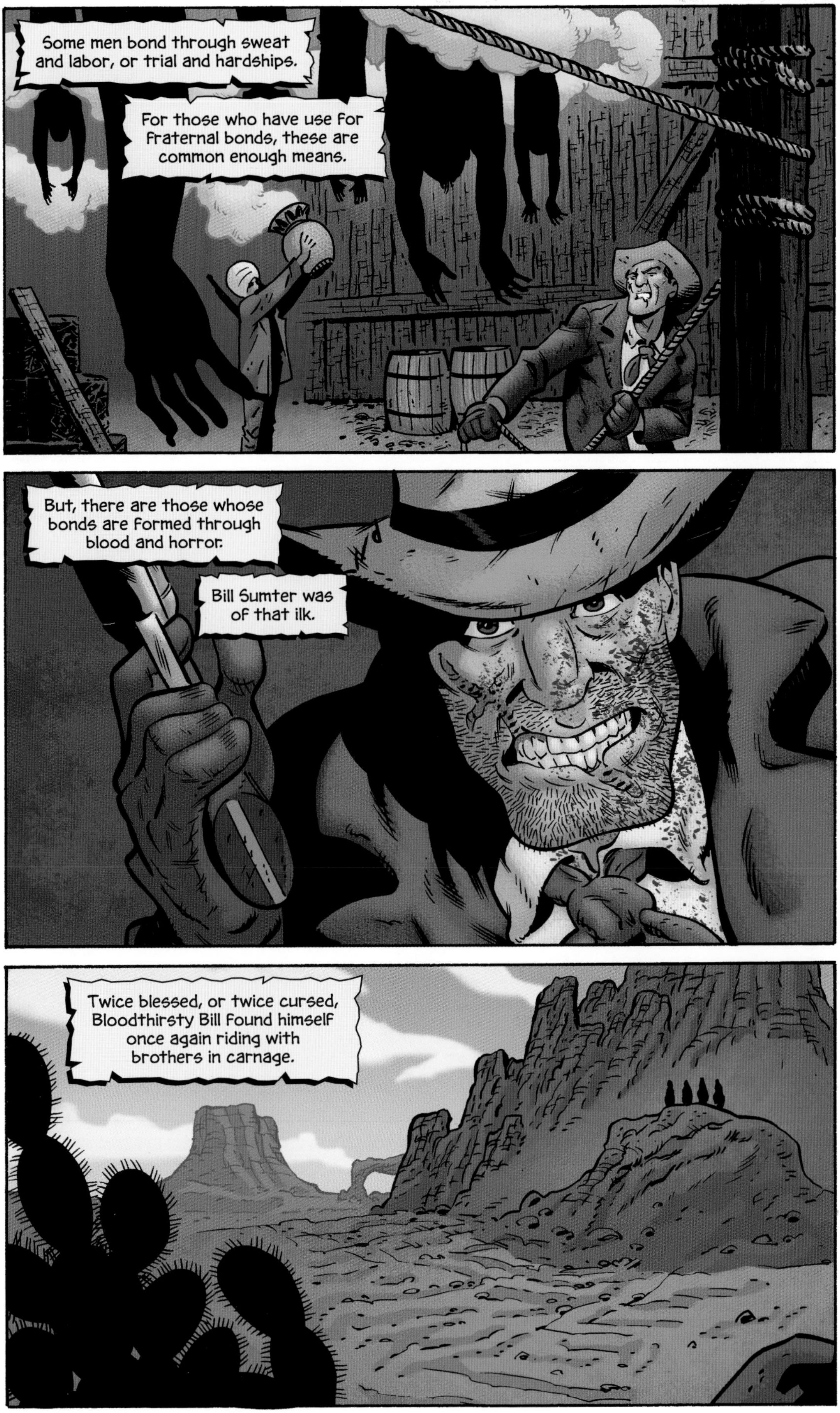
Some men bond through sweat and labor, or trial and hardships.
For those who have use for fraternal bonds, these are common enough means.
But, there are those whose bonds are formed through blood and horror.
Bill Sumter was of that ilk.
Twice blessed, or twice cursed, Bloodthirsty Bill found himself once again riding with brothers in carnage.

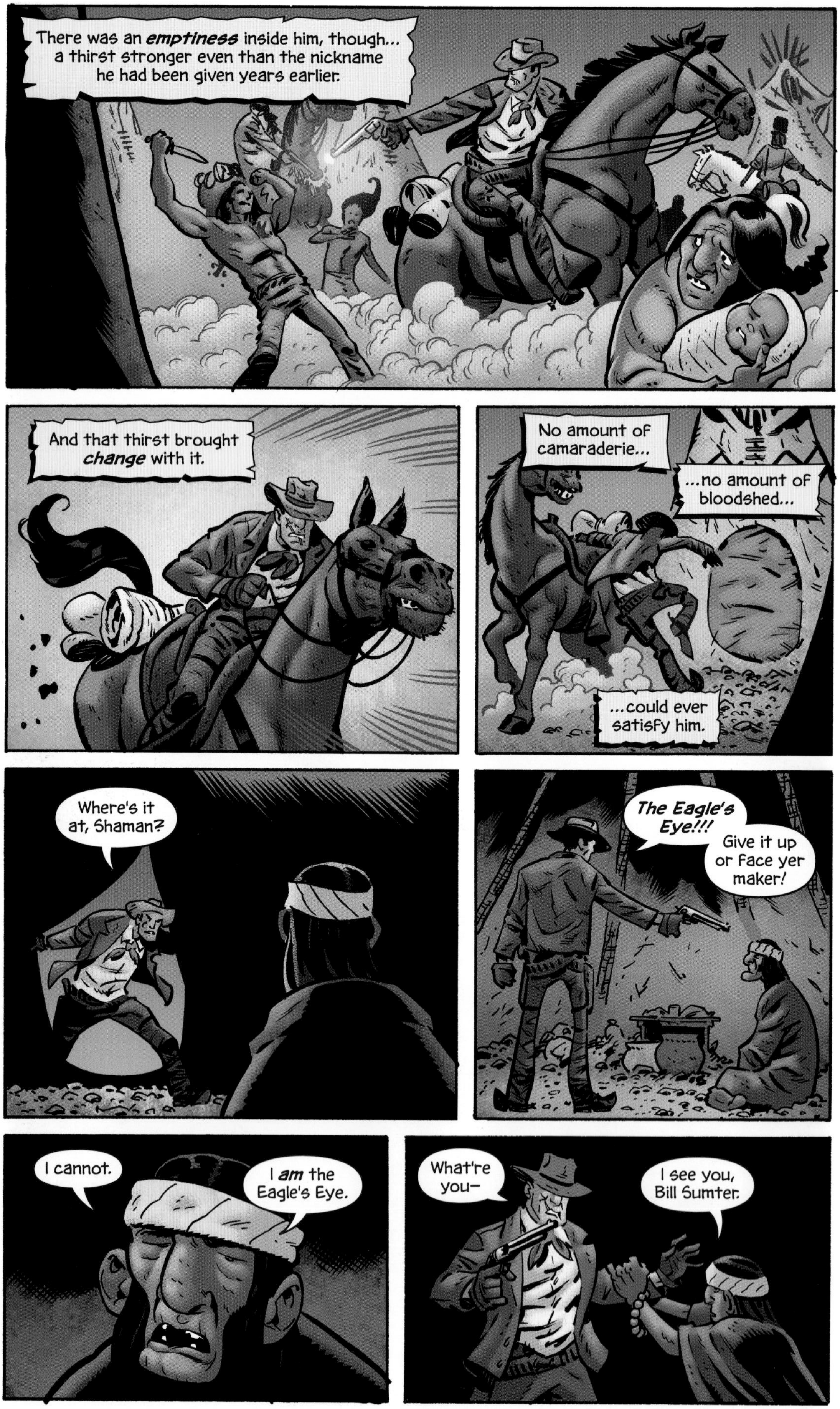
There was an *emptiness* inside him, though... a thirst stronger even than the nickname he had been given years earlier.
And that thirst brought *change* with it.
No amount of camaraderie...
...no amount of bloodshed...
...could ever satisfy him.
Where's it at, Shaman?
The Eagle's Eye!!!
Give it up or face yer maker!
I cannot.
I *am* the Eagle's Eye.
What're you—
I see you, Bill Sumter.

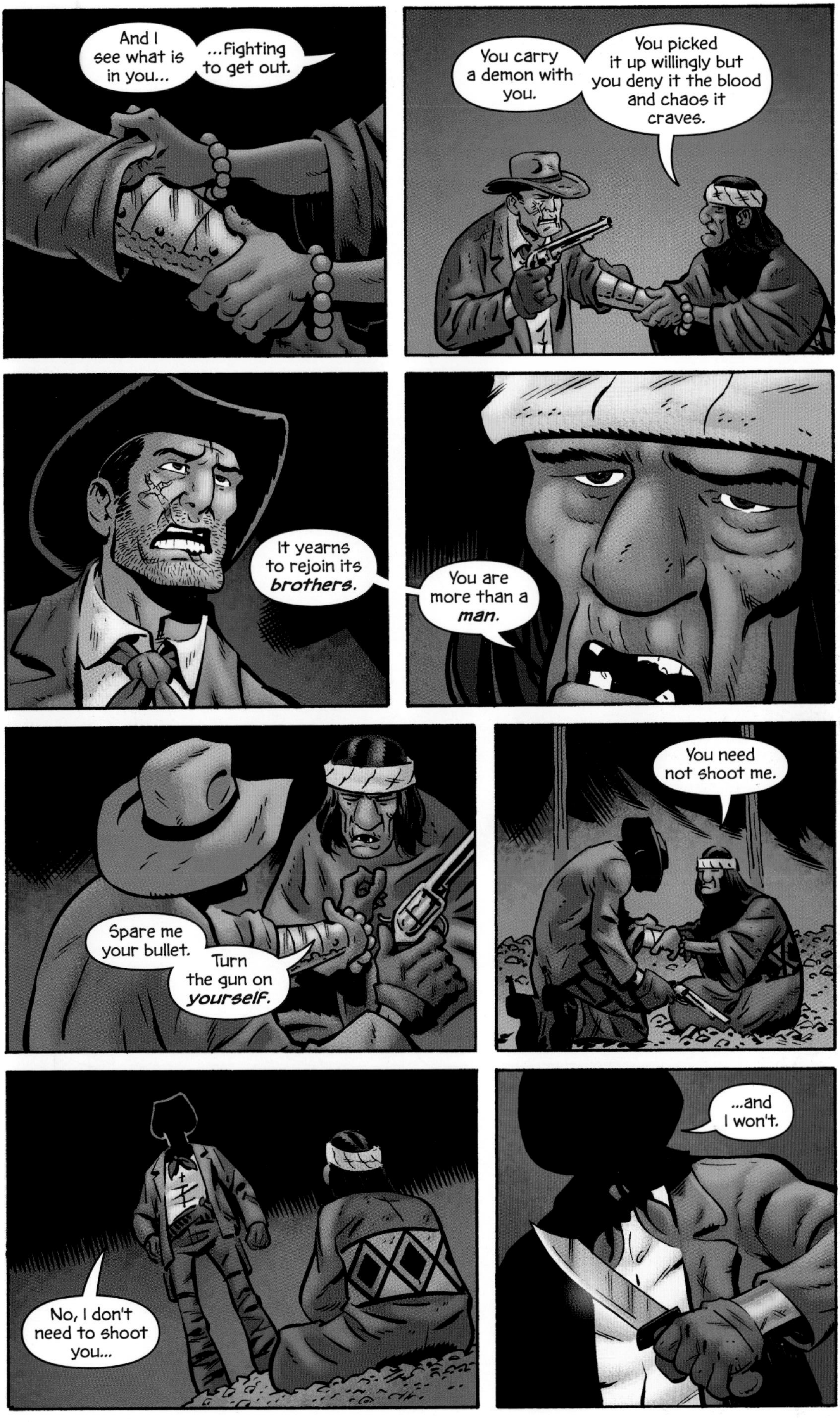

And I see what is in you...
...fighting to get out.
You carry a demon with you.
You picked it up willingly but you deny it the blood and chaos it craves.
It yearns to rejoin its ***brothers.***
You are more than a ***man.***
Spare me your bullet.
Turn the gun on ***yourself.***
You need not shoot me.
No, I don't need to shoot you...
...and I won't.

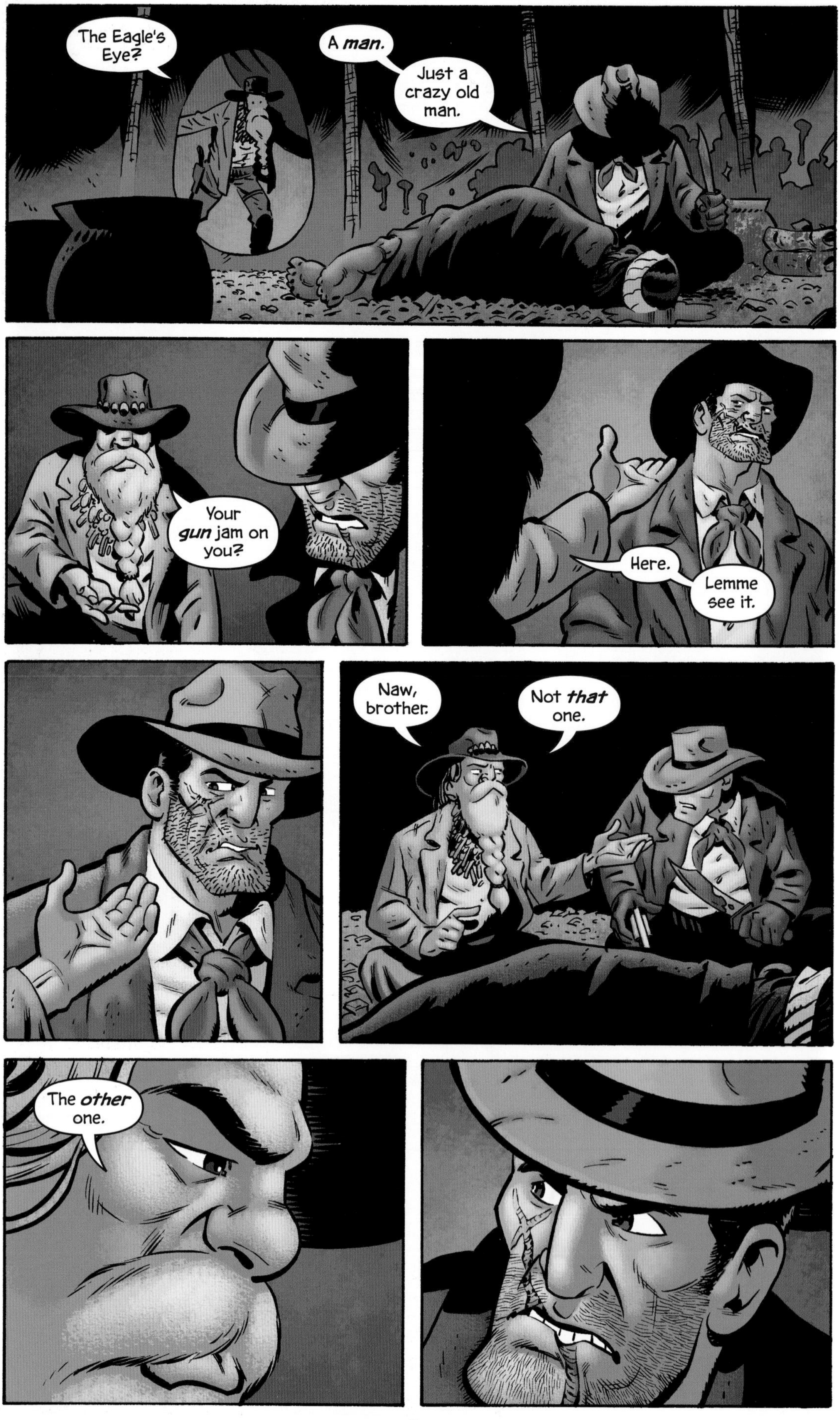
The Eagle's Eye?
A *man*.
Just a crazy old man.
Your *gun* jam on you?
Here.
Lemme see it.
Naw, brother.
Not *that* one.
The *other* one.

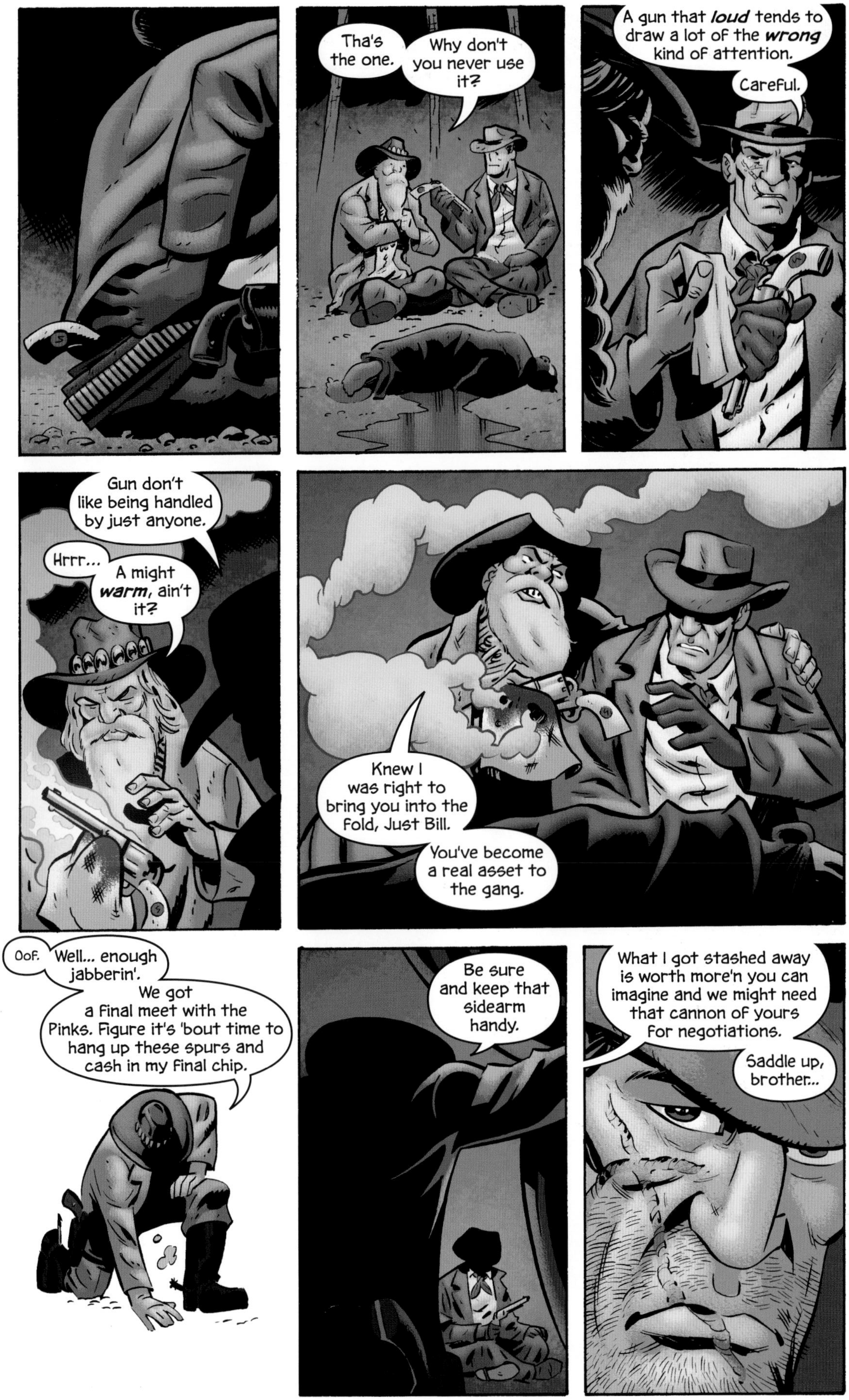

Tha's the one.
Why don't you never use it?
A gun that *loud* tends to draw a lot of the ***wrong*** kind of attention.
Careful.
Gun don't like being handled by just anyone.
Hrrr...
A might ***warm,*** ain't it?
Knew I was right to bring you into the fold, Just Bill.
You've become a real asset to the gang.
Oof.
Well... enough jabberin'.
We got a final meet with the Pinks. Figure it's 'bout time to hang up these spurs and cash in my final chip.
Be sure and keep that sidearm handy.
What I got stashed away is worth more'n you can imagine and we might need that cannon of yours for negotiations.
Saddle up, brother...

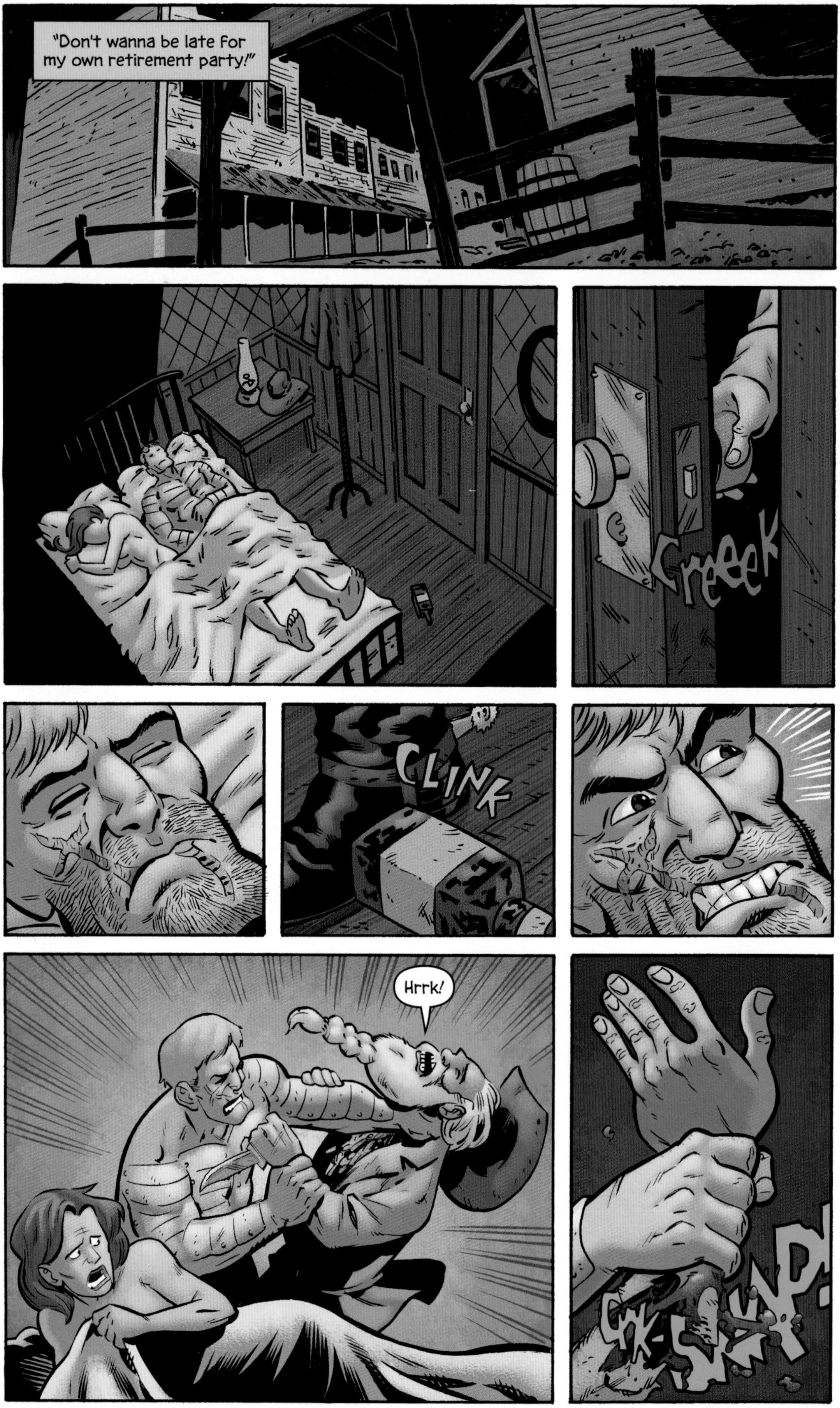
"Don't wanna be late for my own retirement party!"
Creeek
CLINK
Hrrk!

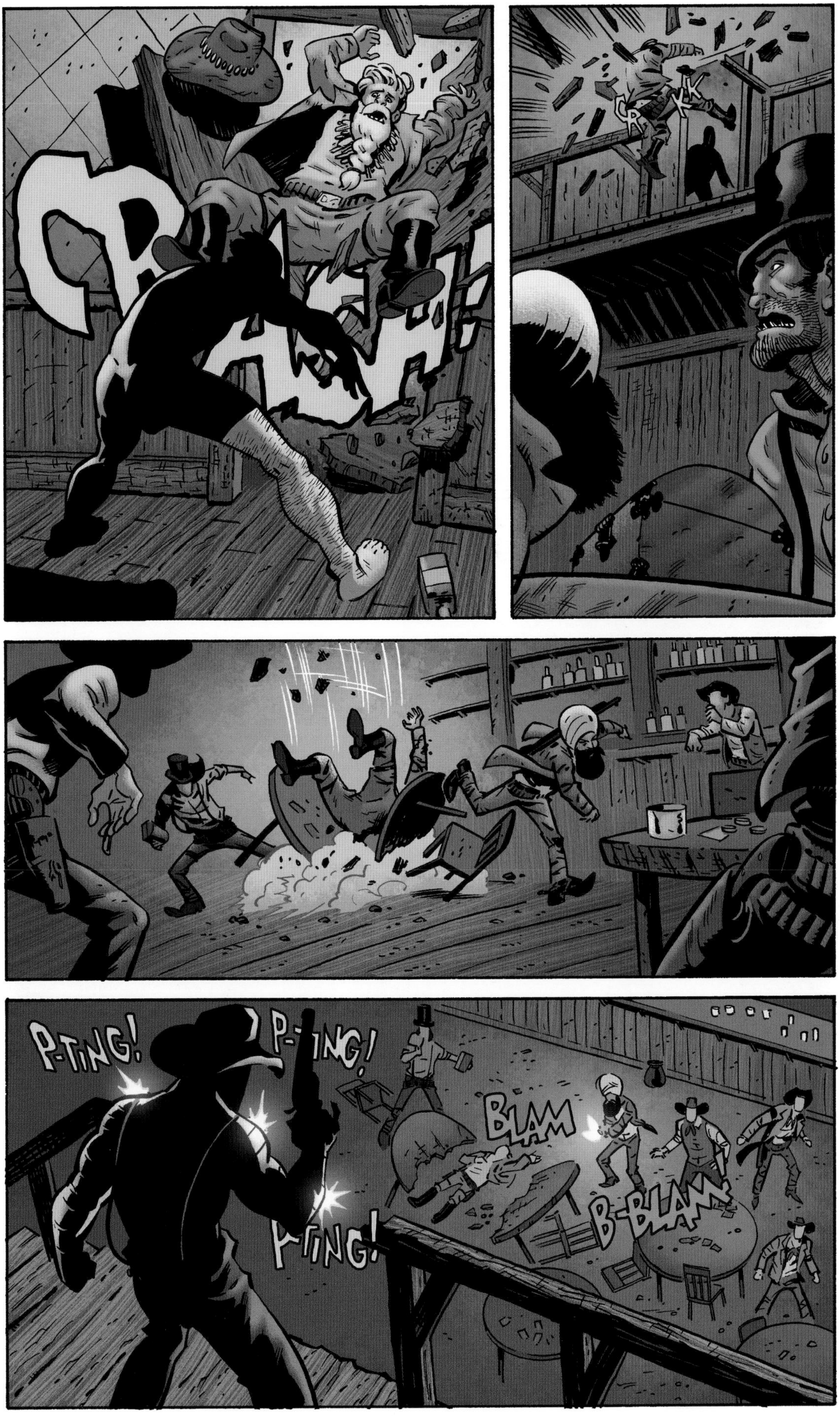
P-TING!
P-TING!
BLAM
B-BLAM
P-TING!

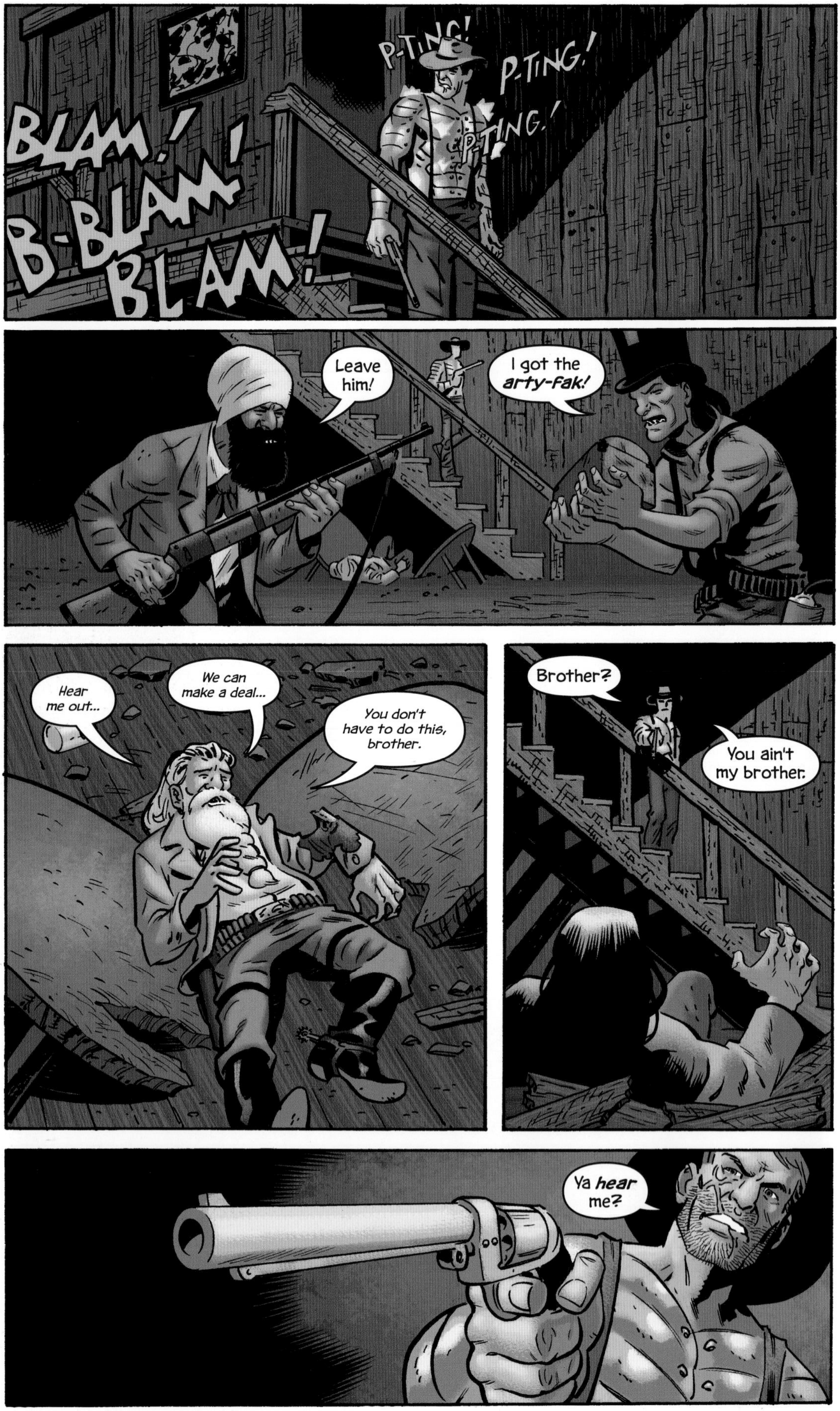

BLAM! B-BLAM! BLAM!
P-TING! P-TING! P-TING!
Leave him!
I got the *arty-fak!*
Hear me out...
We can make a deal...
You don't have to do this, brother.
Brother?
You ain't my brother.
Ya *hear* me?

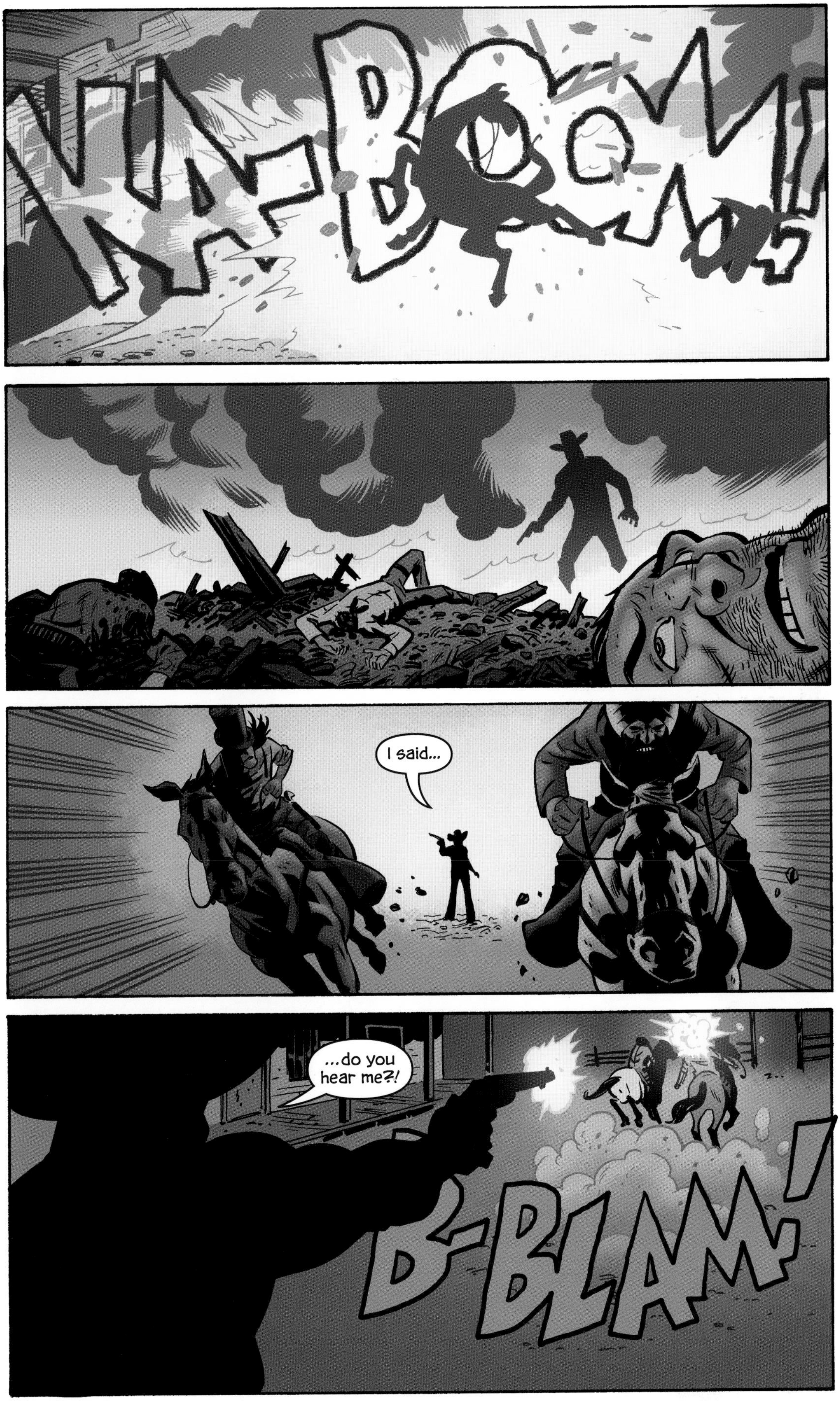
KA-BOOM!
I said...
...do you hear me?!
B-BLAM!

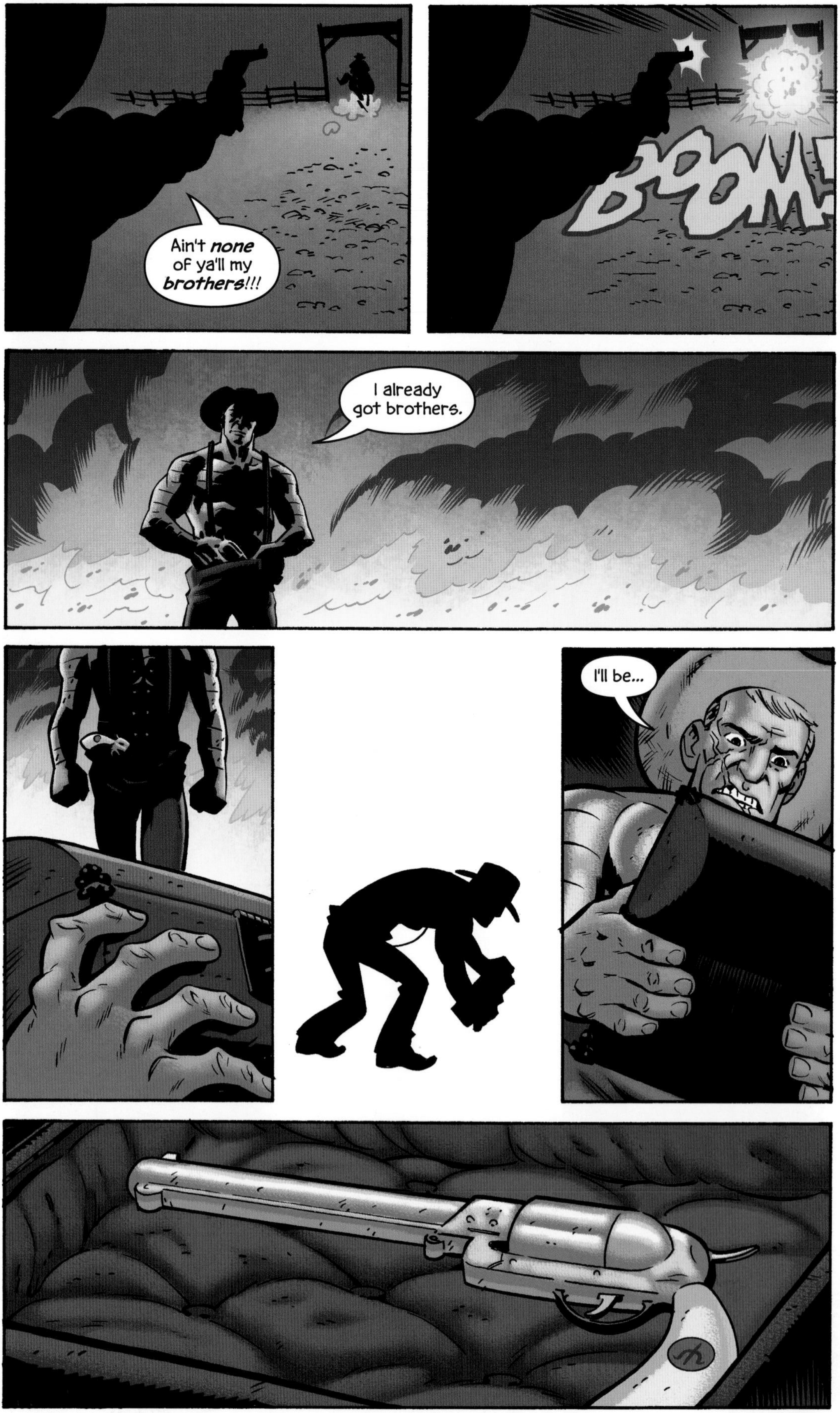
Ain't *none* of ya'll my ***brothers!!!***
BOOM!
I already got brothers.
I'll be...

CHAPTER TWO

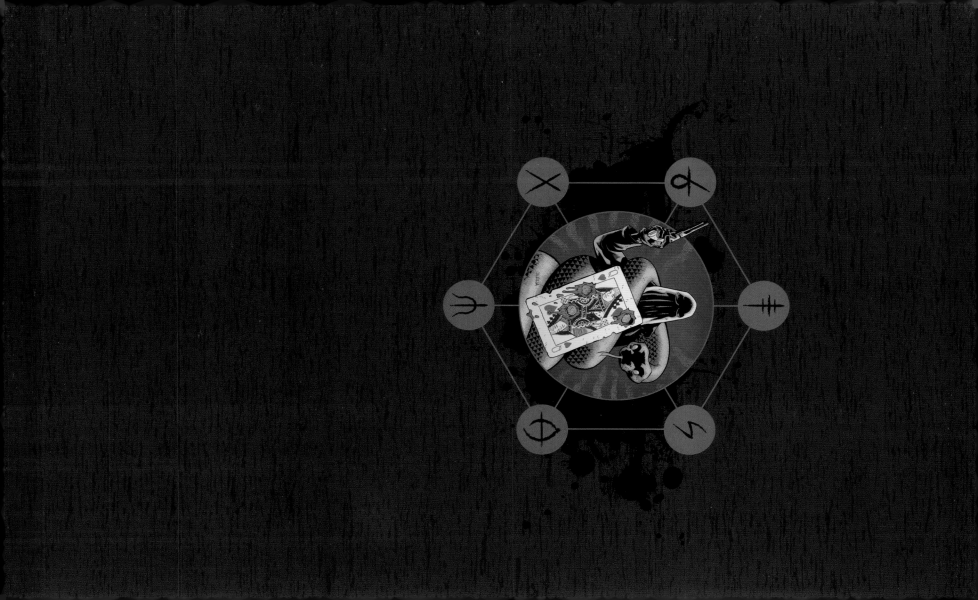

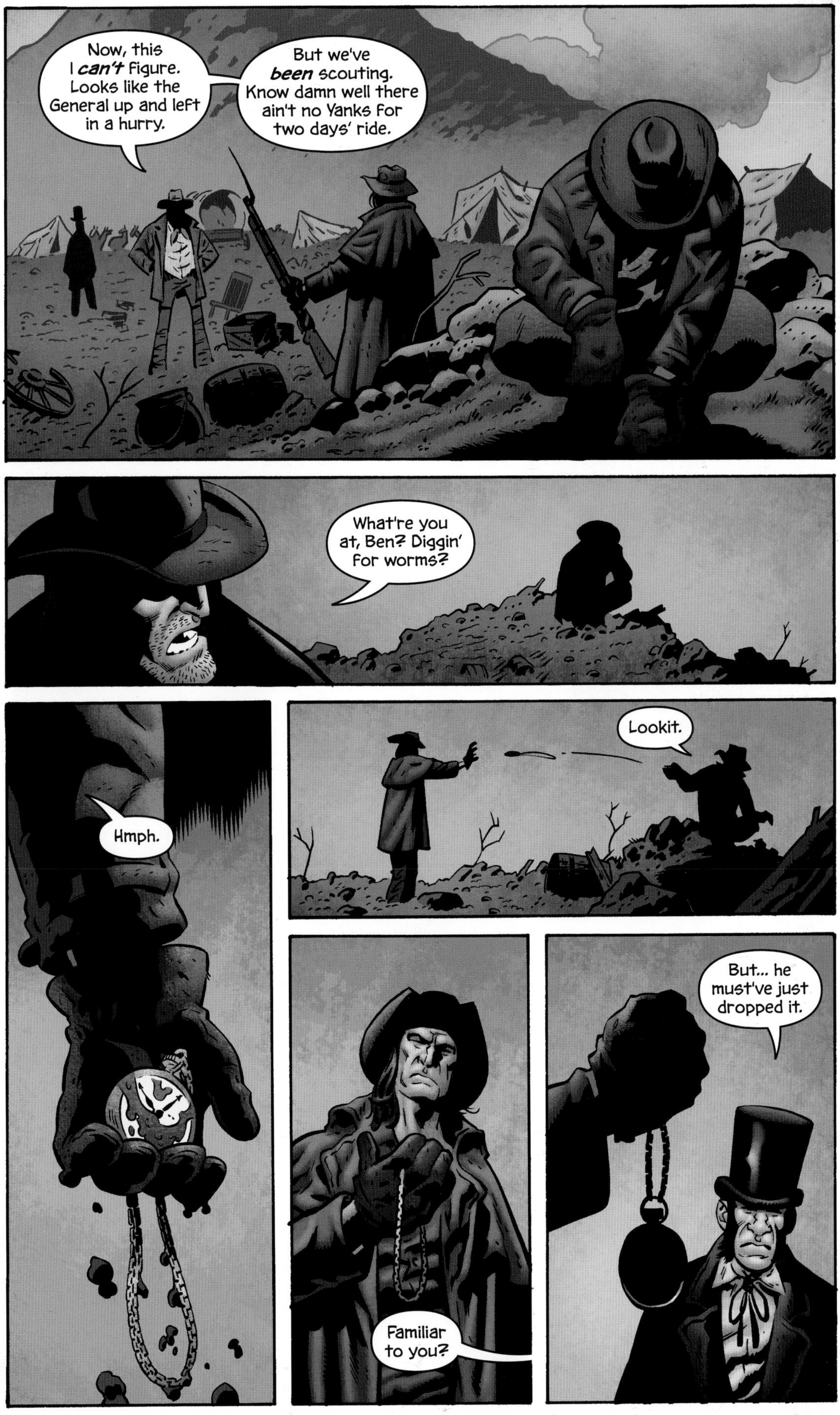
Now, this I *can't* figure. Looks like the General up and left in a hurry.
But we've *been* scouting. Know damn well there ain't no Yanks for two days' ride.
What're you at, Ben? Diggin' for worms?
Lookit.
Hmph.
Familiar to you?
But... he must've just dropped it.

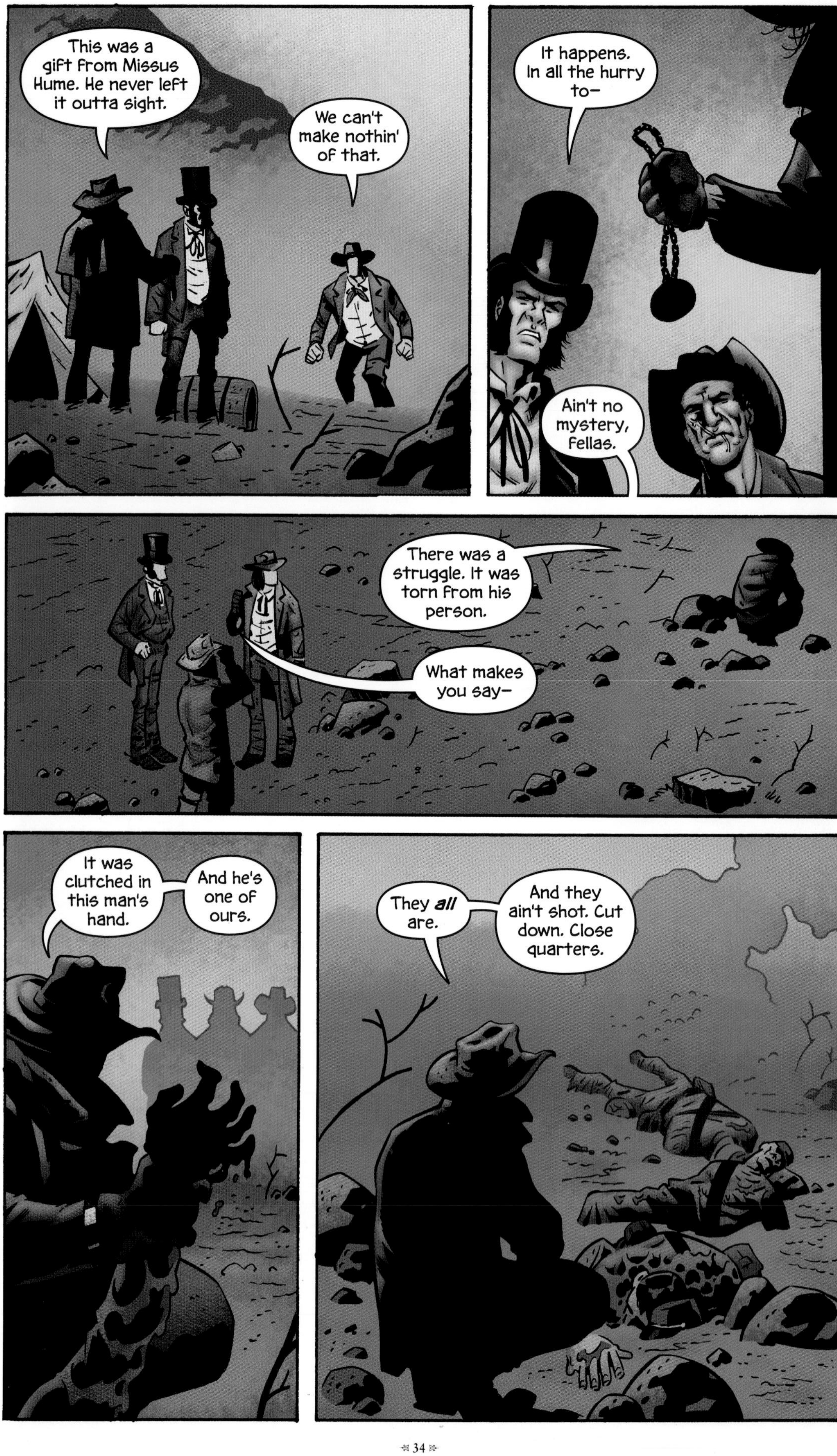
This was a gift from Missus Hume. He never left it outta sight.
We can't make nothin' of that.
It happens. In all the hurry to–
Ain't no mystery, fellas.
There was a struggle. It was torn from his person.
What makes you say–
It was clutched in this man's hand.
And he's one of ours.
They *all* are.
And they ain't shot. Cut down. Close quarters.

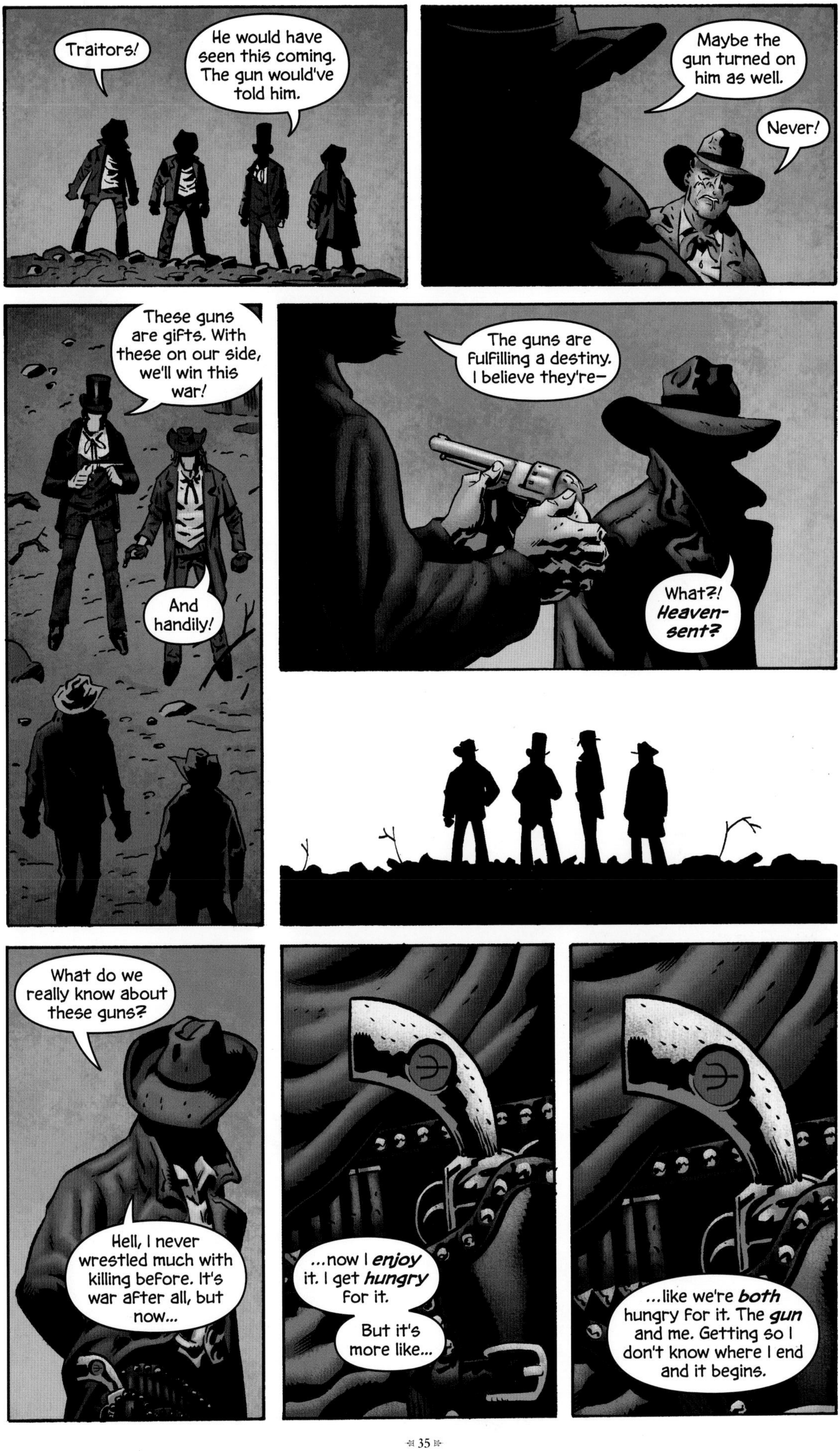
Traitors!
He would have seen this coming. The gun would've told him.
Maybe the gun turned on him as well.
Never!
These guns are gifts. With these on our side, we'll win this war!
And handily!
The guns are fulfilling a destiny. I believe they're—
What?! *Heaven-sent?*
What do we really know about these guns?
Hell, I never wrestled much with killing before. It's war after all, but now...
...now I *enjoy* it. I get *hungry* for it.
But it's more like...
...like we're *both* hungry for it. The *gun* and me. Getting so I don't know where I end and it begins.

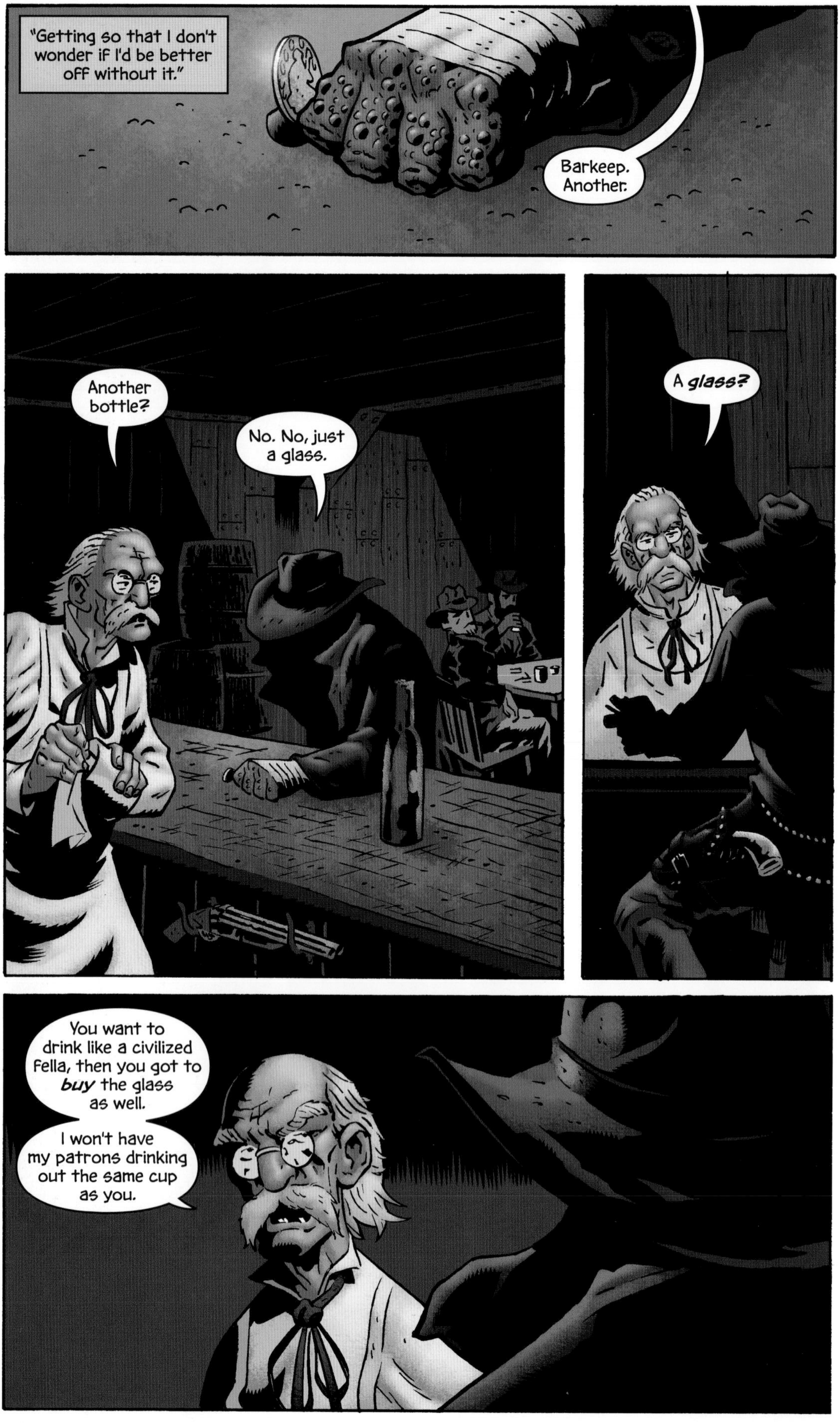
"Getting so that I don't wonder if I'd be better off without it."
Barkeep. Another.
Another bottle?
No. No, just a glass.
A *glass?*
You want to drink like a civilized fella, then you got to *buy* the glass as well.
I won't have my patrons drinking out the same cup as you.

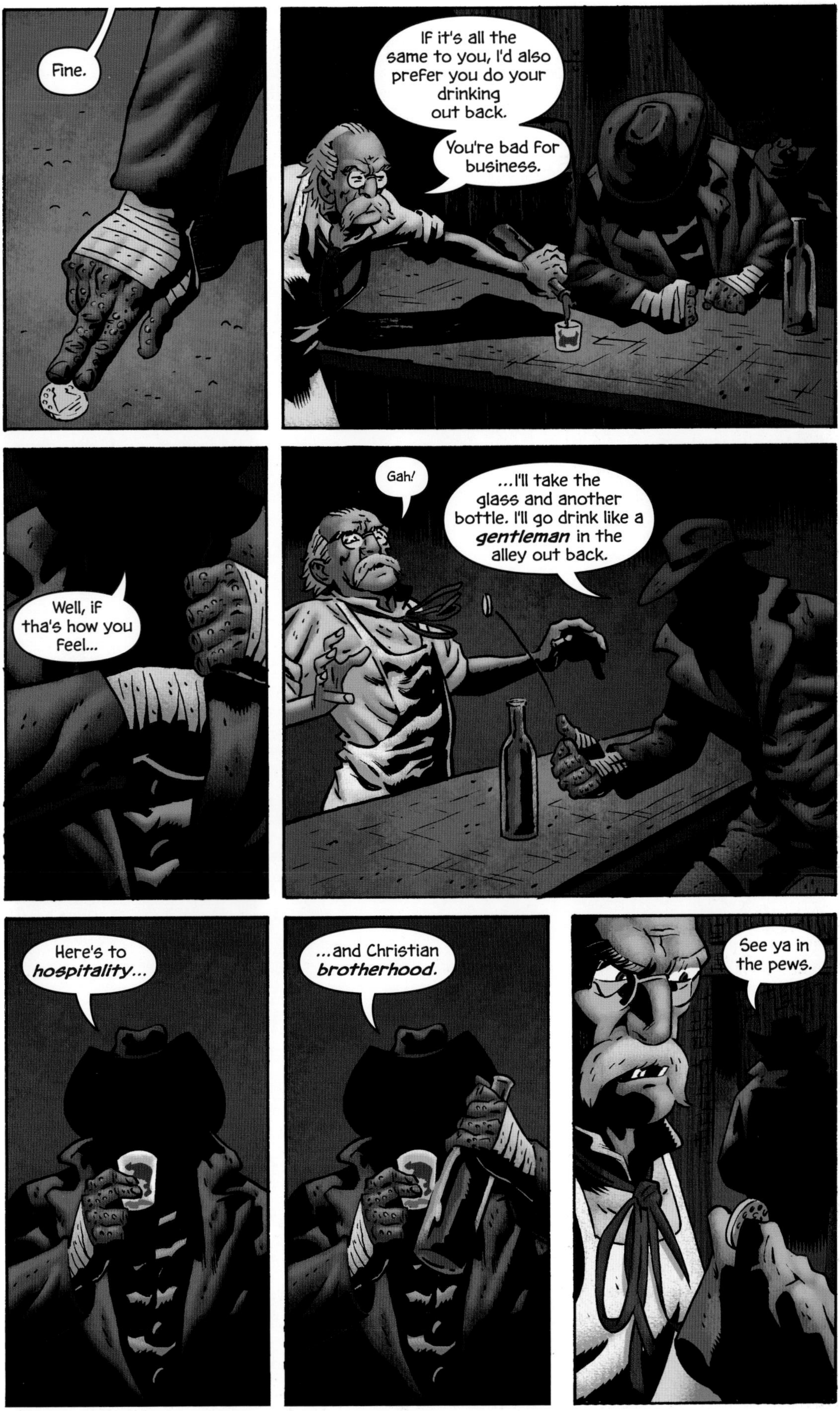
Fine.
If it's all the same to you, I'd also prefer you do your drinking out back.
You're bad for business.
Well, if tha's how you feel...
Gah!
...I'll take the glass and another bottle. I'll go drink like a **gentleman** in the alley out back.
Here's to **hospitality**...
...and Christian **brotherhood**.
See ya in the pews.

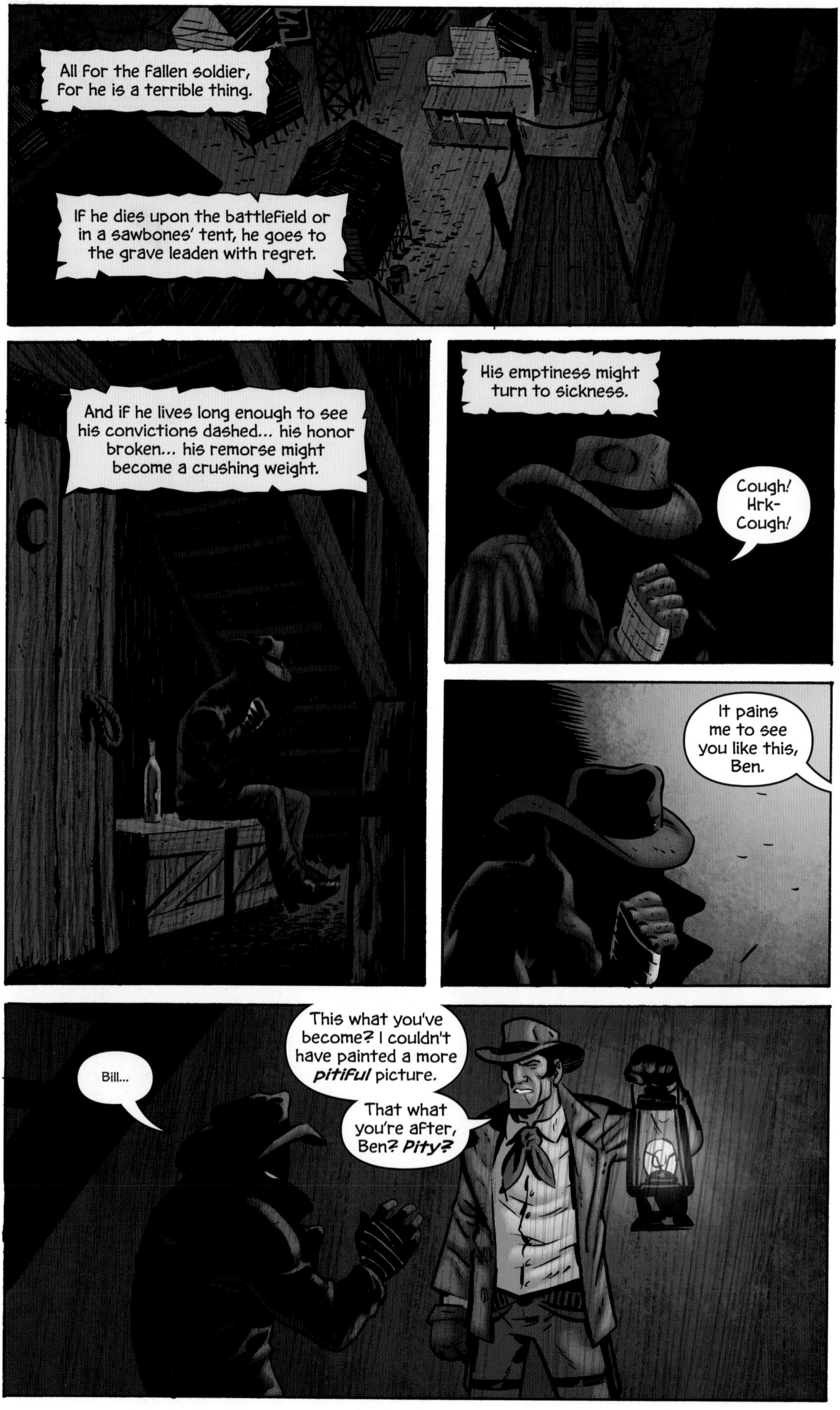
All for the fallen soldier, for he is a terrible thing.
If he dies upon the battlefield or in a sawbones' tent, he goes to the grave leaden with regret.
And if he lives long enough to see his convictions dashed... his honor broken... his remorse might become a crushing weight.
His emptiness might turn to sickness.
Cough! Hrk- Cough!
It pains me to see you like this, Ben.
Bill...
This what you've become? I couldn't have painted a more *pitiful* picture.
That what you're after, Ben? *Pity?*

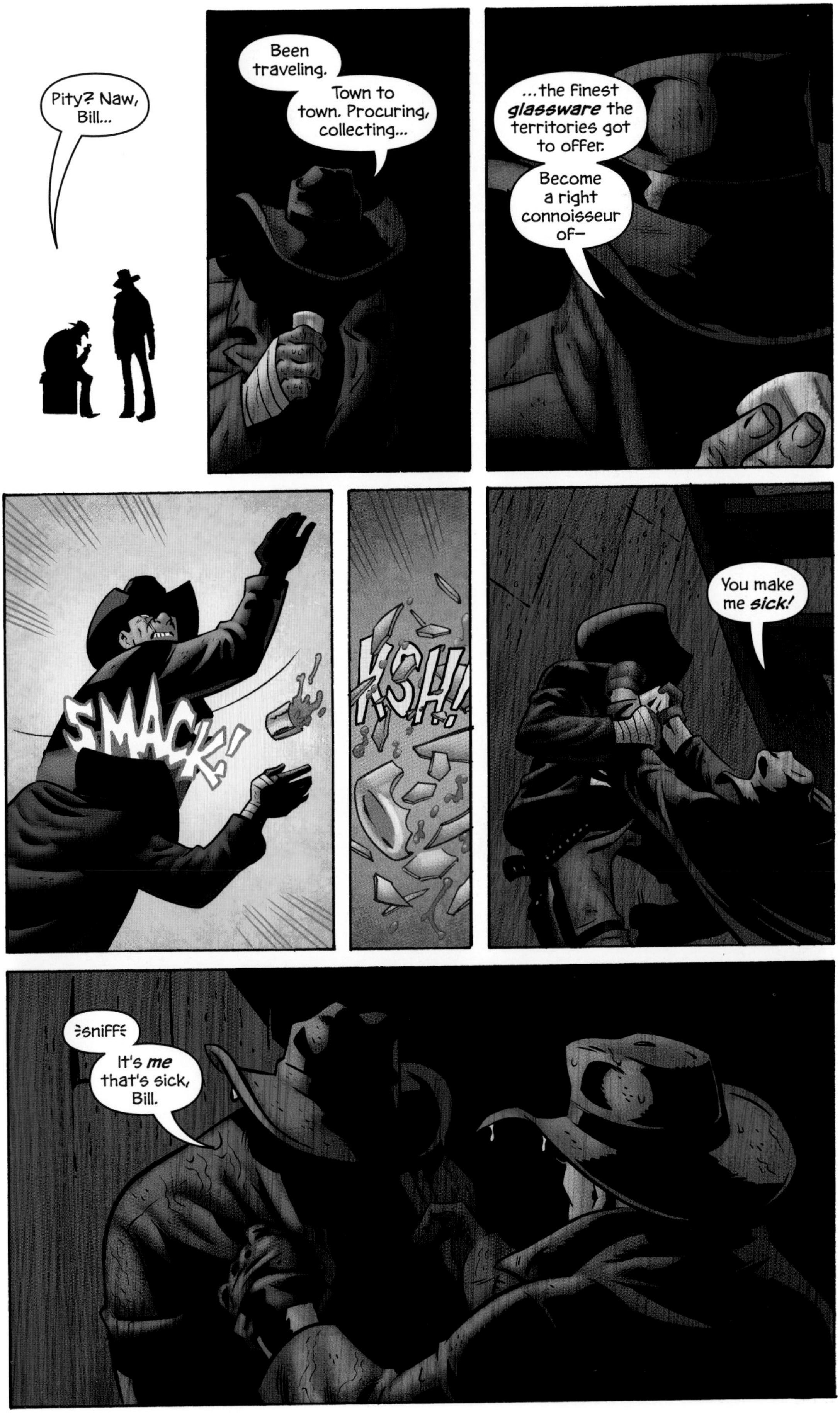
Pity? Naw, Bill...
Been traveling.
Town to town. Procuring, collecting...
...the finest glassware the territories got to offer.
Become a right connoisseur of–
SMACK!
KSH!
You make me sick!
≷sniff≶
It's me that's sick, Bill.

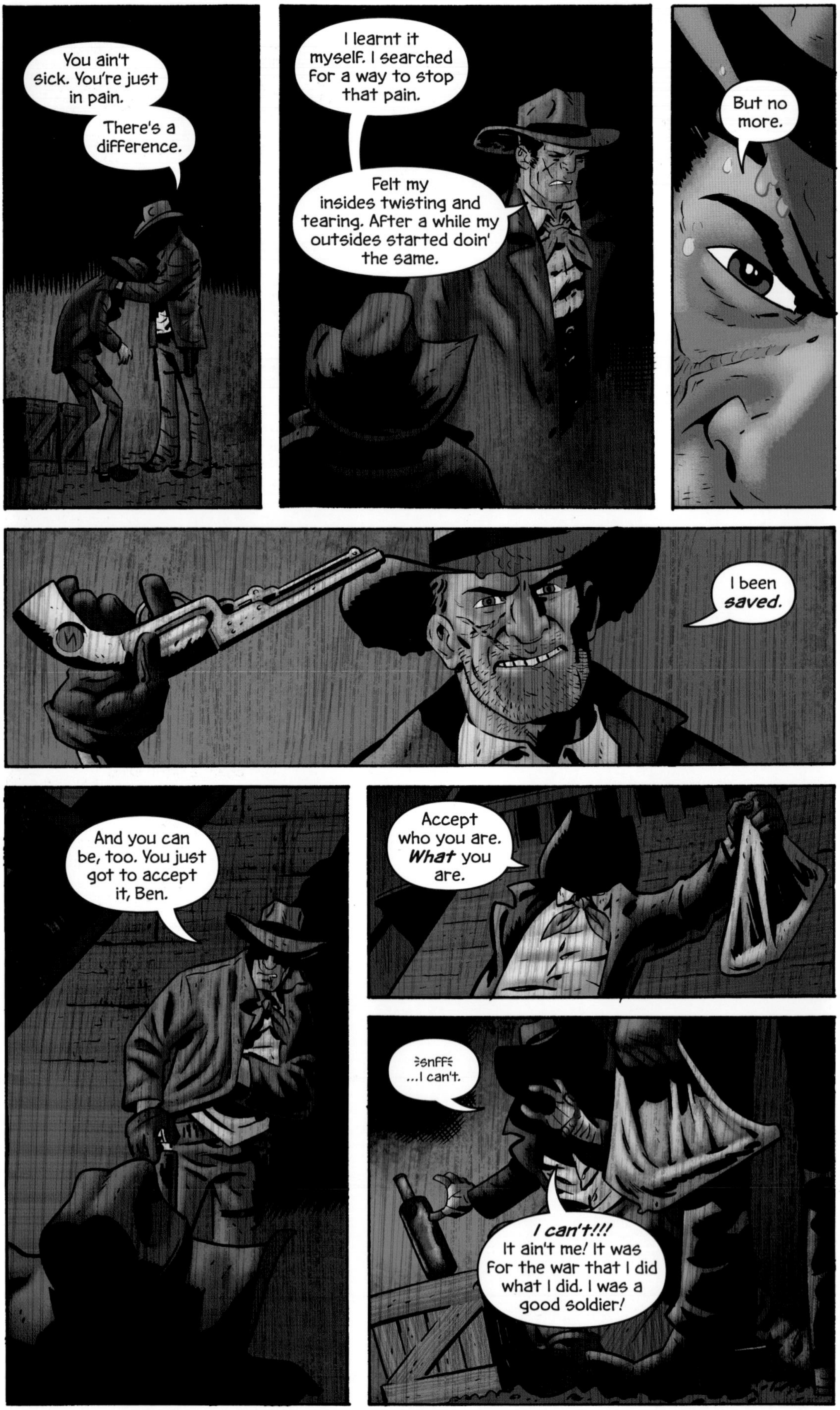
You ain't sick. You're just in pain.
There's a difference.
I learnt it myself. I searched for a way to stop that pain.
Felt my insides twisting and tearing. After a while my outsides started doin' the same.
But no more.
I been *saved.*
And you can be, too. You just got to accept it, Ben.
Accept who you are. *What* you are.
≶snff≶ ...I can't.
I can't!!! It ain't me! It was for the war that I did what I did. I was a good soldier!

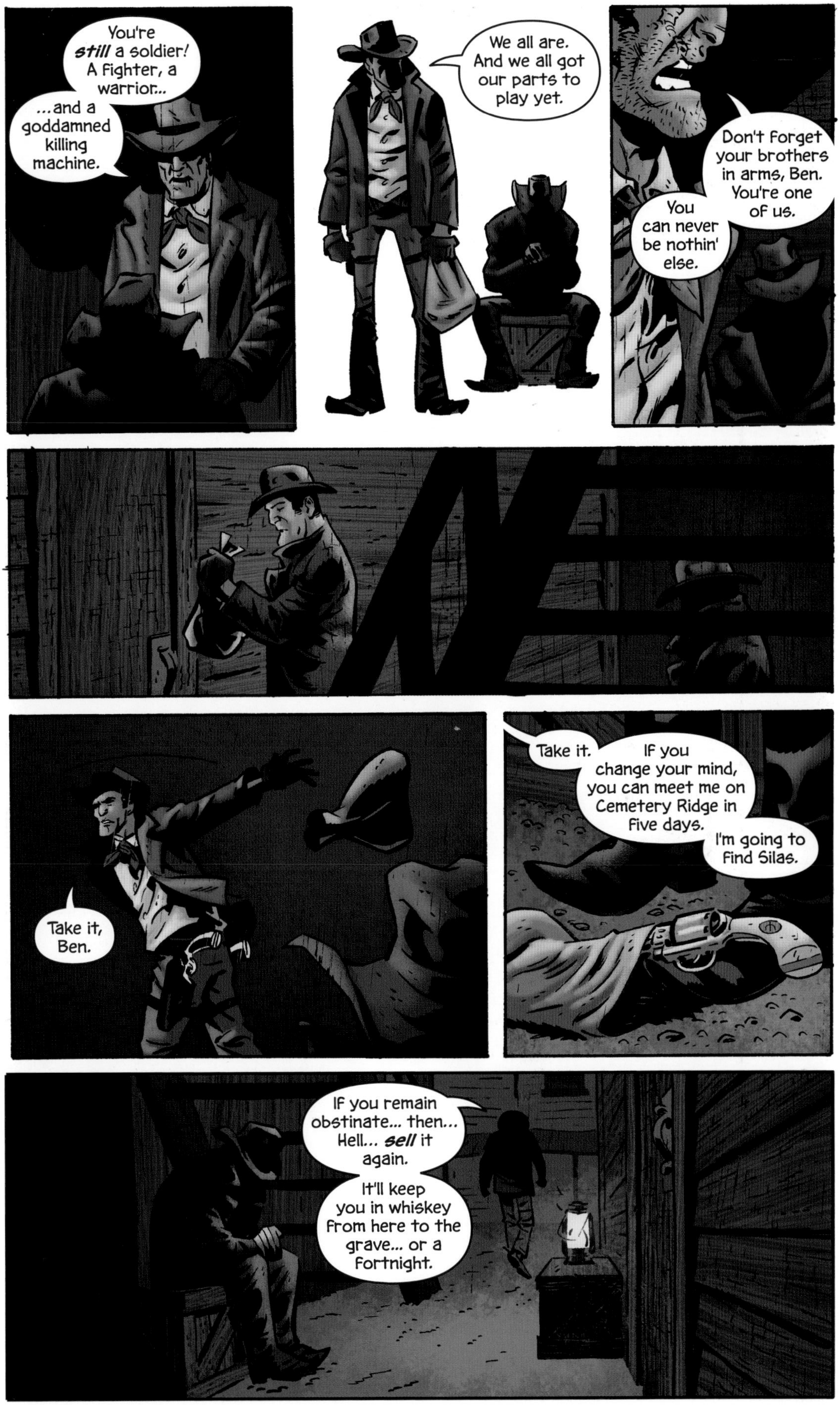
You're *still* a soldier! A fighter, a warrior...
...and a goddamned killing machine.
We all are. And we all got our parts to play yet.
Don't forget your brothers in arms, Ben. You're one of us.
You can never be nothin' else.
Take it, Ben.
Take it.
If you change your mind, you can meet me on Cemetery Ridge in five days.
I'm going to find Silas.
If you remain obstinate... then... Hell... *sell* it again.
It'll keep you in whiskey from here to the grave... or a fortnight.

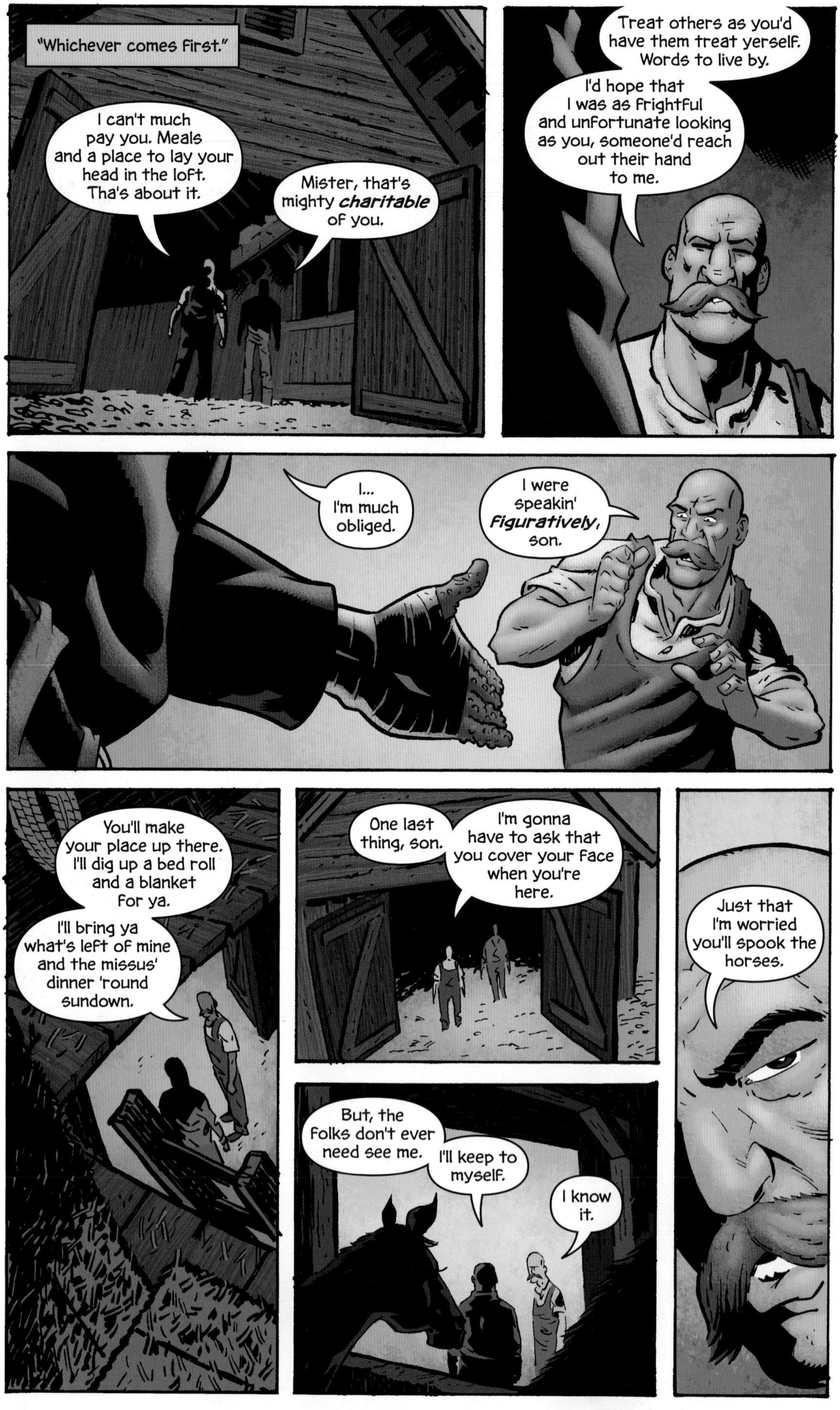
"Whichever comes first."
I can't much pay you. Meals and a place to lay your head in the loft. Tha's about it.
Mister, that's mighty *charitable* of you.
Treat others as you'd have them treat yerself. Words to live by.
I'd hope that I was as frightful and unfortunate looking as you, someone'd reach out their hand to me.
I... I'm much obliged.
I were speakin' *figuratively*, son.
You'll make your place up there. I'll dig up a bed roll and a blanket for ya.
I'll bring ya what's left of mine and the missus' dinner 'round sundown.
One last thing, son.
I'm gonna have to ask that you cover your face when you're here.
But, the folks don't ever need see me.
I'll keep to myself.
I know it.
Just that I'm worried you'll spook the horses.

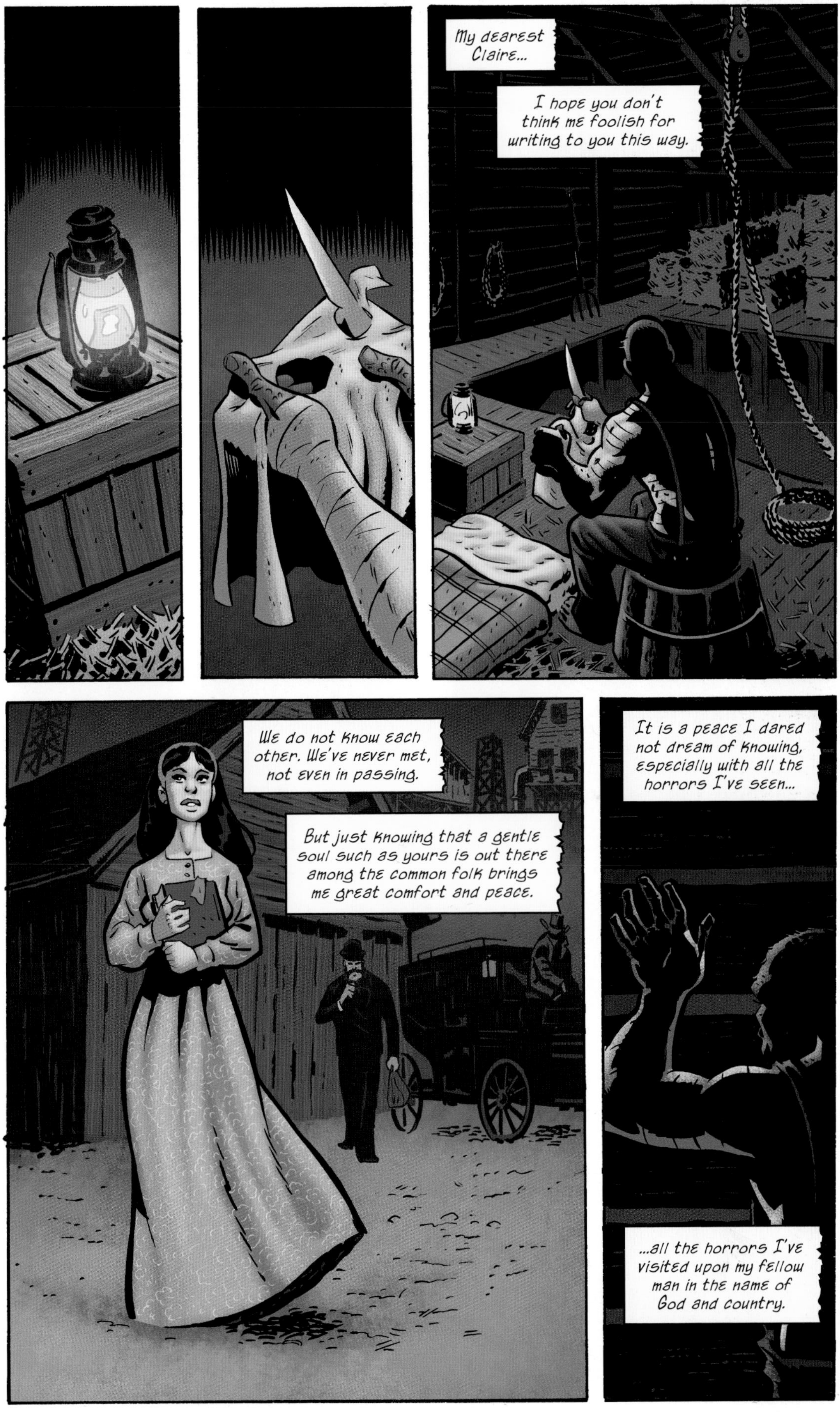

My dearest Claire...
I hope you don't think me foolish for writing to you this way.
We do not know each other. We've never met, not even in passing.
But just knowing that a gentle soul such as yours is out there among the common folk brings me great comfort and peace.
It is a peace I dared not dream of knowing, especially with all the horrors I've seen...
...all the horrors I've visited upon my fellow man in the name of God and country.

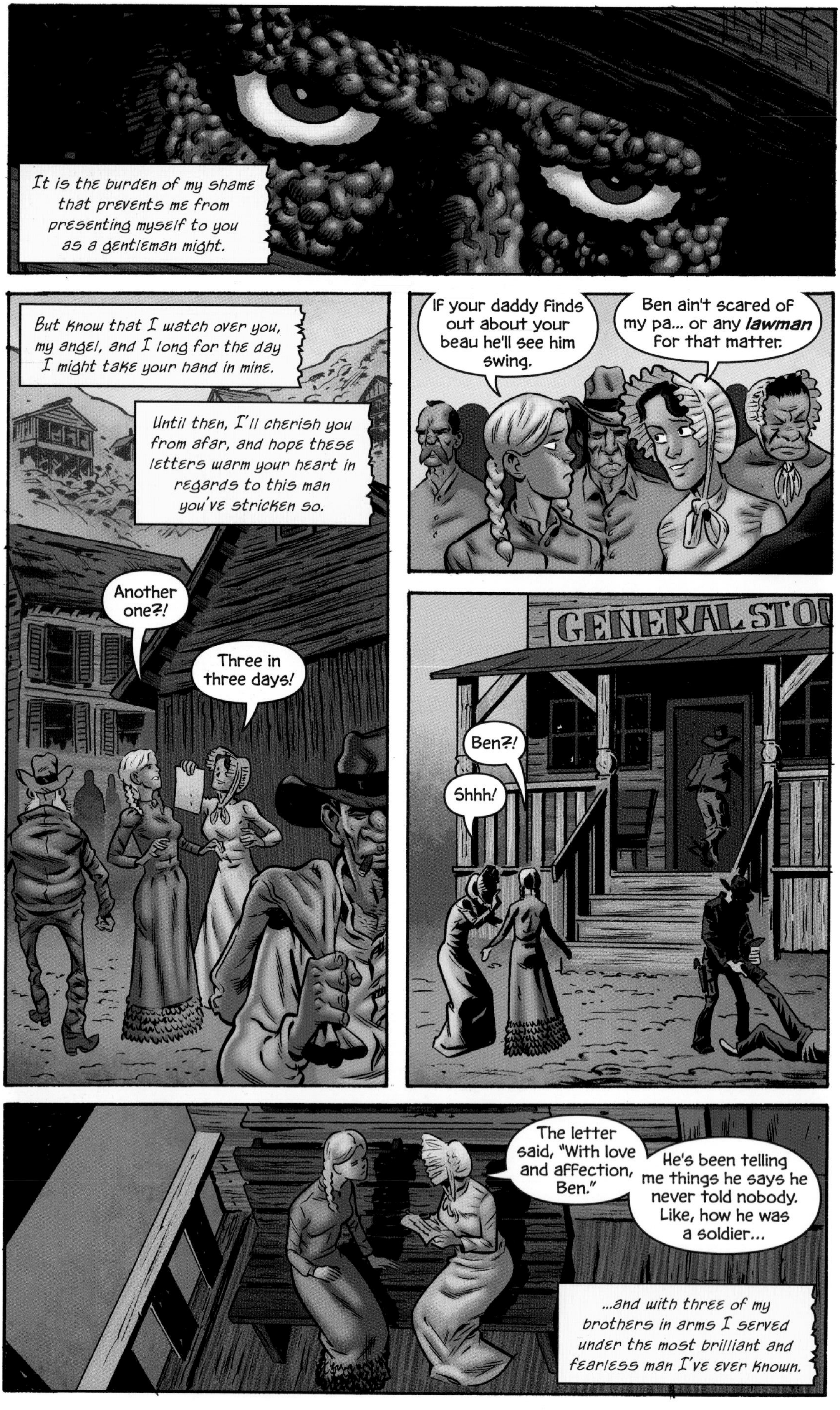
It is the burden of my shame that prevents me from presenting myself to you as a gentleman might.
But know that I watch over you, my angel, and I long for the day I might take your hand in mine.
Until then, I'll cherish you from afar, and hope these letters warm your heart in regards to this man you've stricken so.
Another one?!
Three in three days!
If your daddy finds out about your beau he'll see him swing.
Ben ain't scared of my pa... or any ***lawman*** for that matter.
GENERAL STO
Ben?!
Shhh!
The letter said, "With love and affection, Ben."
He's been telling me things he says he never told nobody. Like, how he was a soldier...
...and with three of my brothers in arms I served under the most brilliant and fearless man I've ever known.

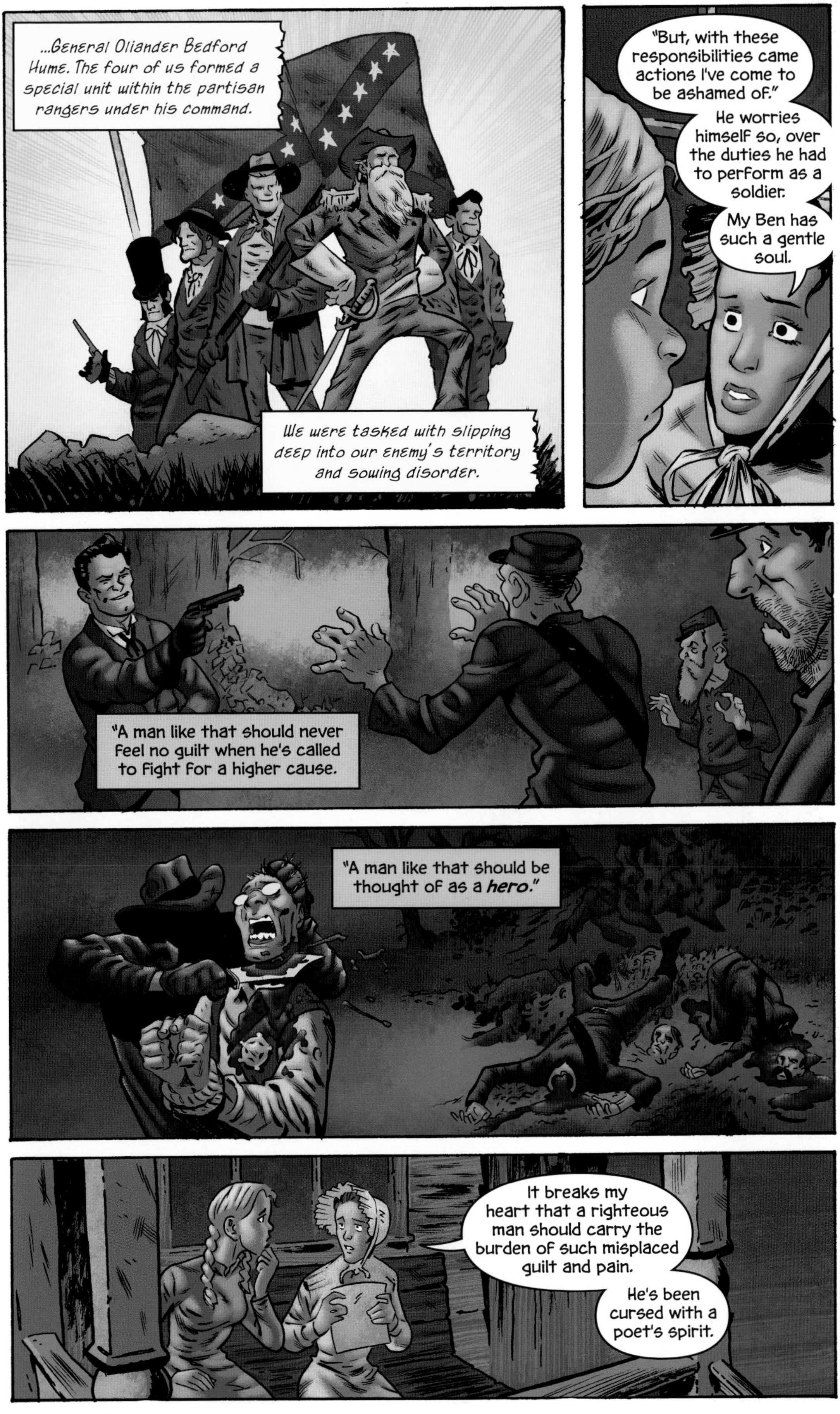
...General Oliander Bedford Hume. The four of us formed a special unit within the partisan rangers under his command.
We were tasked with slipping deep into our enemy's territory and sowing disorder.
"But, with these responsibilities came actions I've come to be ashamed of."
He worries himself so, over the duties he had to perform as a soldier.
My Ben has such a gentle soul.
"A man like that should never feel no guilt when he's called to fight for a higher cause.
"A man like that should be thought of as a *hero*."
It breaks my heart that a righteous man should carry the burden of such misplaced guilt and pain.
He's been cursed with a poet's spirit.

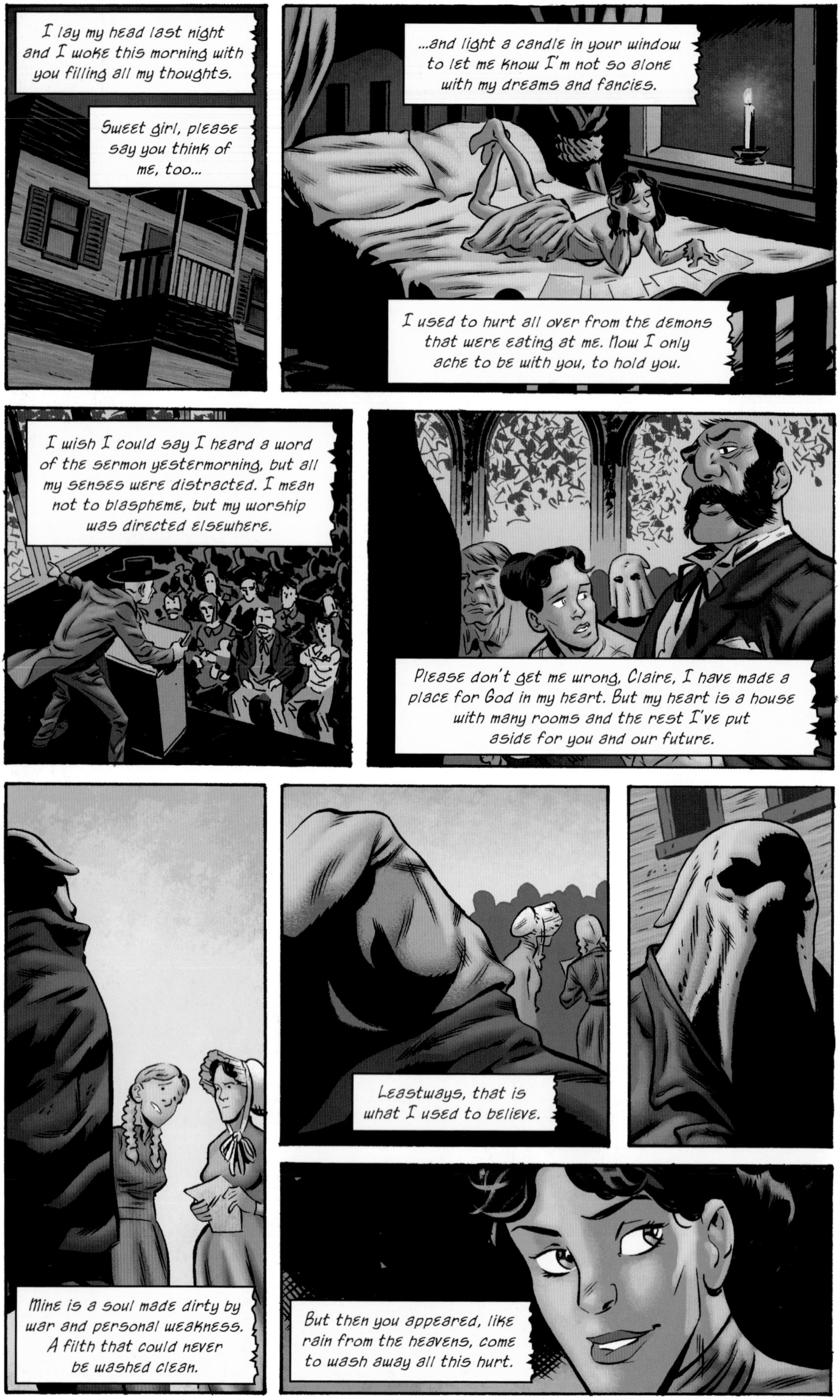
I lay my head last night and I woke this morning with you filling all my thoughts.
Sweet girl, please say you think of me, too...
...and light a candle in your window to let me know I'm not so alone with my dreams and fancies.
I used to hurt all over from the demons that were eating at me. Now I only ache to be with you, to hold you.
I wish I could say I heard a word of the sermon yestermorning, but all my senses were distracted. I mean not to blaspheme, but my worship was directed elsewhere.
Please don't get me wrong, Claire, I have made a place for God in my heart. But my heart is a house with many rooms and the rest I've put aside for you and our future.
Mine is a soul made dirty by war and personal weakness. A filth that could never be washed clean.
Leastways, that is what I used to believe.
But then you appeared, like rain from the heavens, come to wash away all this hurt.

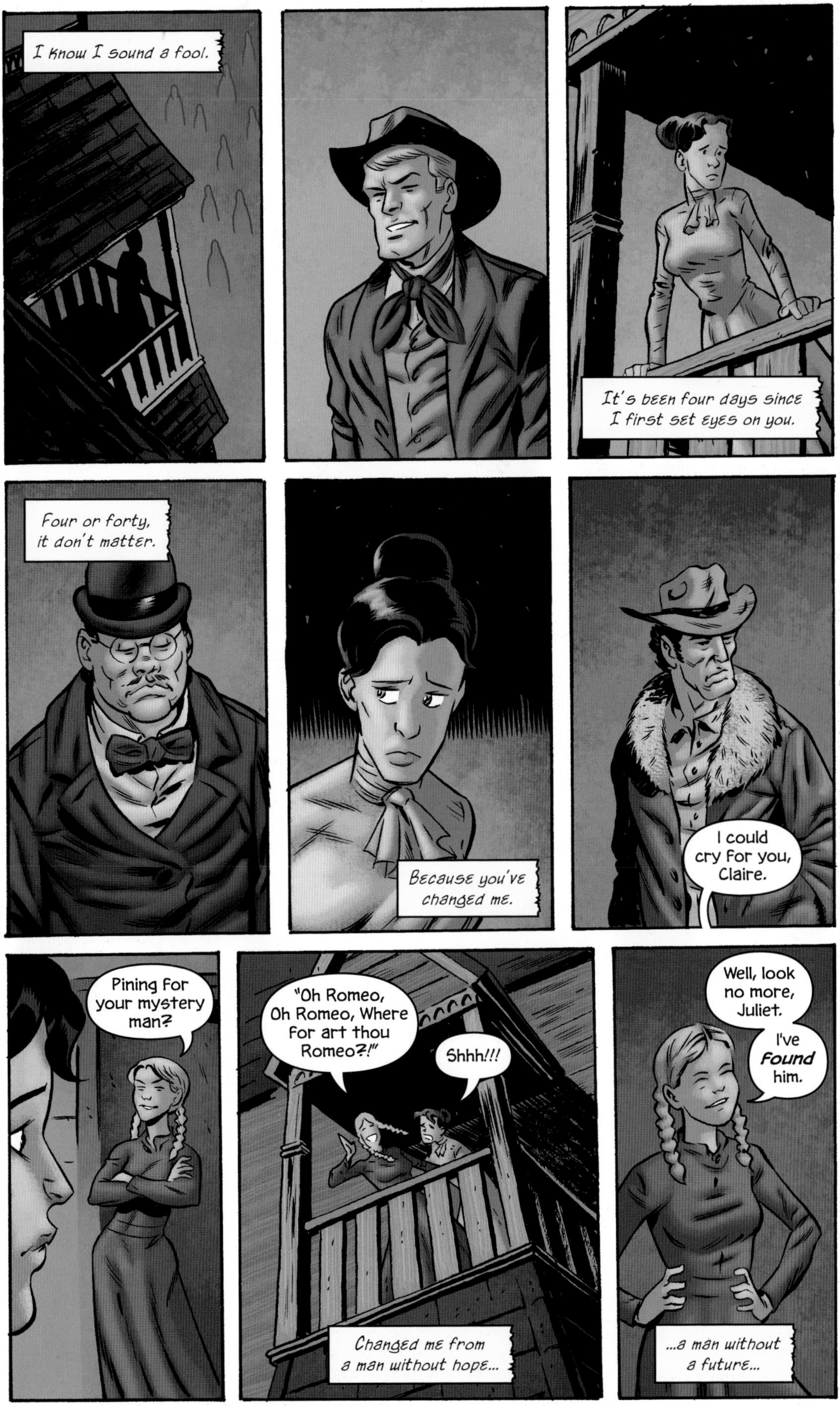
I know I sound a fool.
It's been four days since I first set eyes on you.
Four or forty, it don't matter.
Because you've changed me.
I could cry for you, Claire.
Pining for your mystery man?
"Oh Romeo, Oh Romeo, Where for art thou Romeo?!"
Shhh!!!
Changed me from a man without hope...
Well, look no more, Juliet.
I've ***found*** him.
...a man without a future...

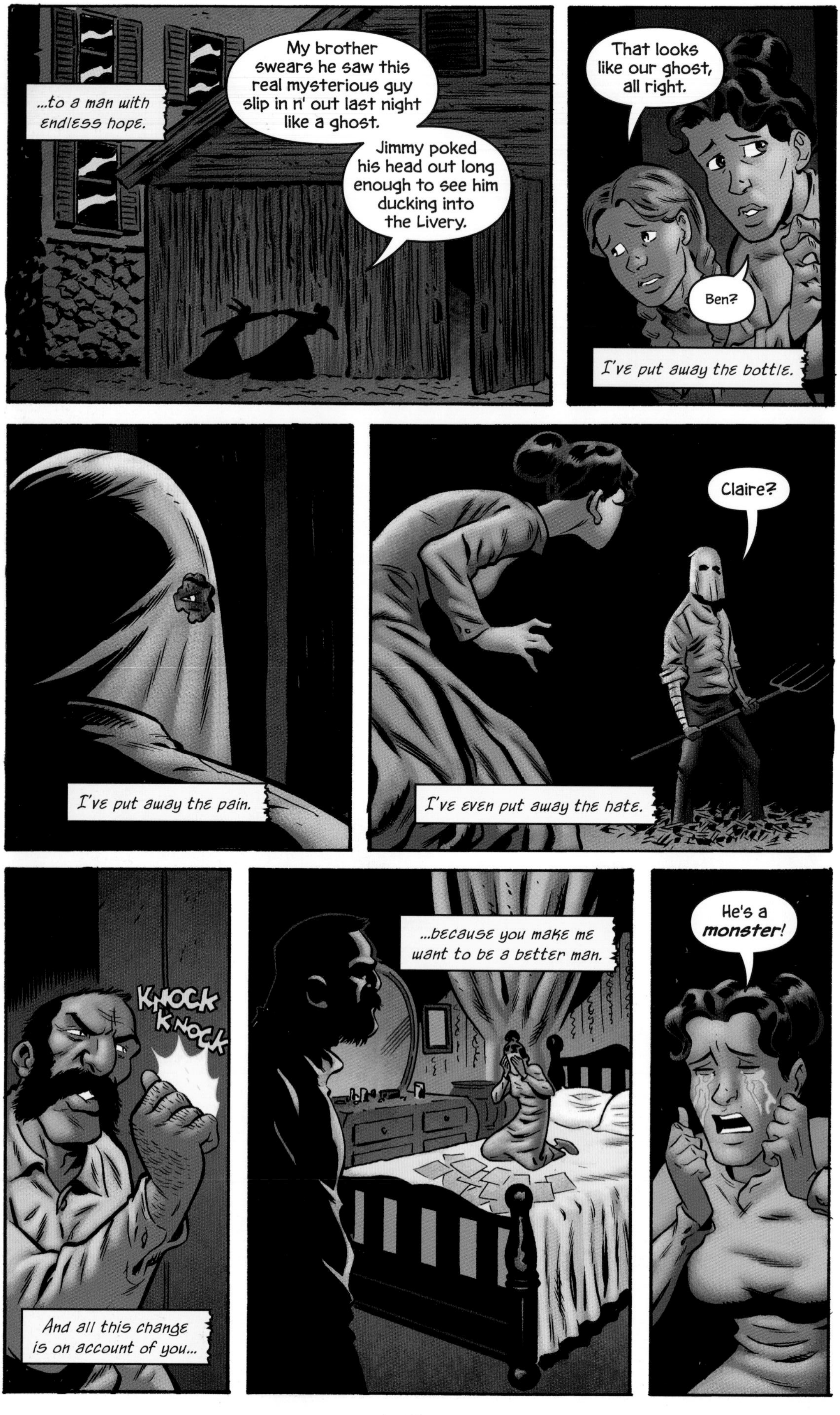
...to a man with endless hope.
My brother swears he saw this real mysterious guy slip in n' out last night like a ghost.
Jimmy poked his head out long enough to see him ducking into the Livery.
That looks like our ghost, all right.
Ben?
I've put away the bottle.
I've put away the pain.
I've even put away the hate.
Claire?
KNOCK KNOCK
And all this change is on account of you...
...because you make me want to be a better man.
He's a **monster**!

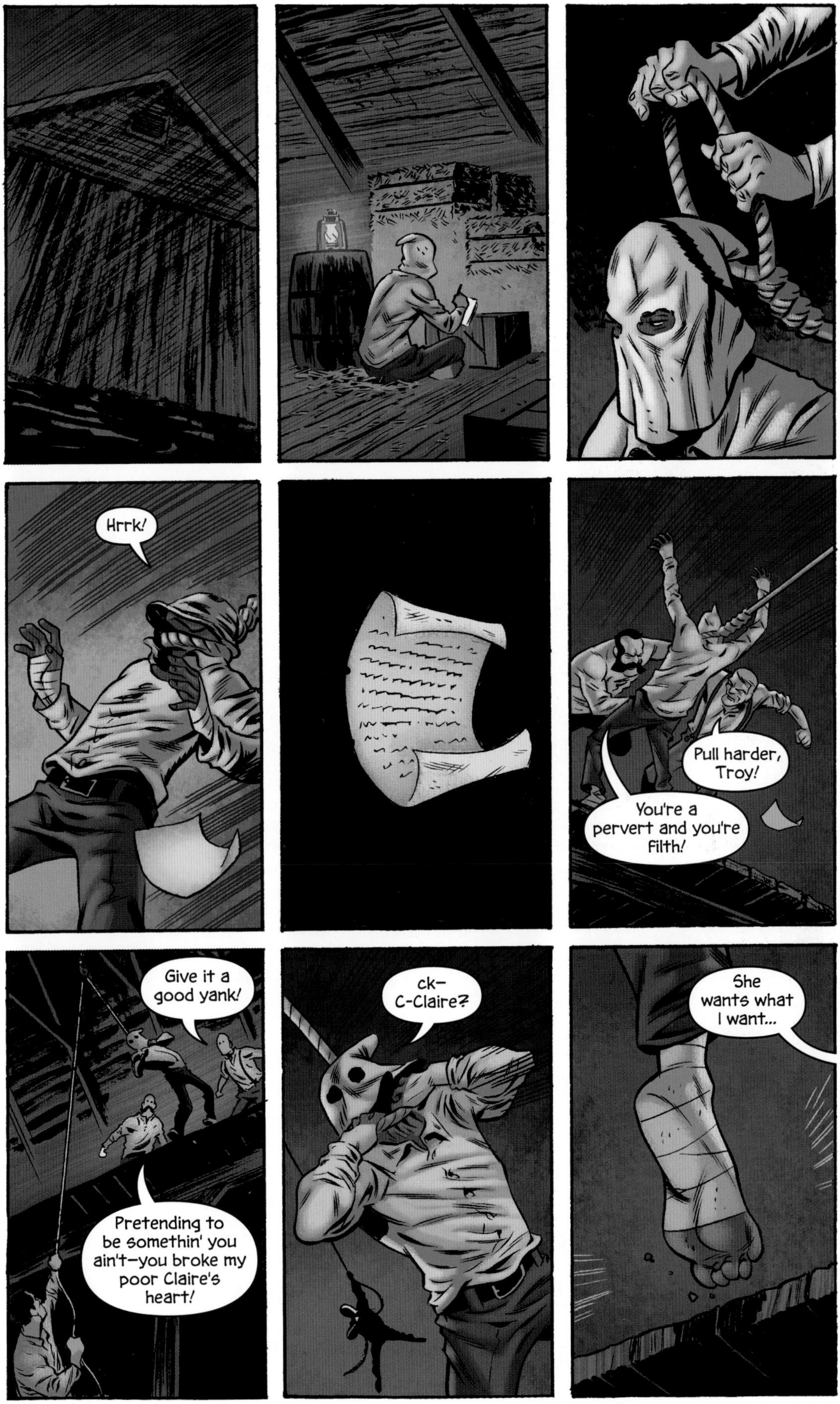
Hrrk!
Pull harder, Troy!
You're a pervert and you're filth!
Give it a good yank!
Pretending to be somethin' you ain't—you broke my poor Claire's heart!
ck— C-Claire?
She wants what I want...

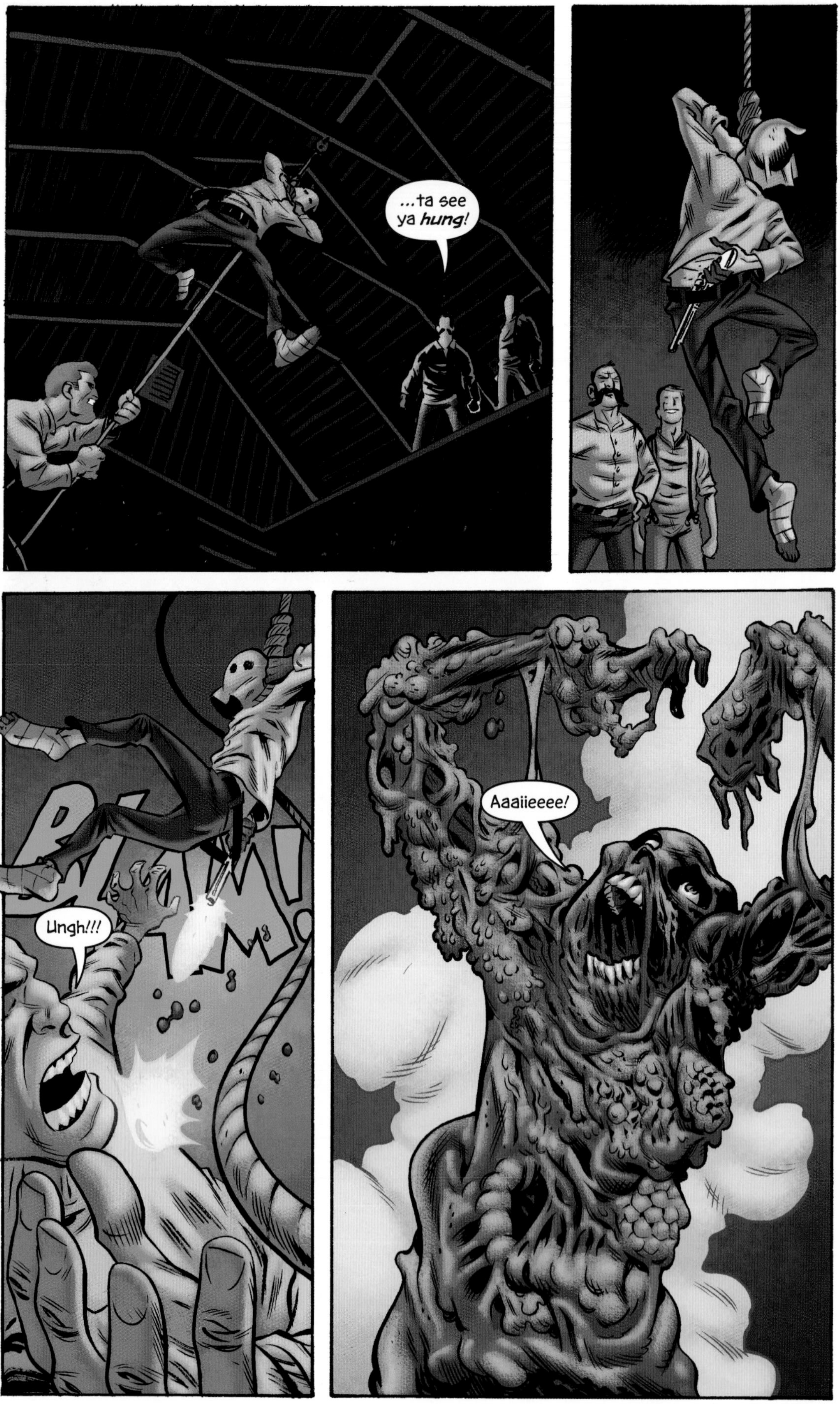
...ta see ya *hung*!
Ungh!!!
Aaaiieeee!

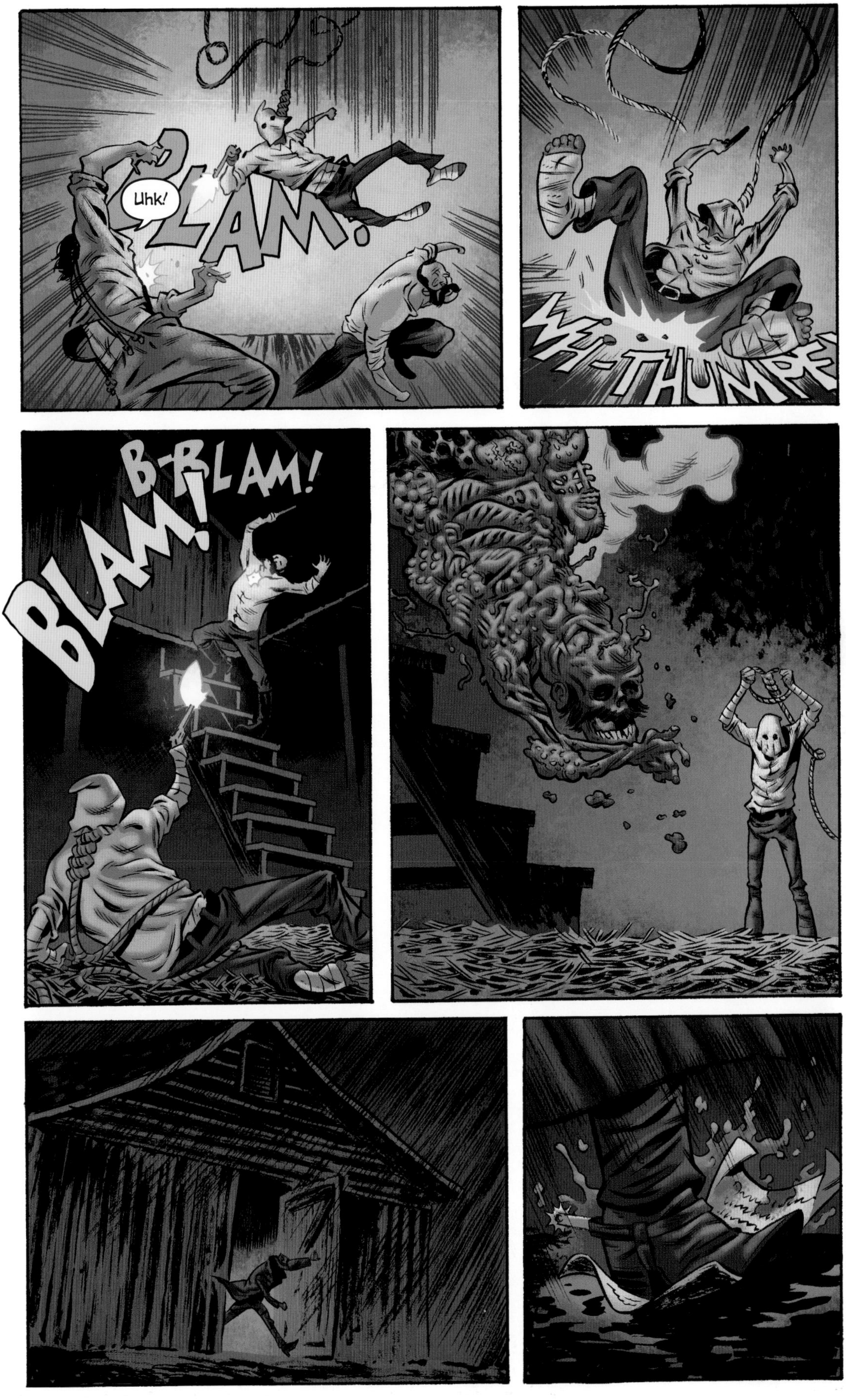
BLAM!
Uhk!
WH-THUMPF!
BLAM! B-BLAM!

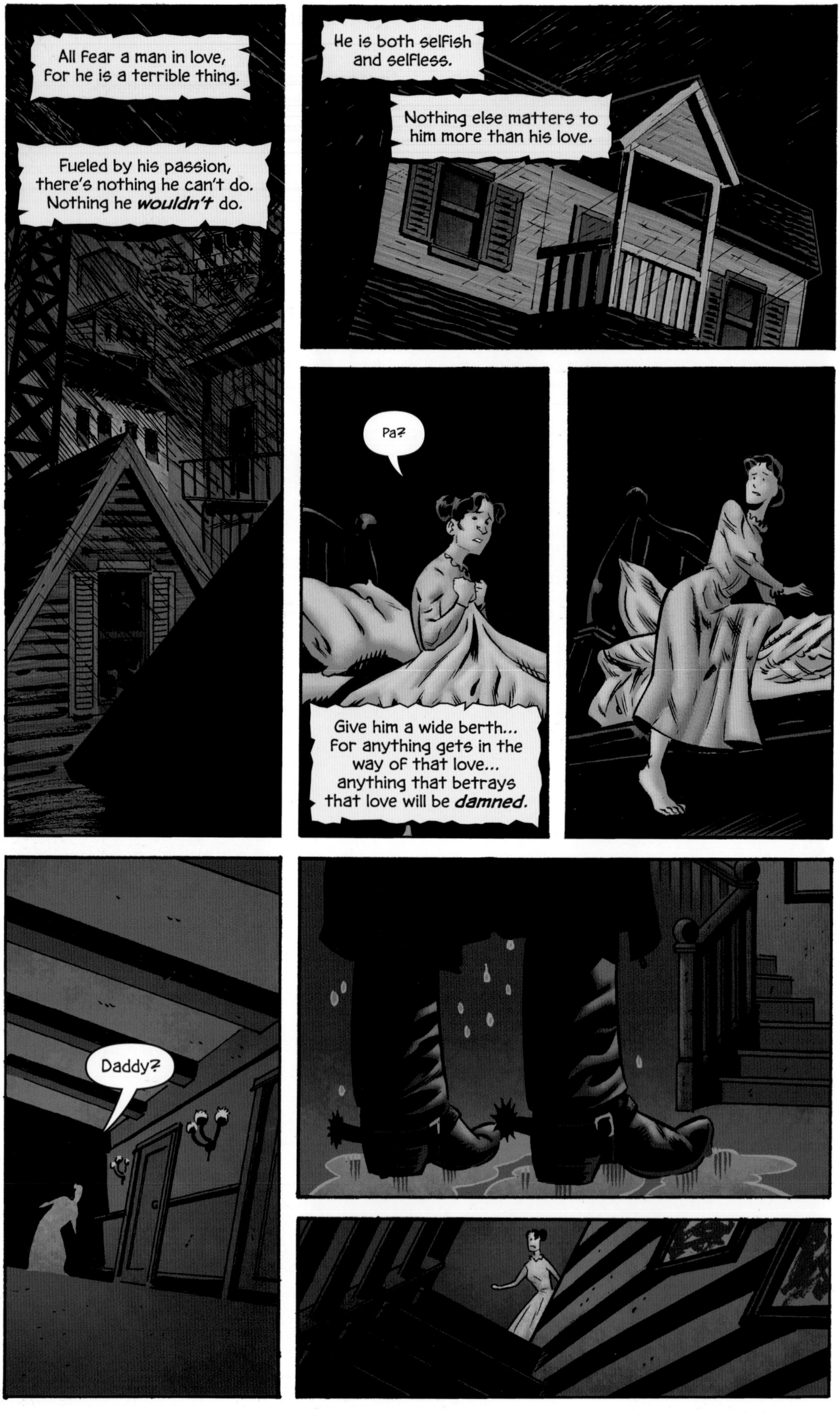
All fear a man in love,
for he is a terrible thing.
Fueled by his passion,
there's nothing he can't do.
Nothing he ***wouldn't*** do.
He is both selfish
and selfless.
Nothing else matters to
him more than his love.
Pa?
Give him a wide berth...
for anything gets in the
way of that love...
anything that betrays
that love will be ***damned.***
Daddy?

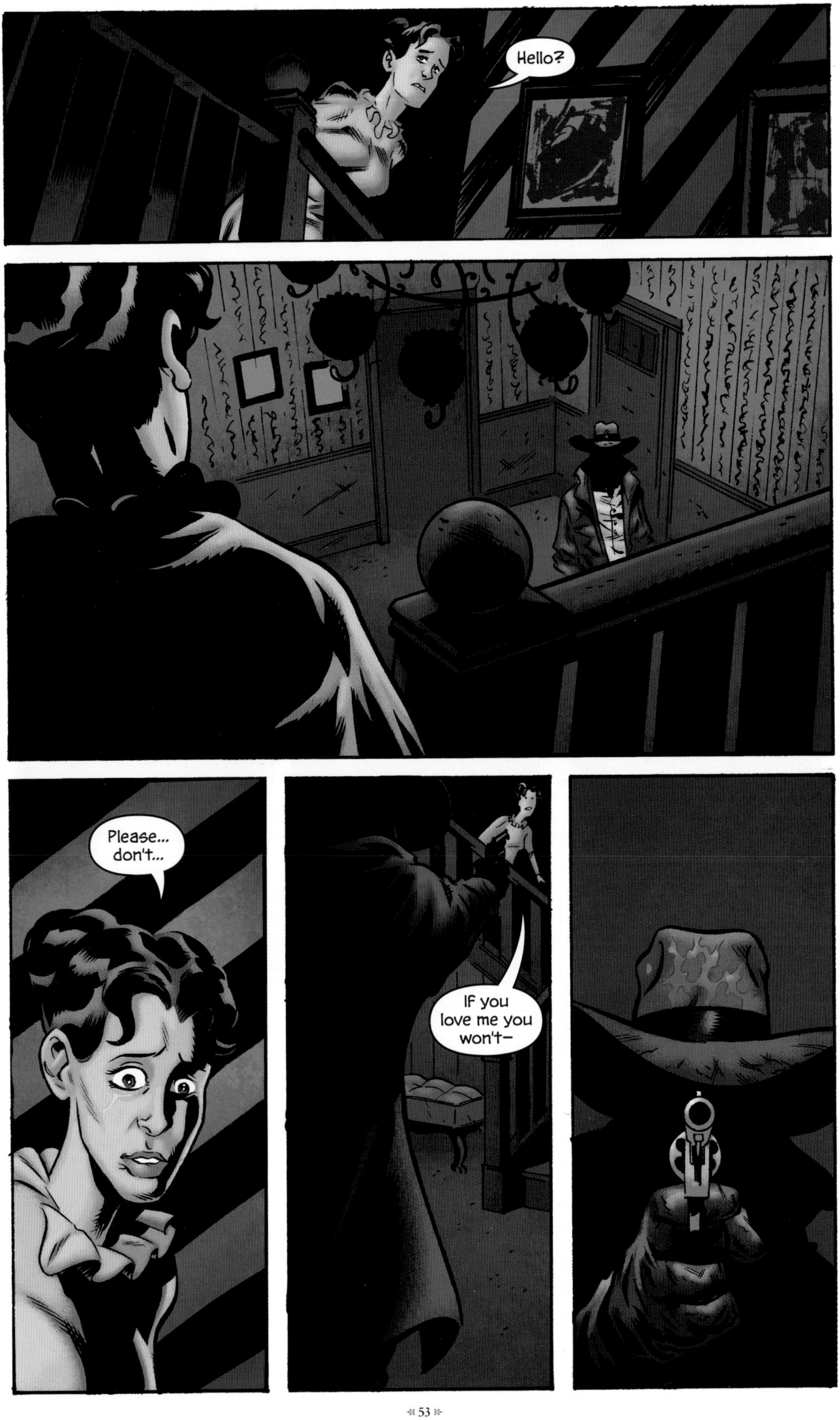
Hello?
Please... don't...
If you love me you won't–

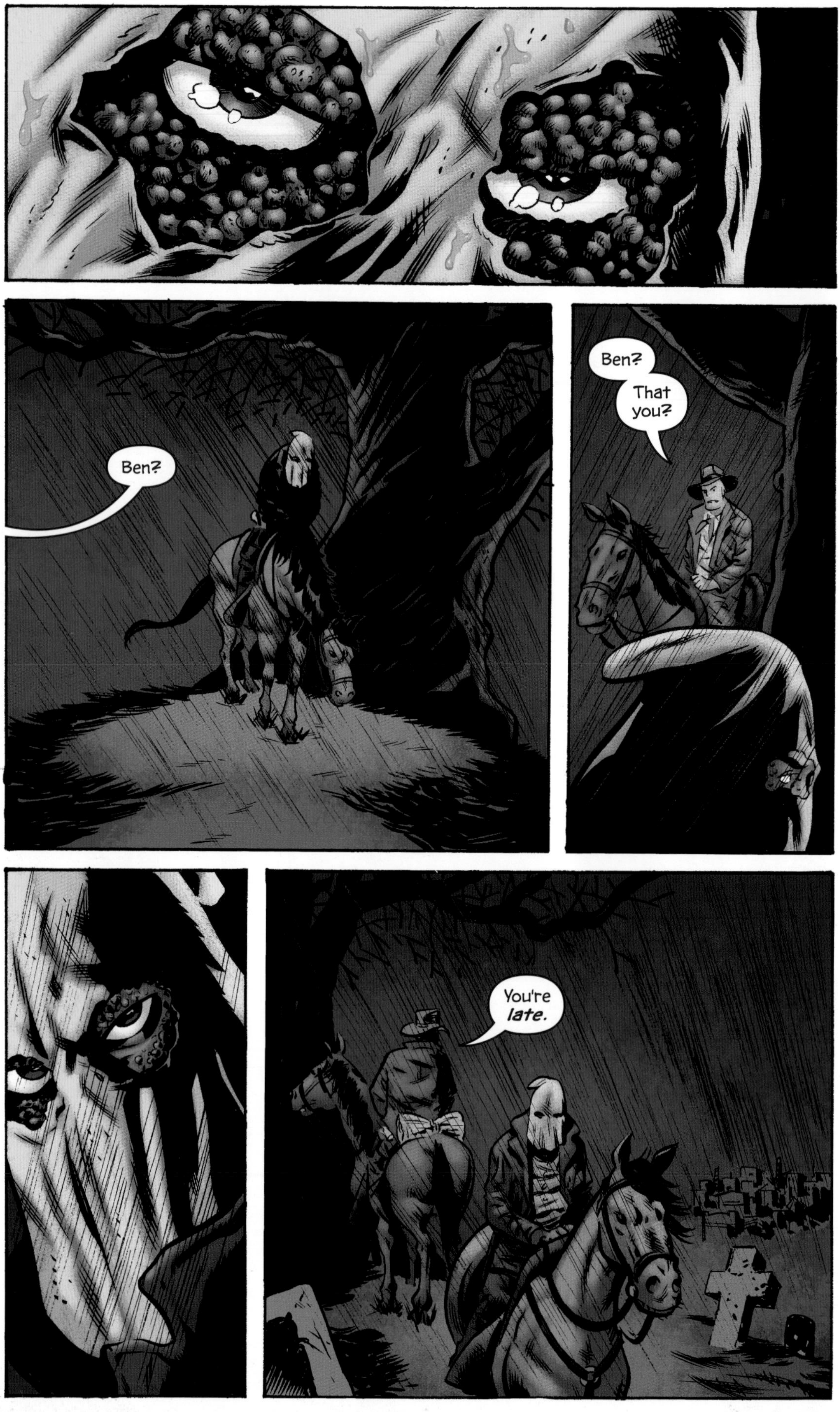
Ben?
Ben?
That you?
You're *late.*

CHAPTER THREE

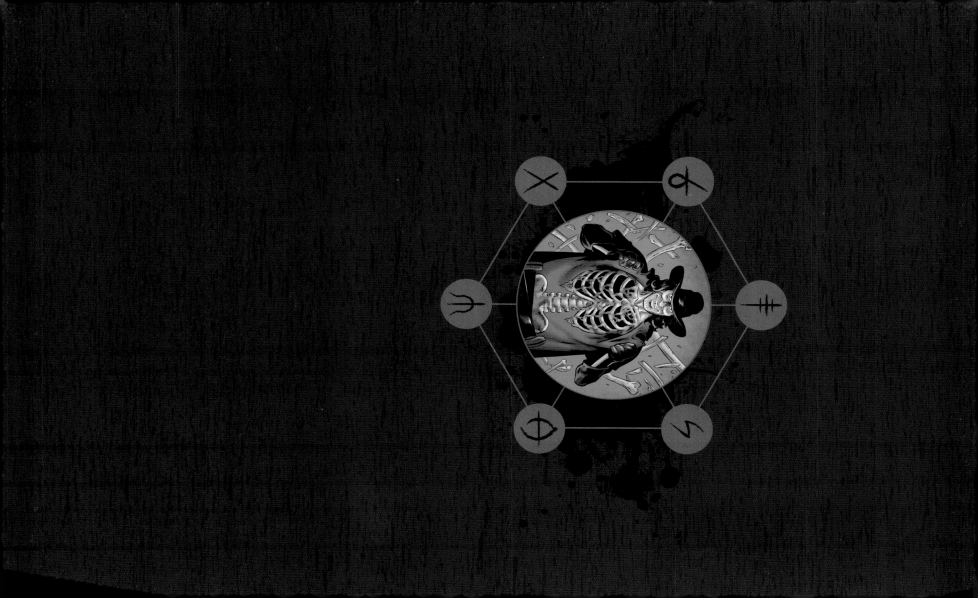

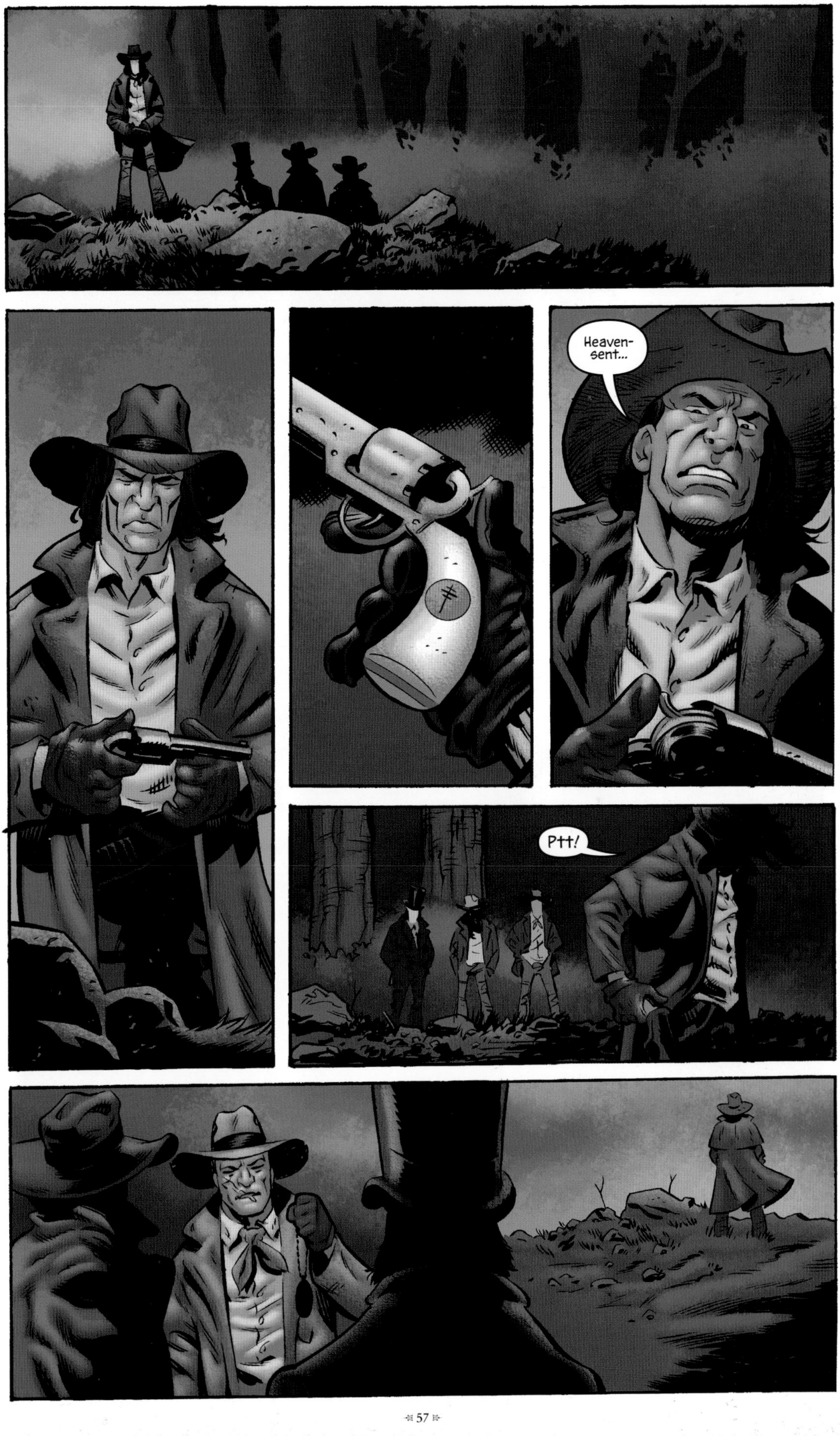
Heaven-sent...
Ptt!

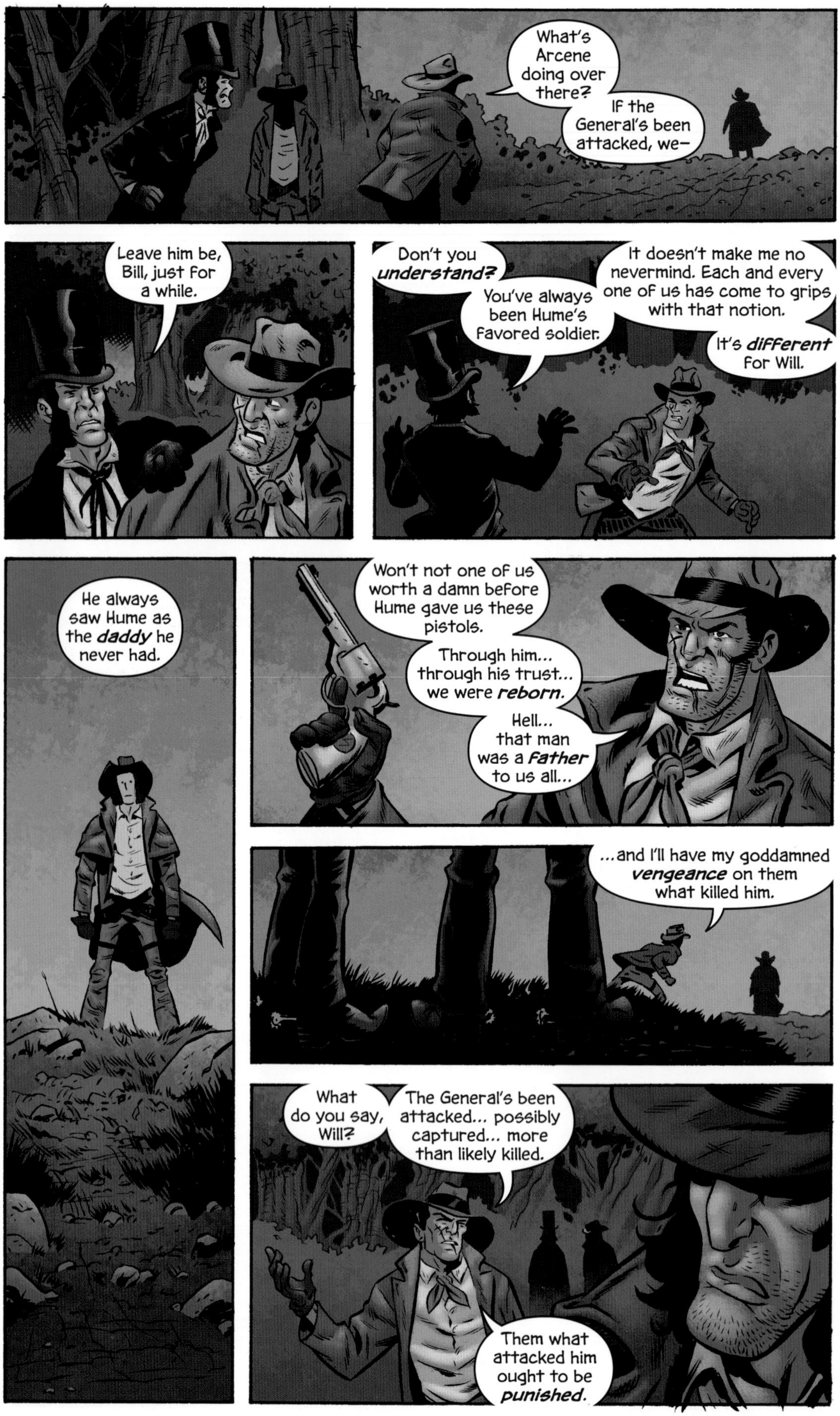
What's Arcene doing over there?
If the General's been attacked, we—
Leave him be, Bill, just for a while.
Don't you *understand?*
You've always been Hume's favored soldier.
It doesn't make me no nevermind. Each and every one of us has come to grips with that notion.
It's *different* for Will.
He always saw Hume as the *daddy* he never had.
Won't not one of us worth a damn before Hume gave us these pistols.
Through him... through his trust... we were *reborn.*
Hell... that man was a *father* to us all...
...and I'll have my goddamned *vengeance* on them what killed him.
What do you say, Will?
The General's been attacked... possibly captured... more than likely killed.
Them what attacked him ought to be *punished.*

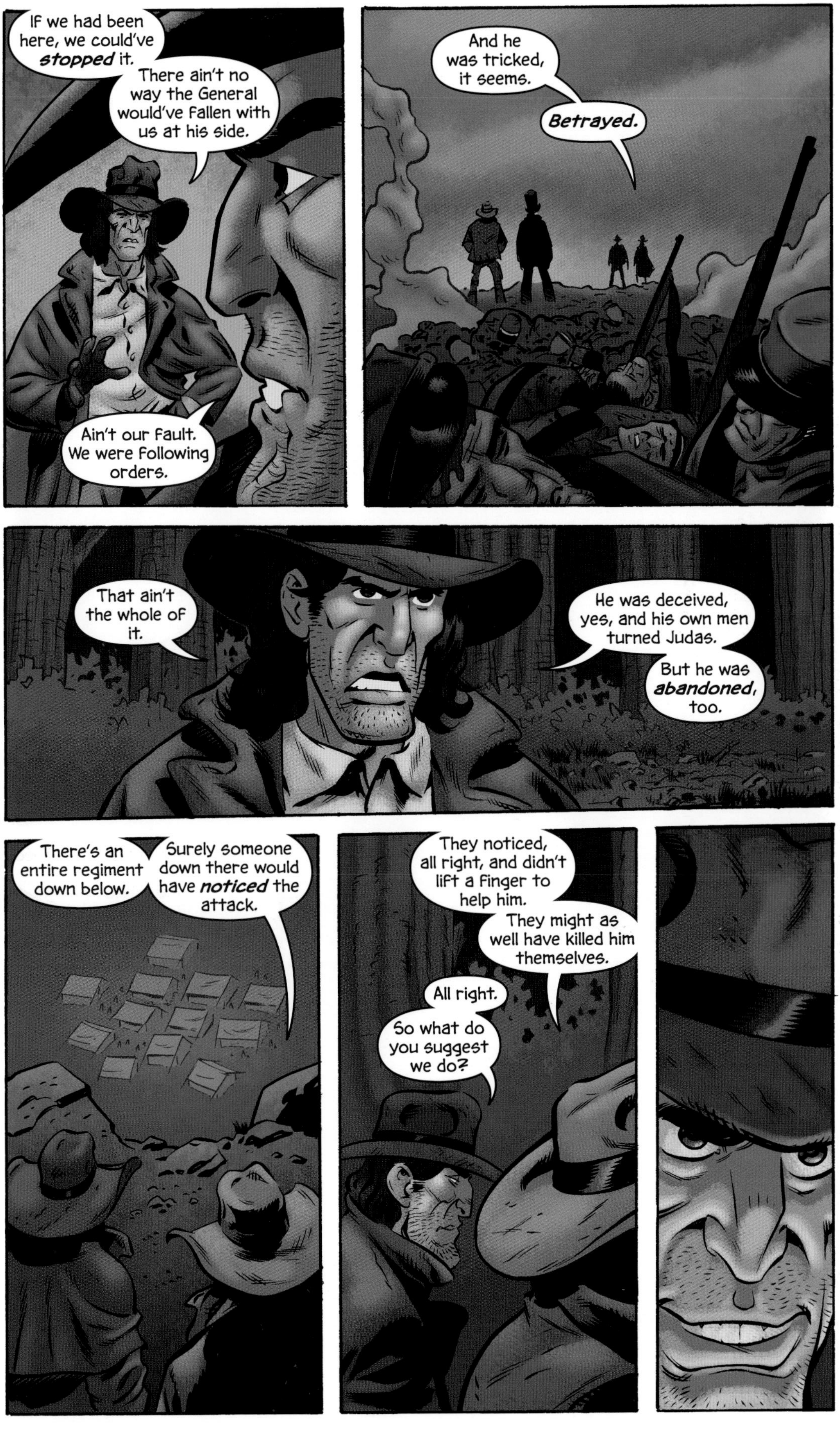
If we had been here, we could've ***stopped*** it.
There ain't no way the General would've fallen with us at his side.
Ain't our fault. We were following orders.
And he was tricked, it seems.
Betrayed.
That ain't the whole of it.
He was deceived, yes, and his own men turned Judas.
But he was ***abandoned,*** too.
There's an entire regiment down below.
Surely someone down there would have ***noticed*** the attack.
They noticed, all right, and didn't lift a finger to help him.
They might as well have killed him themselves.
All right.
So what do you suggest we do?

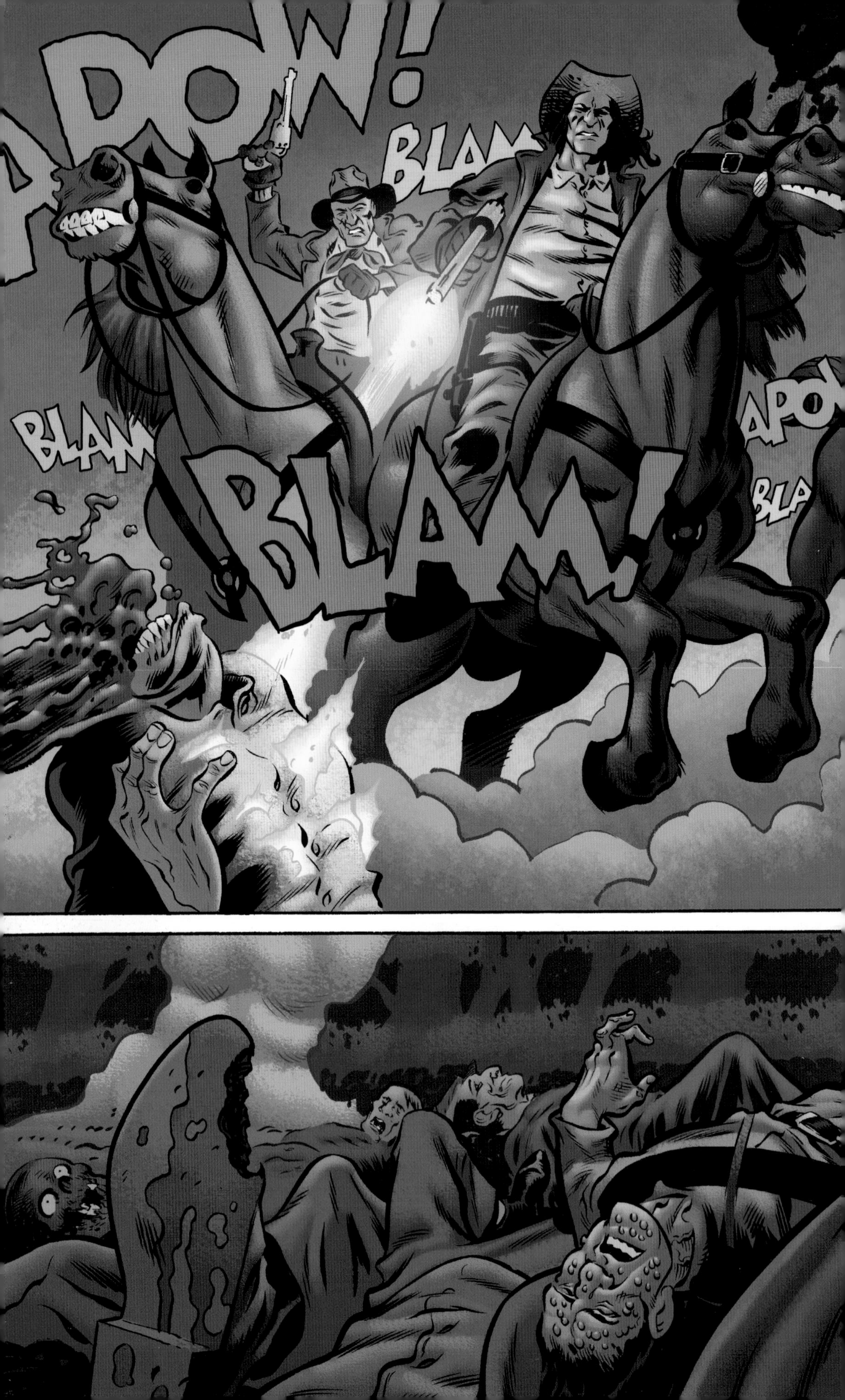
DOW!
BLAM
BLAM
BLAM!
APO
BLA

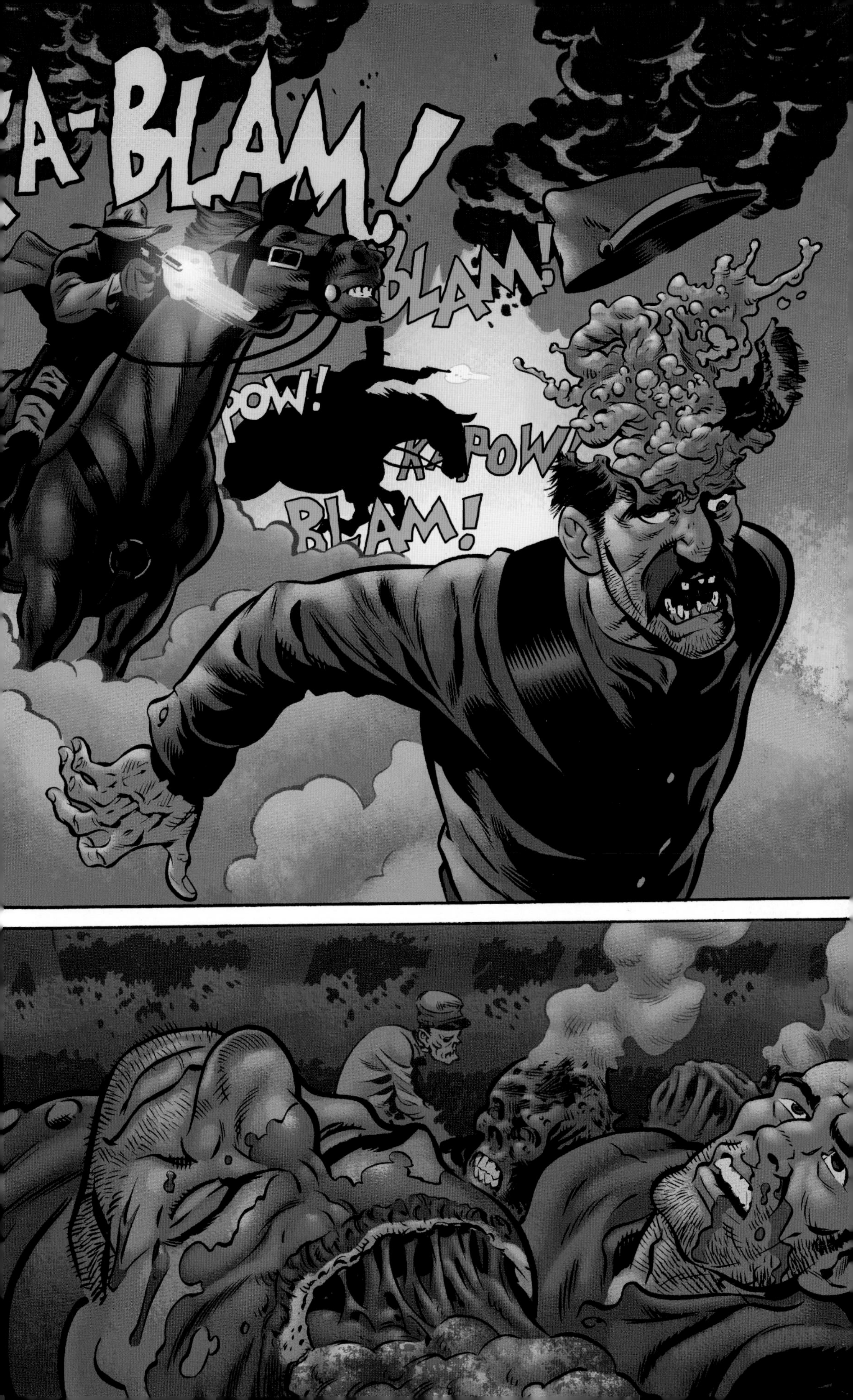

A-BLAM!
BLAM!
POW!
KA-POW!
BLAM!

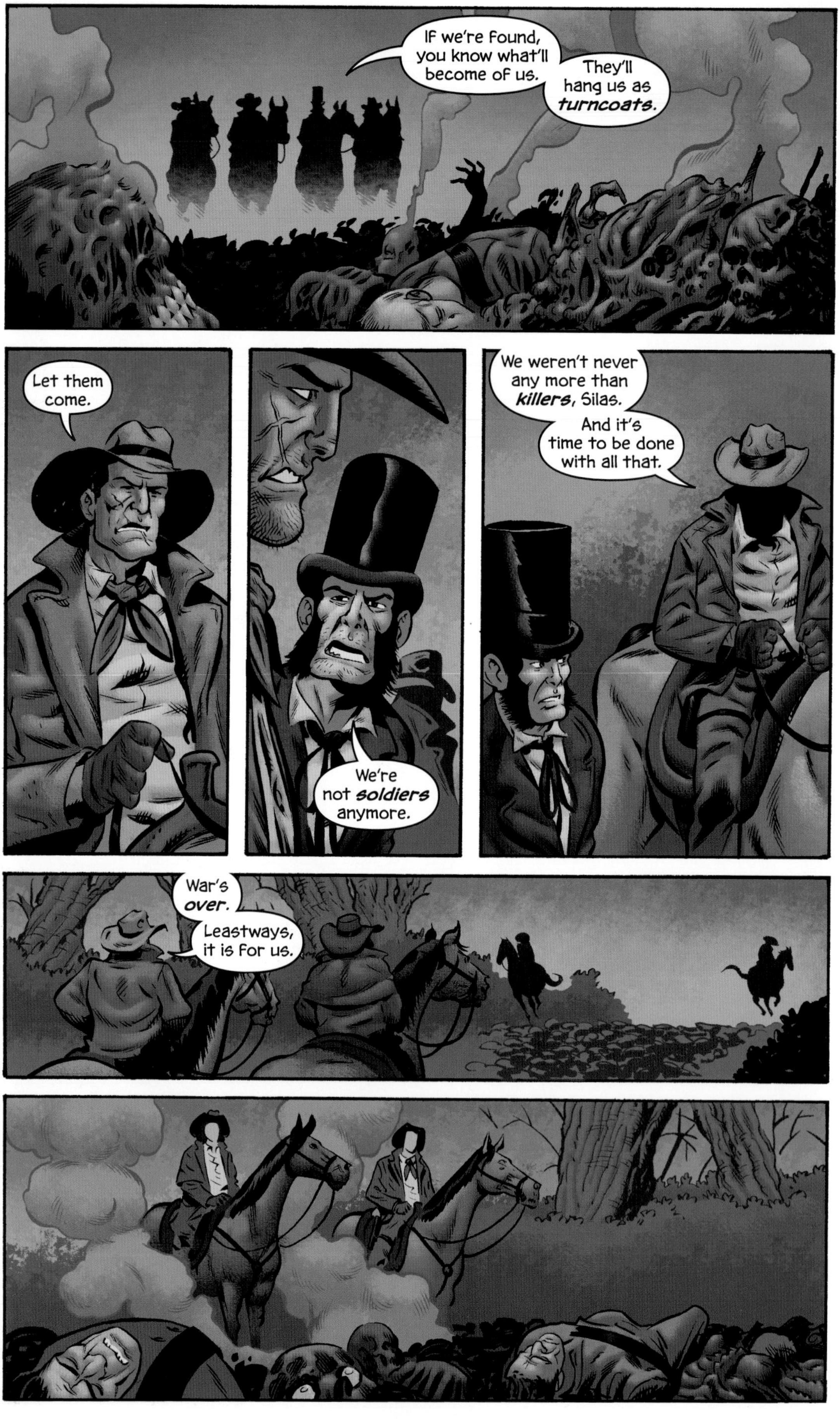
If we're found, you know what'll become of us.
They'll hang us as *turncoats*.
Let them come.
We're not *soldiers* anymore.
We weren't never any more than *killers*, Silas.
And it's time to be done with all that.
War's *over*.
Leastways, it is for us.

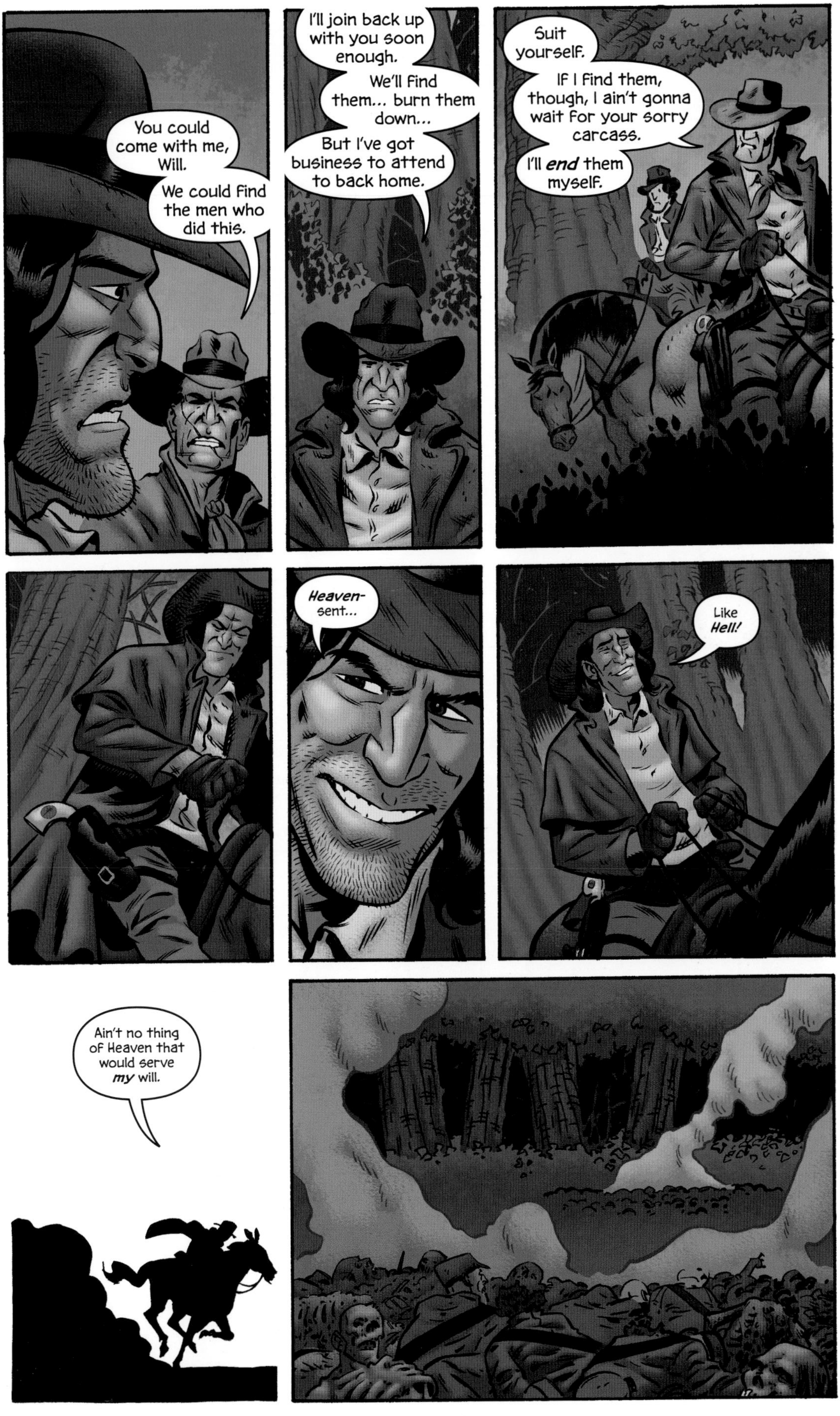
You could come with me, Will.
We could find the men who did this.
I'll join back up with you soon enough.
We'll find them... burn them down...
But I've got business to attend to back home.
Suit yourself.
If I find them, though, I ain't gonna wait for your sorry carcass.
I'll *end* them myself.
Heaven-sent...
Like *Hell!*
Ain't no thing of Heaven that would serve *my* will.

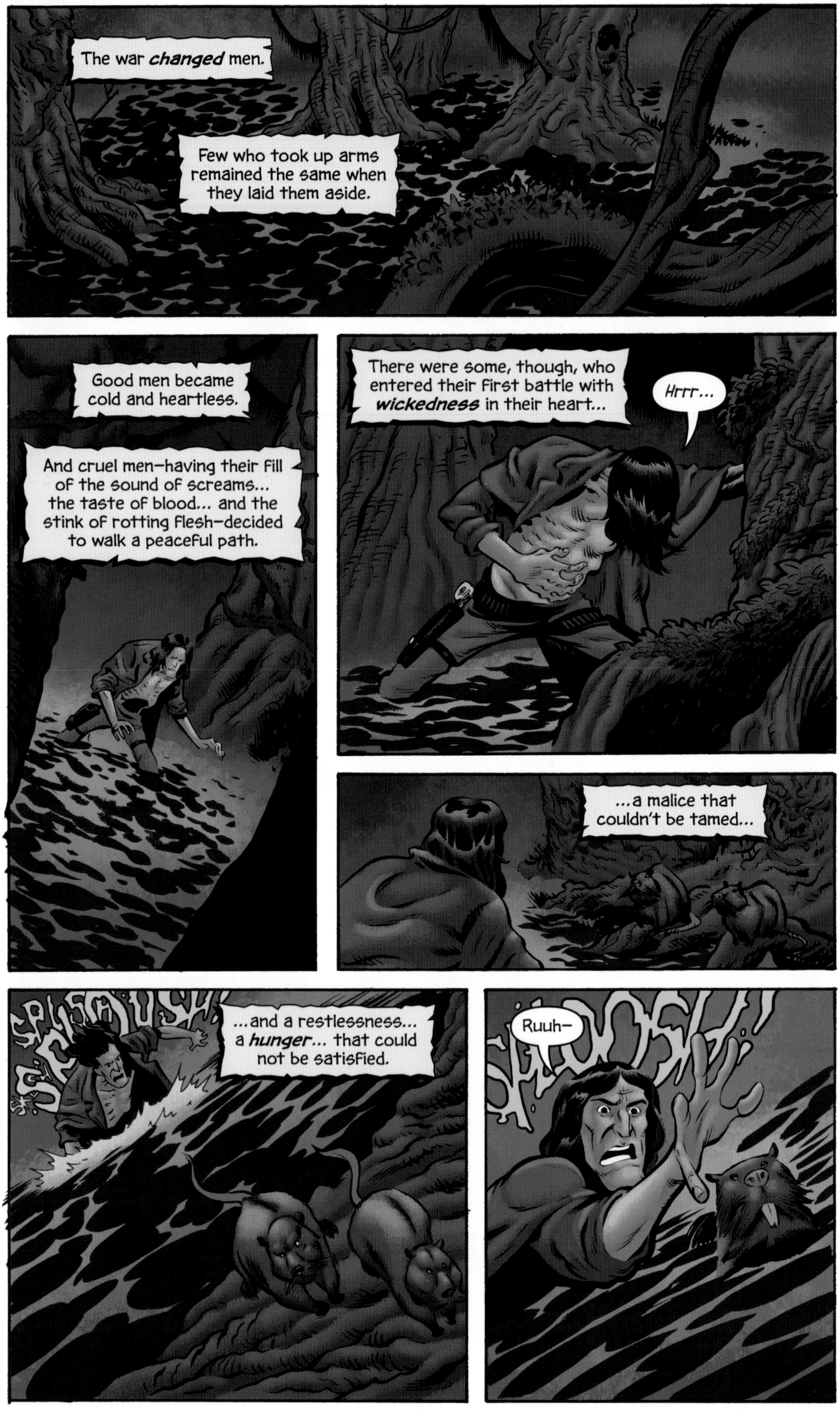
The war *changed* men.
Few who took up arms remained the same when they laid them aside.
Good men became cold and heartless.
And cruel men—having their fill of the sound of screams... the taste of blood... and the stink of rotting flesh—decided to walk a peaceful path.
There were some, though, who entered their first battle with *wickedness* in their heart...
Hrrr...
...a malice that couldn't be tamed...
...and a restlessness... a *hunger*... that could not be satisfied.
Ruuh—

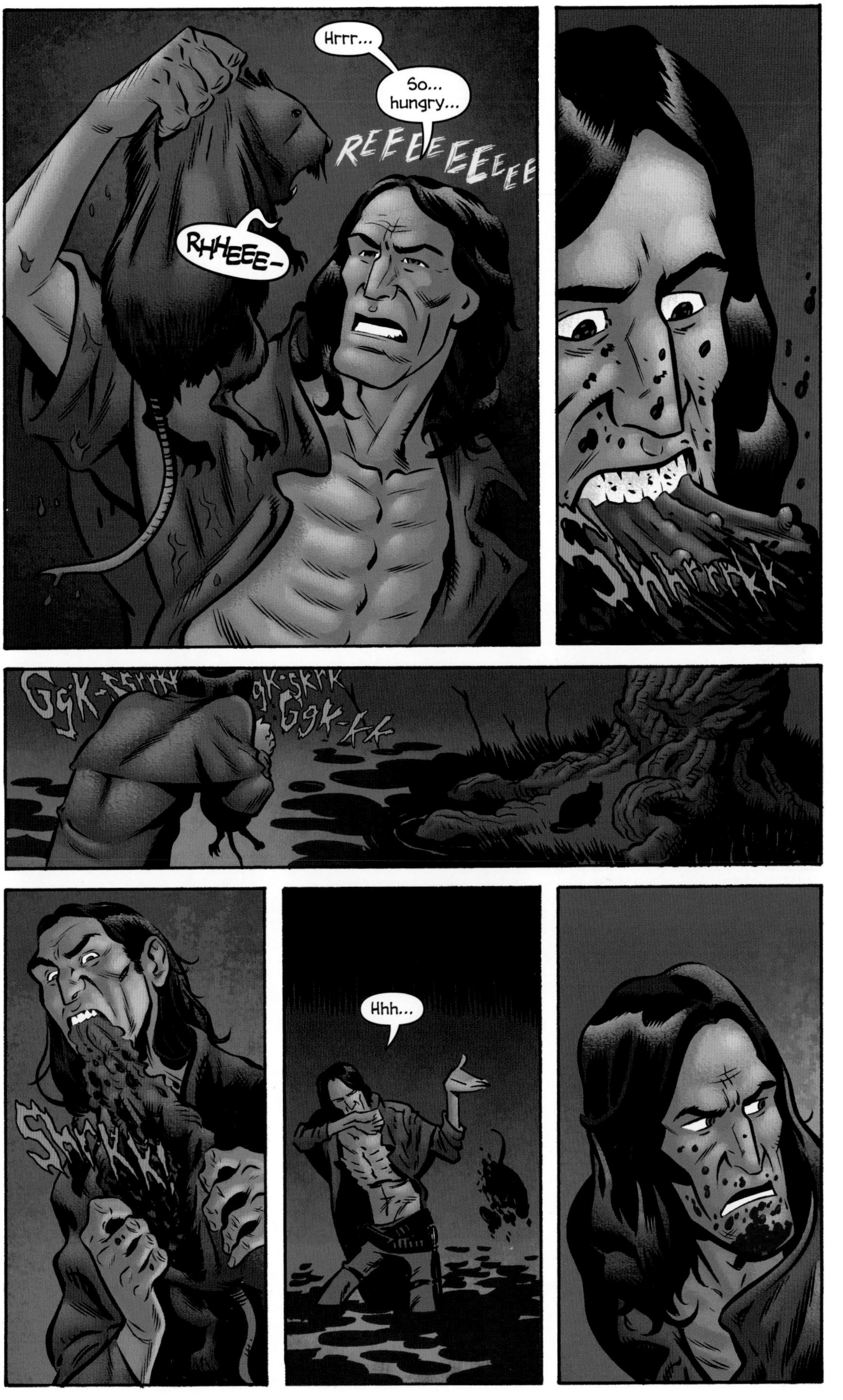
Hrrr...
So... hungry...
RHHEEE-
Hhh...

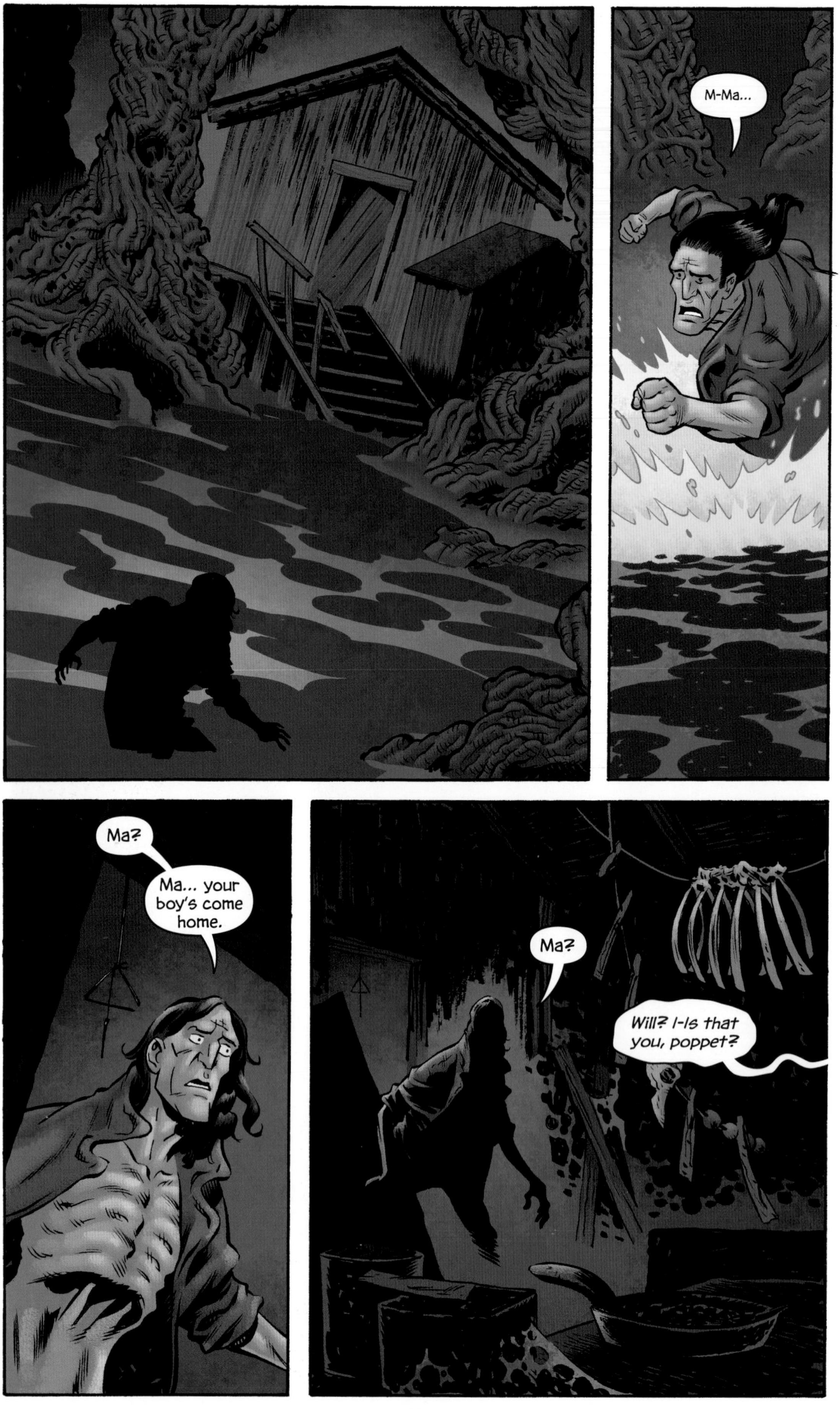
M-Ma...
Ma?
Ma... your boy's come home.
Ma?
Will? I-Is that you, poppet?

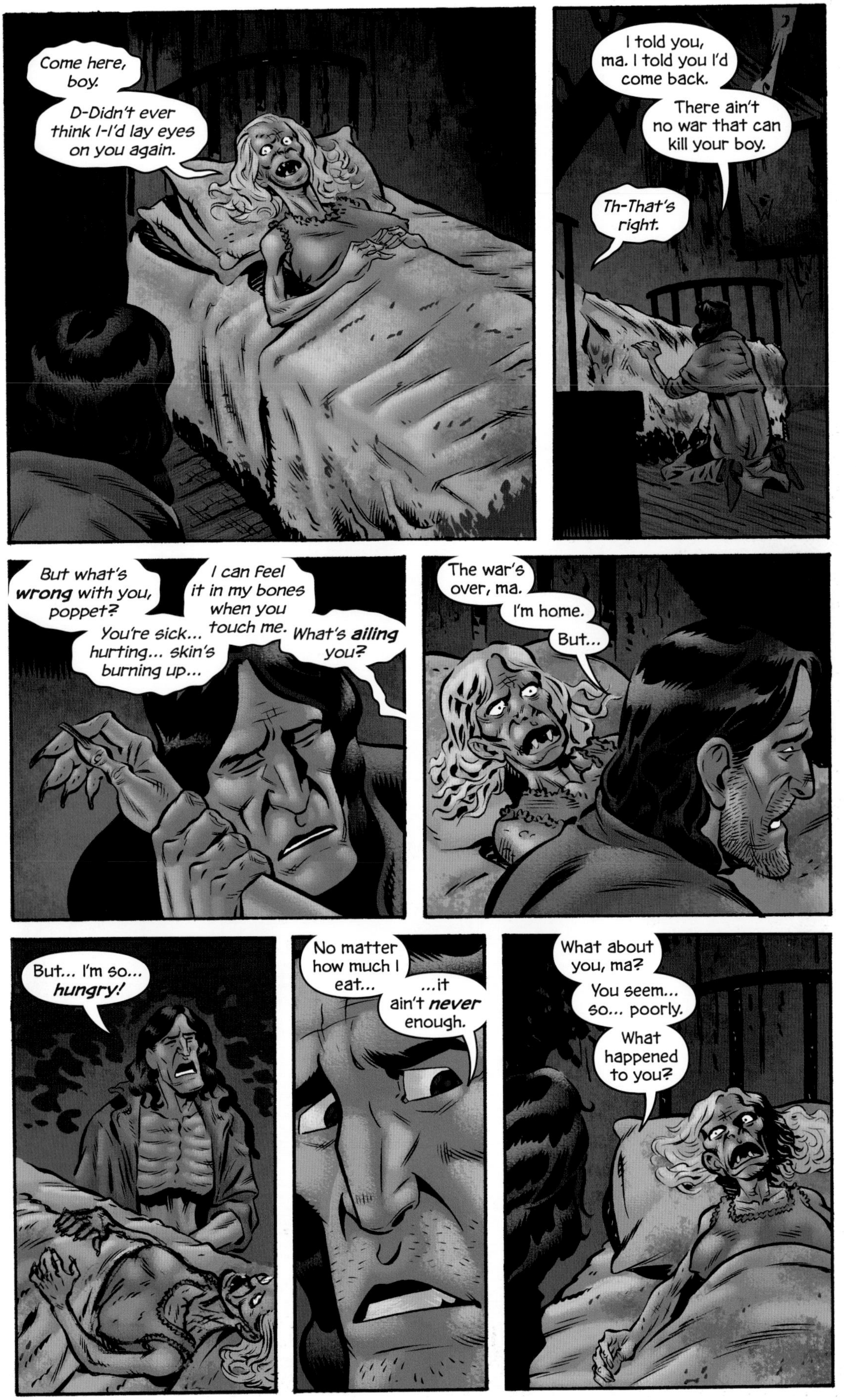
Come here, boy.
D-Didn't ever think I-I'd lay eyes on you again.
I told you, ma. I told you I'd come back.
There ain't no war that can kill your boy.
Th-That's right.
But what's **wrong** with you, poppet?
You're sick... hurting... skin's burning up...
I can feel it in my bones when you touch me.
What's **ailing** you?
The war's over, ma.
I'm home.
But...
But... I'm so... **hungry!**
No matter how much I eat...
...it ain't **never** enough.
What about you, ma?
You seem... so... poorly.
What happened to you?

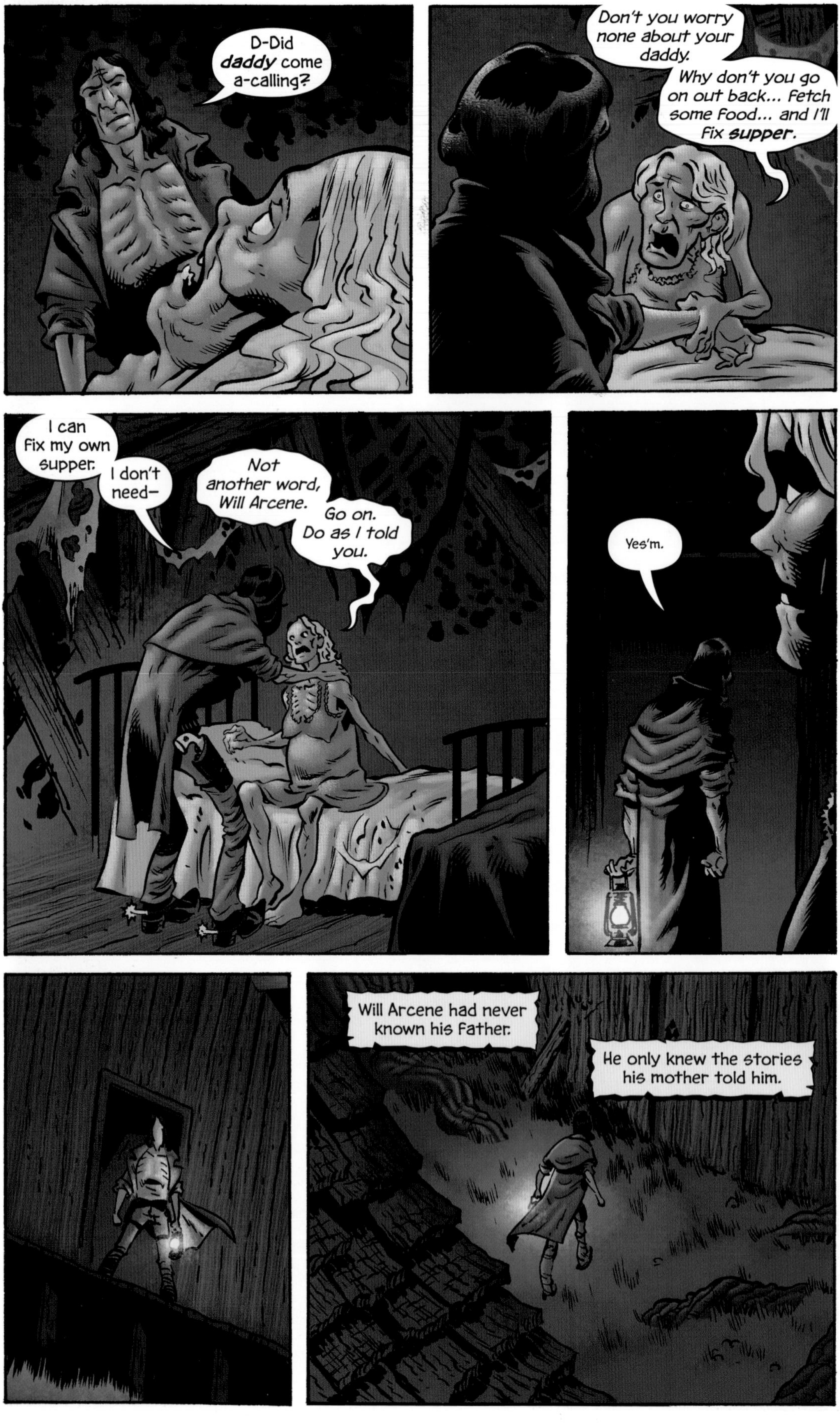
D-Did *daddy* come a-calling?
Don't you worry none about your daddy.
Why don't you go on out back... Fetch some food... and I'll fix **supper**.
I can fix my own supper.
I don't need—
Not another word, Will Arcene.
Go on. Do as I told you.
Yes'm.
Will Arcene had never known his father.
He only knew the stories his mother told him.

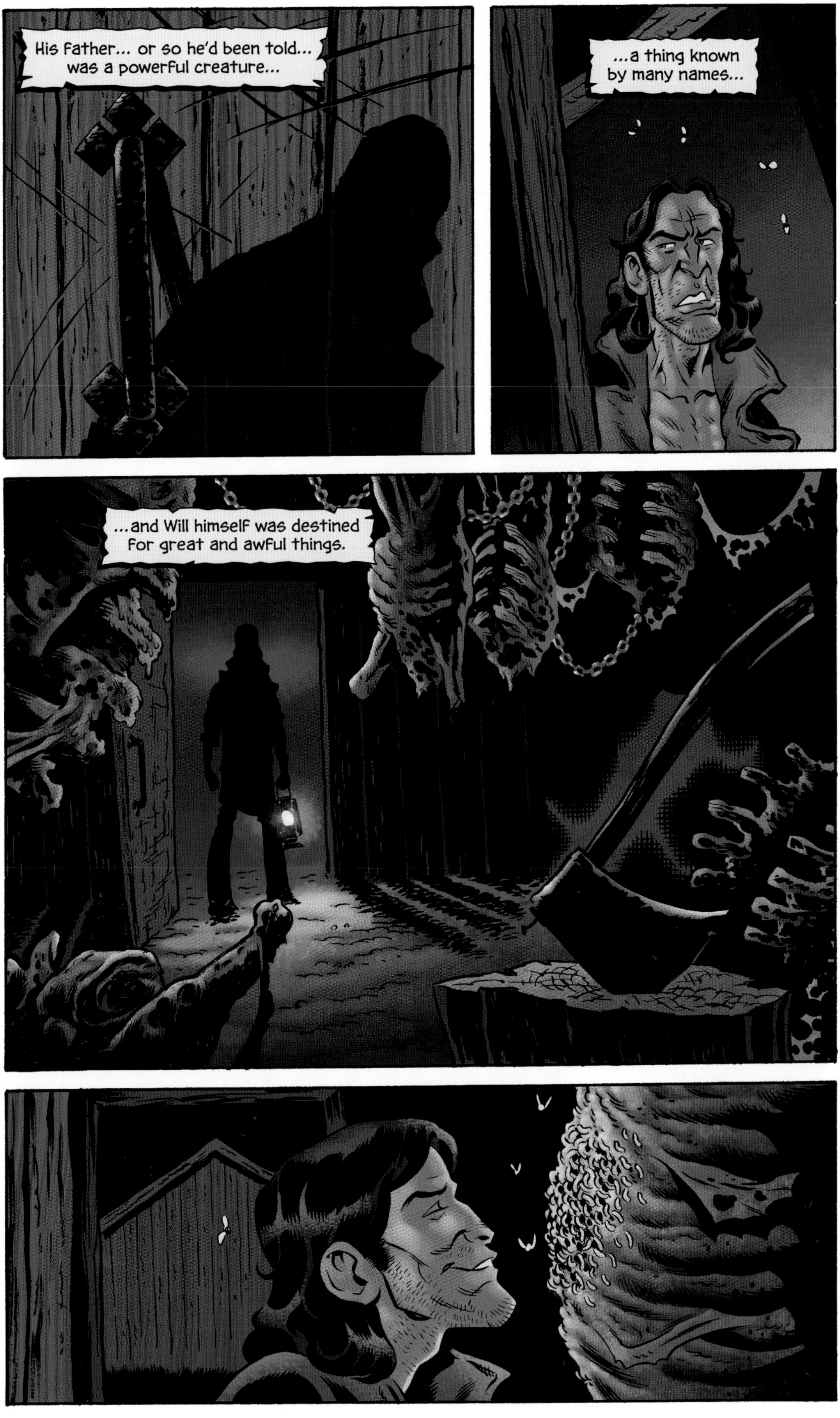
His Father... or so he'd been told... was a powerful creature...
...a thing known by many names...
...and Will himself was destined for great and awful things.

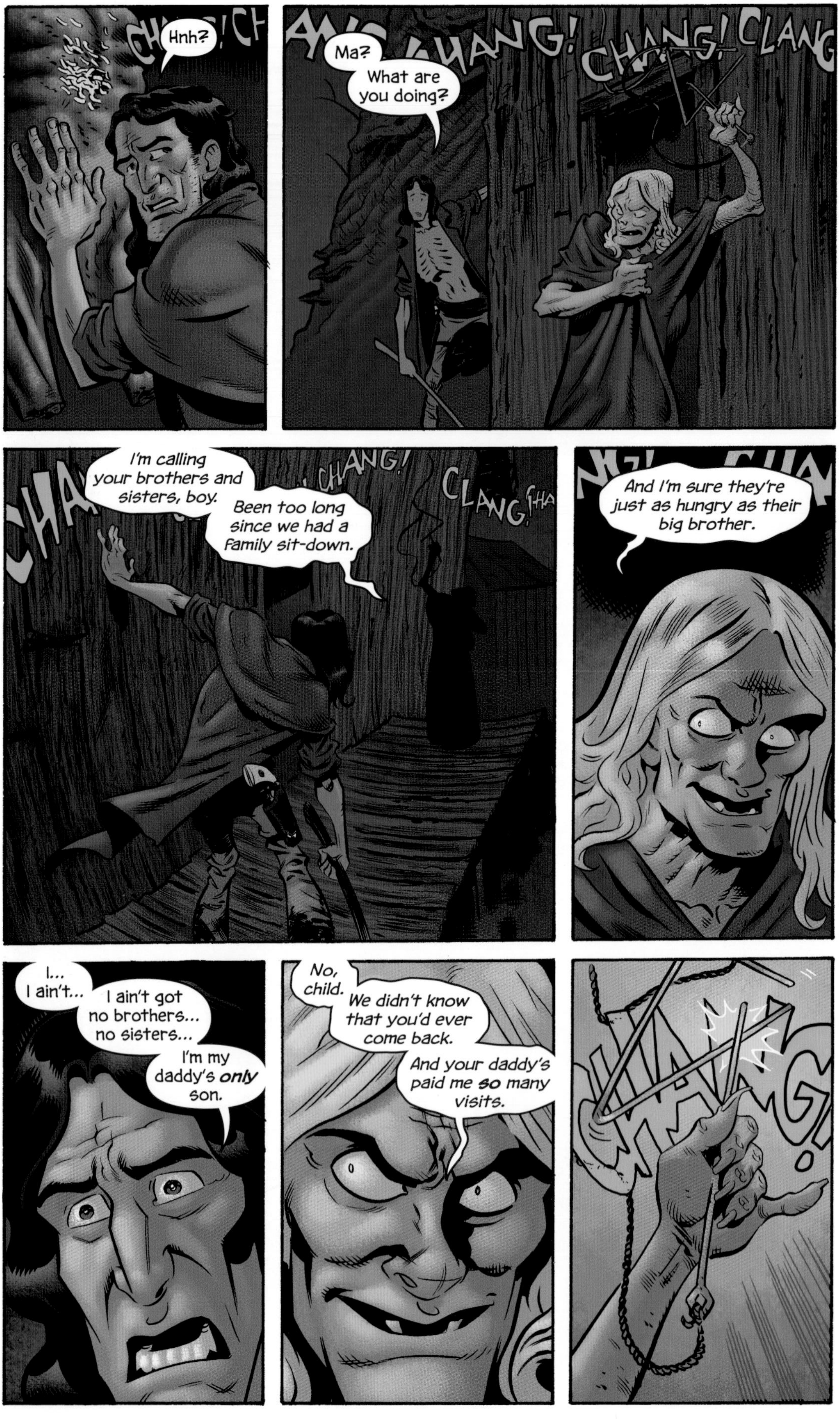
Hnh?
Ma?
What are you doing?
CHANG! CHANG! CLANG
I'm calling your brothers and sisters, boy.
Been too long since we had a family sit-down.
CHANG! CLANG!
And I'm sure they're just as hungry as their big brother.
I... I ain't...
I ain't got no brothers... no sisters...
I'm my daddy's **only** son.
No, child.
We didn't know that you'd ever come back.
And your daddy's paid me **so** many visits.
CHANG!

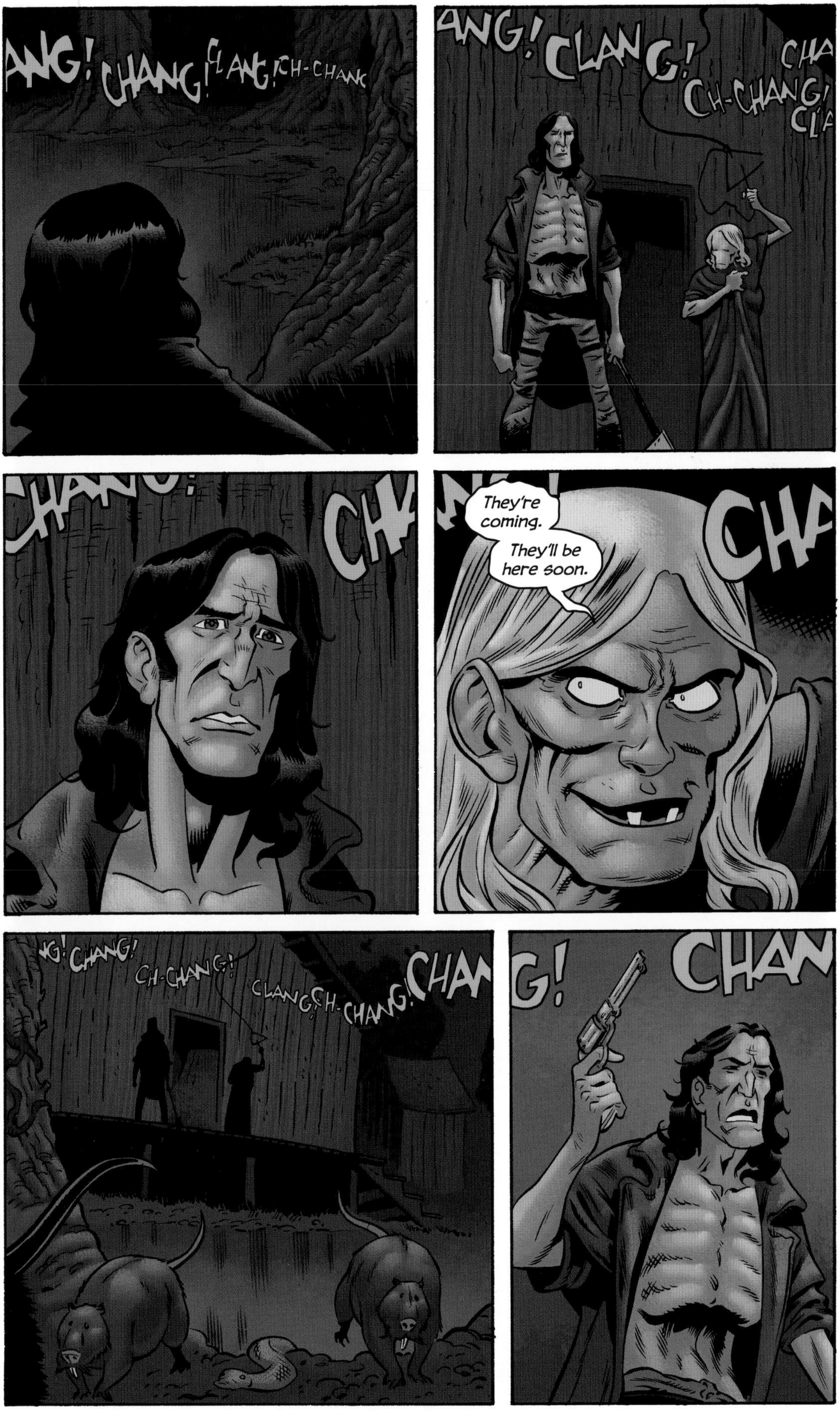
ANG! CHANG! CLANG! CH-CHANG
ANG! CLANG!
CHA
CH-CHANG!
CL'A
CHANG!
CHA
They're coming.
They'll be here soon.
CHA
NG! CHANG!
CH-CHANG!
CLANG! CH-CHANG! CHANG!
CHAN

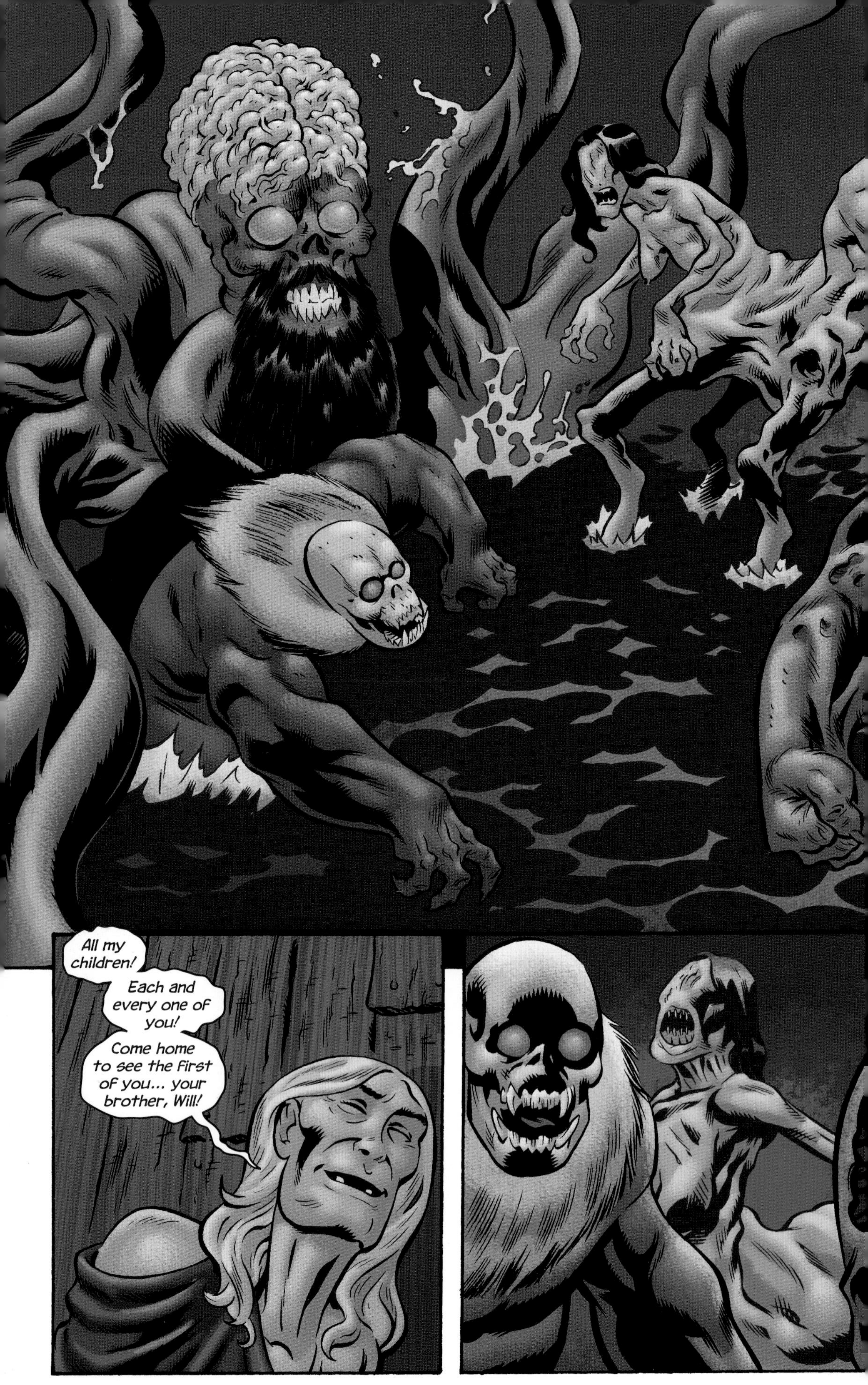
All my children!
Each and every one of you!
Come home to see the first of you... your brother, Will!

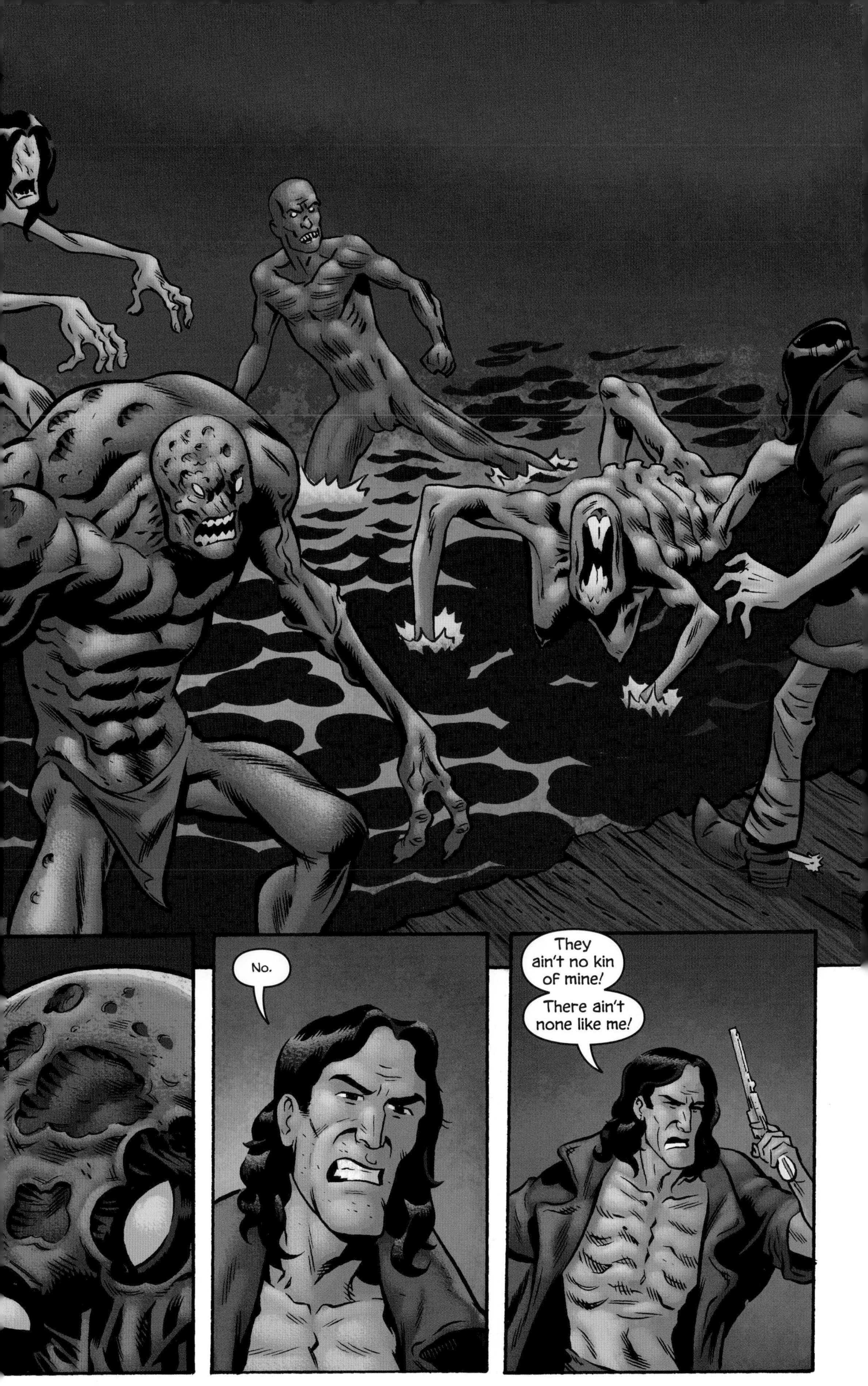
No.
They ain't no kin of mine!
There ain't none like me!

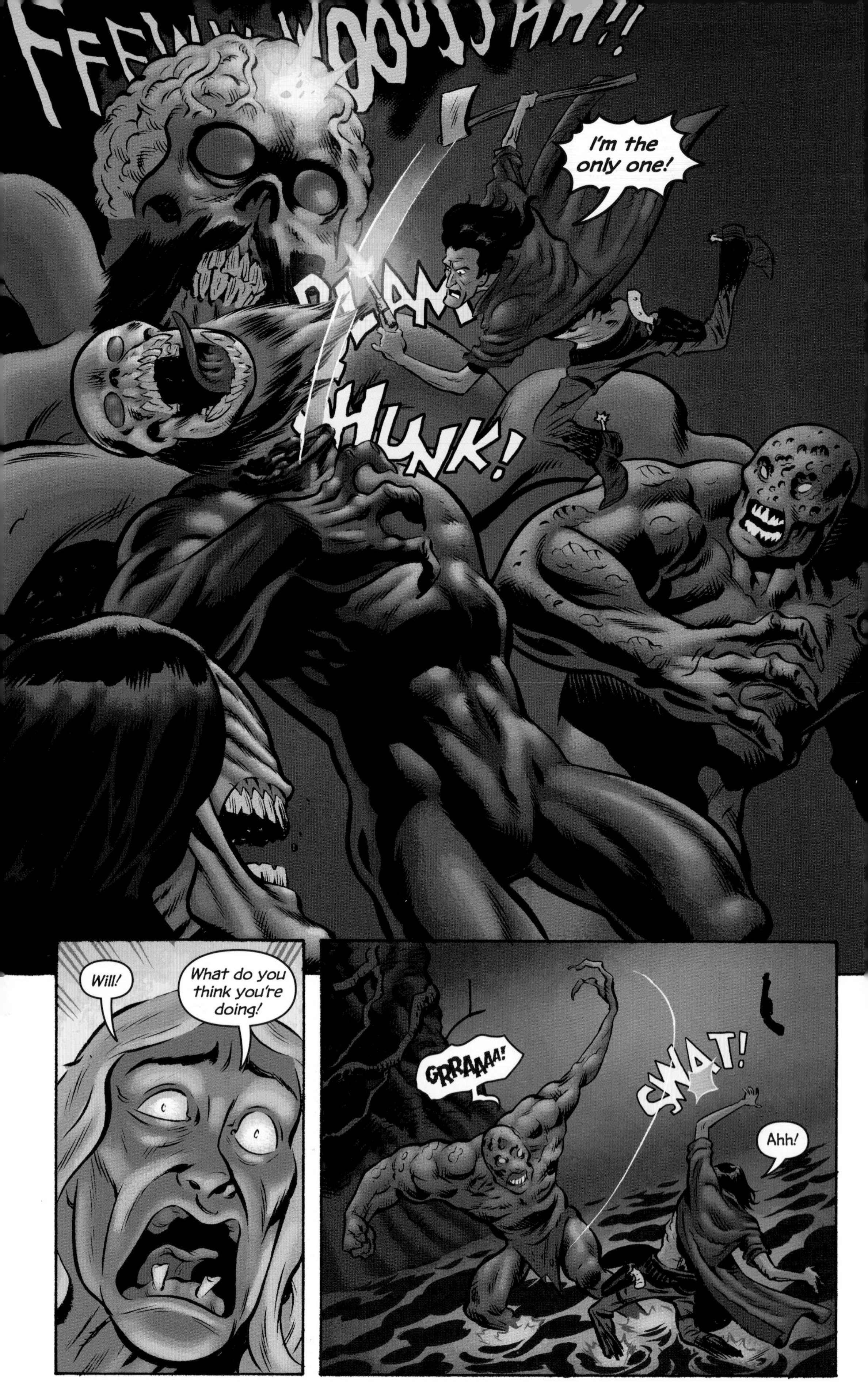
I'm the only one!
Will!
What do you think you're doing!
GRRAAAA!
Ahh!

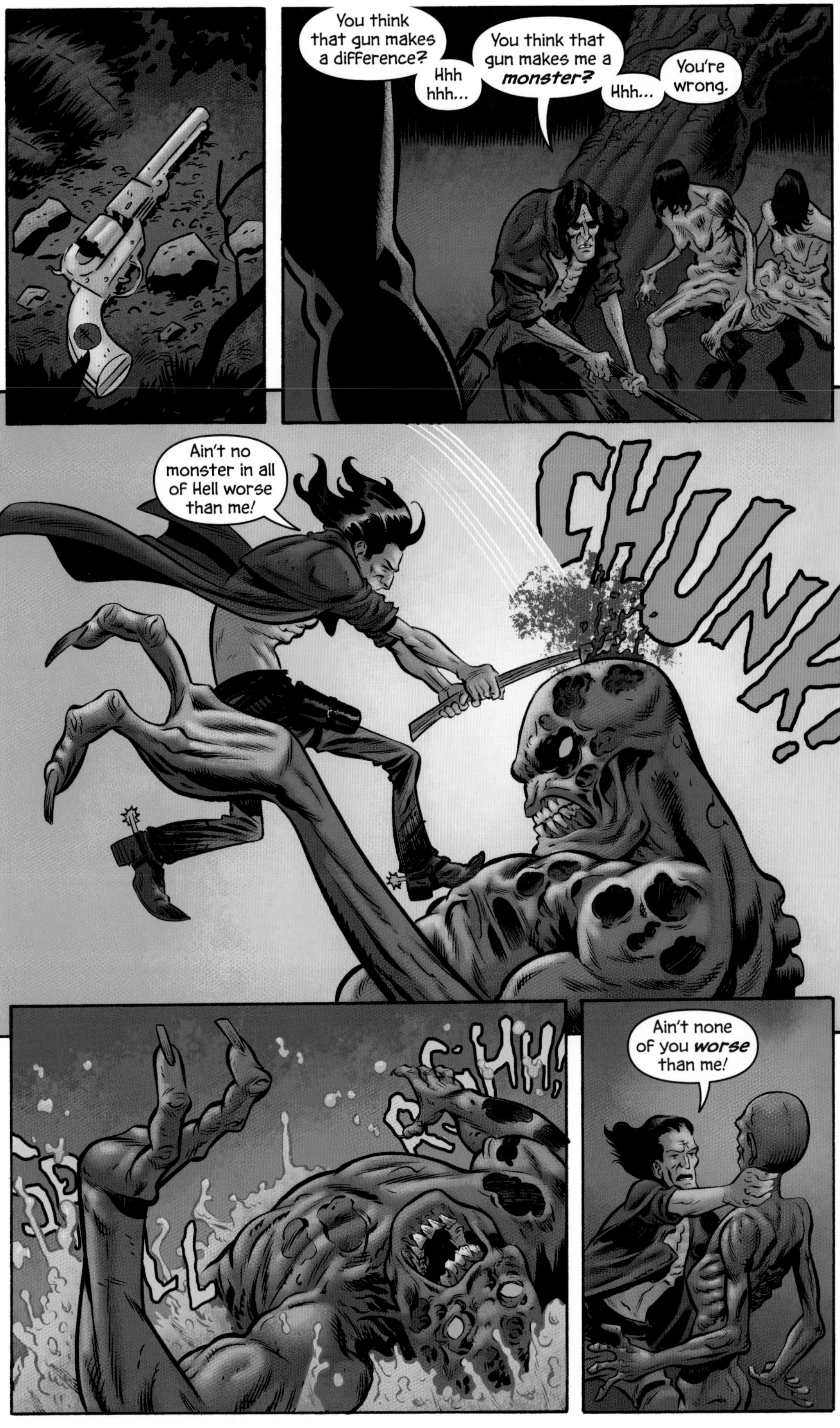
You think that gun makes a difference?
Hhh hhh...
You think that gun makes me a **monster?**
Hhh...
You're wrong.
Ain't no monster in all of Hell worse than me!
CHUNK!!
Ain't none of you **worse** than me!

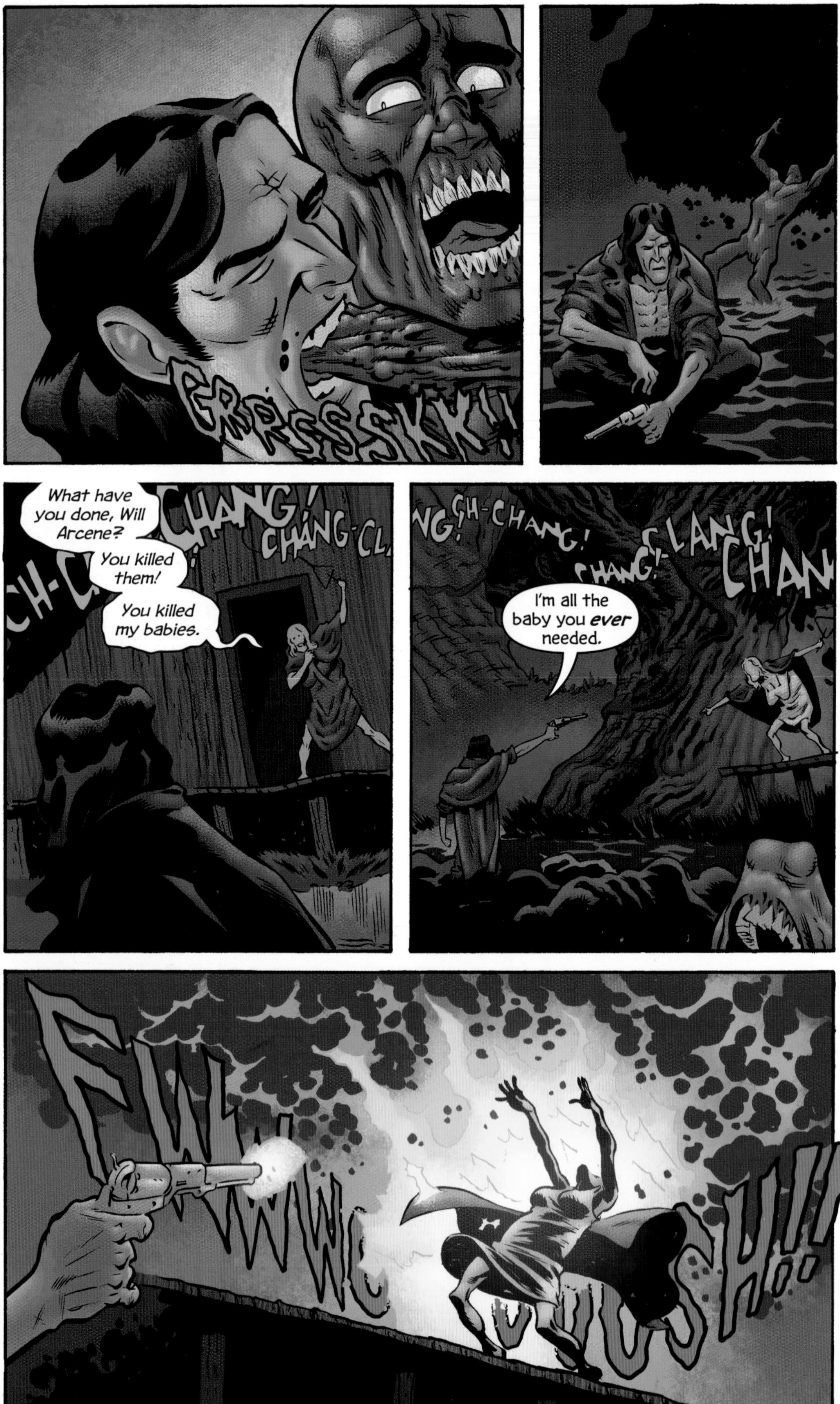
GRRSSSKK!!
What have you done, Will Arcene?
CHANG!
CHANG-CL
CH-C
You killed them!
You killed my babies.
NG!
CH-CHANG!
CHANG!
CLANG!
CHAN
I'm all the baby you ***ever*** needed.
FWWWOOOSH!!

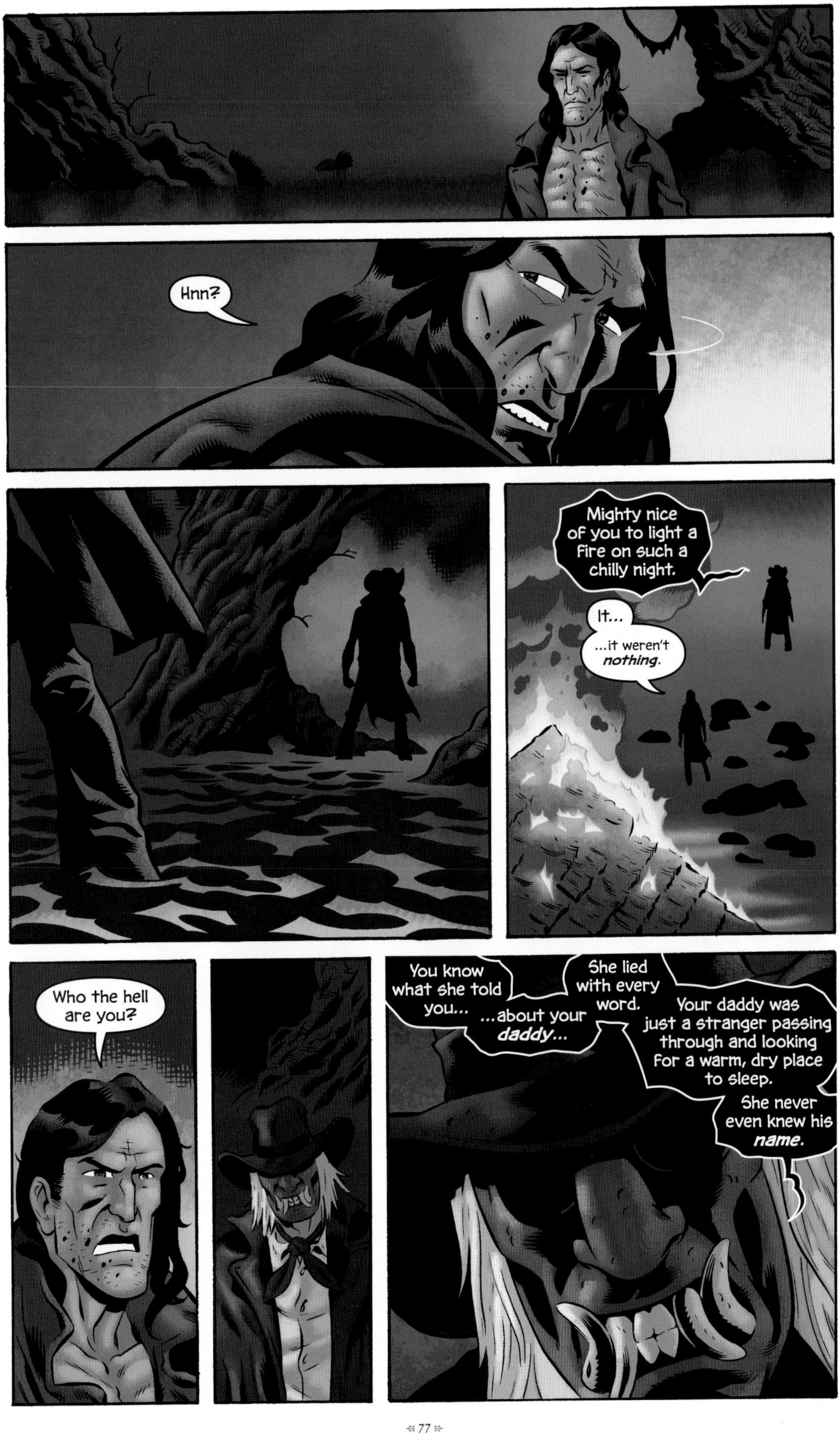
Hnn?
Mighty nice of you to light a fire on such a chilly night.
It...
...it weren't *nothing*.
Who the hell are you?
You know what she told you...
...about your *daddy*...
She lied with every word.
Your daddy was just a stranger passing through and looking for a warm, dry place to sleep.
She never even knew his *name*.

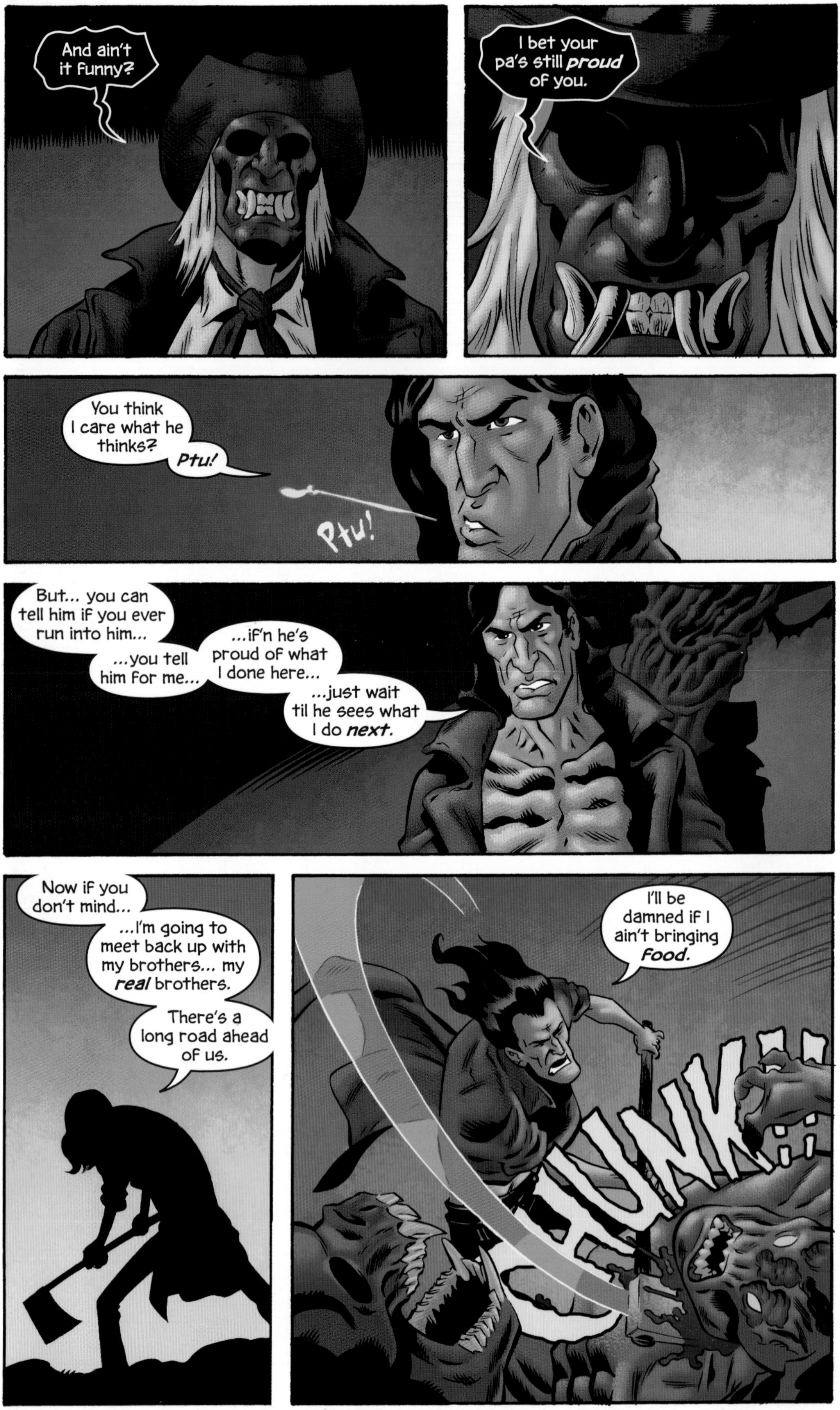

And ain't it funny?
I bet your pa's still *proud* of you.
You think I care what he thinks? *Ptu!*
Ptu!
But... you can tell him if you ever run into him...
...you tell him for me...
...if'n he's proud of what I done here...
...just wait til he sees what I do *next*.
Now if you don't mind...
...I'm going to meet back up with my brothers... my *real* brothers.
There's a long road ahead of us.
I'll be damned if I ain't bringing *food*.
CHUNK!!

CHAPTER FOUR

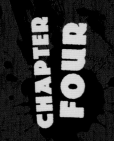

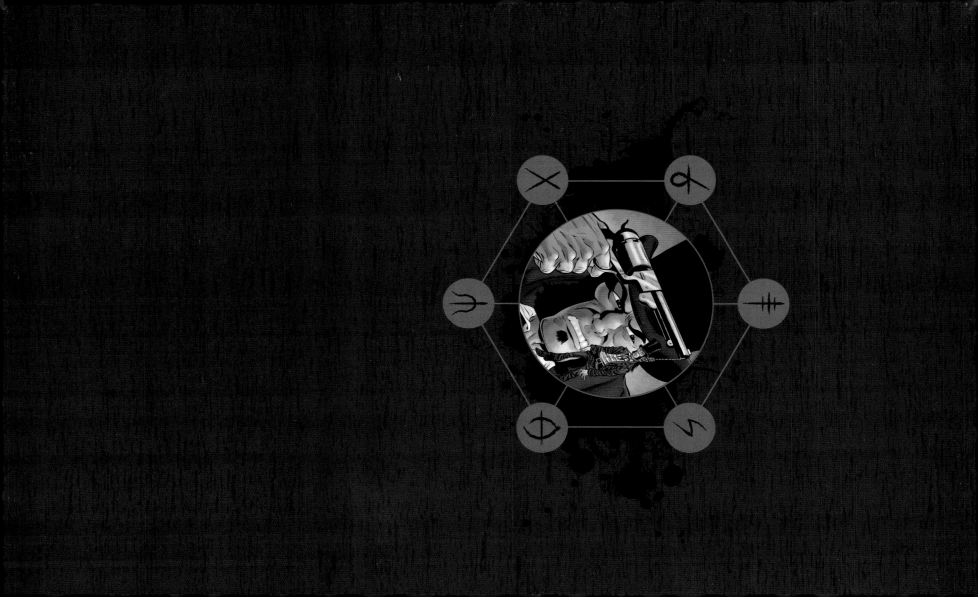

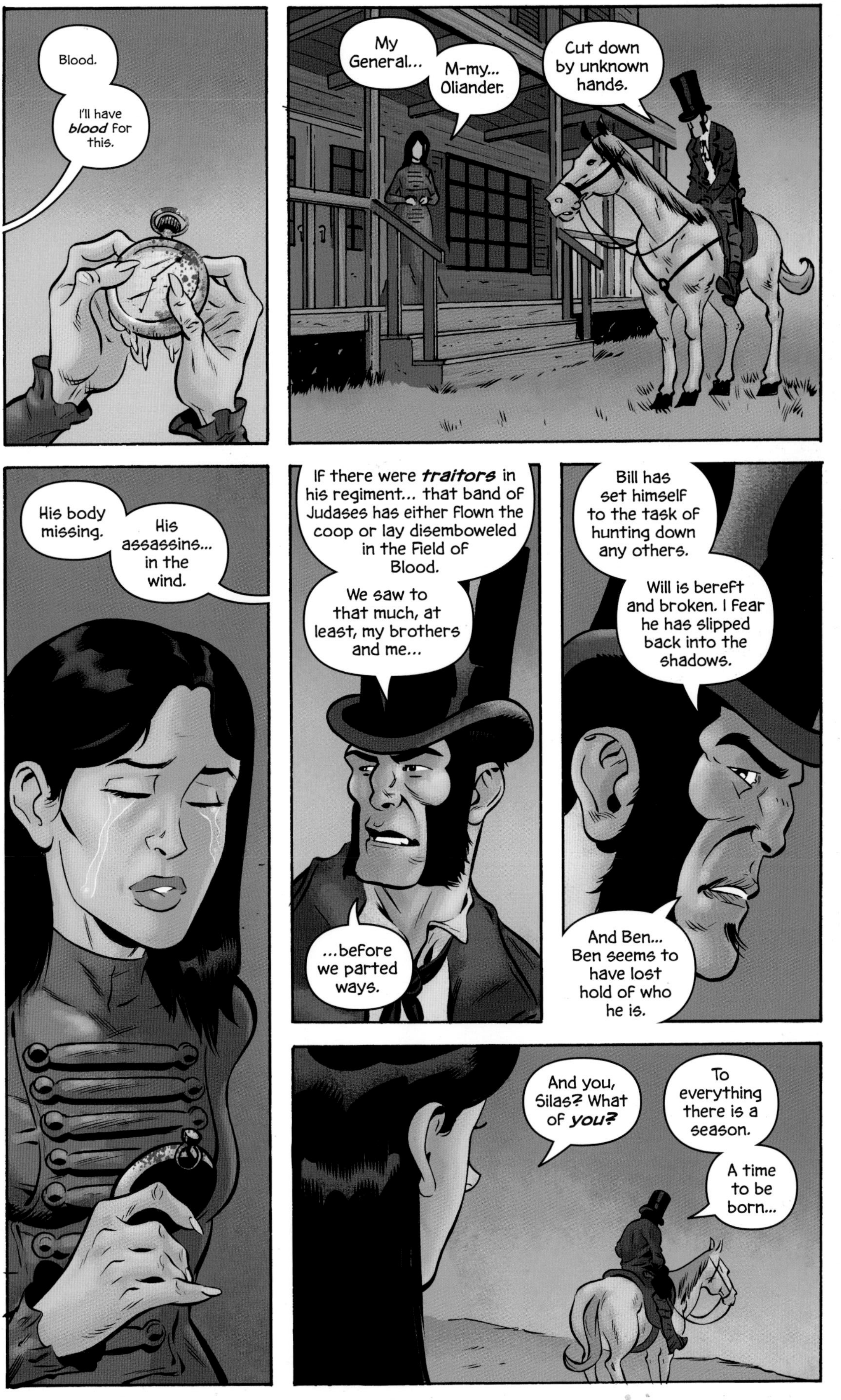
Blood.
I'll have *blood* for this.
My General...
M-my... Oliander.
Cut down by unknown hands.
His body missing.
His assassins... in the wind.
If there were *traitors* in his regiment... that band of Judases has either flown the coop or lay disemboweled in the Field of Blood.
We saw to that much, at least, my brothers and me...
...before we parted ways.
Bill has set himself to the task of hunting down any others.
Will is bereft and broken. I fear he has slipped back into the shadows.
And Ben... Ben seems to have lost hold of who he is.
And you, Silas? What of *you?*
To everything there is a season.
A time to be born...

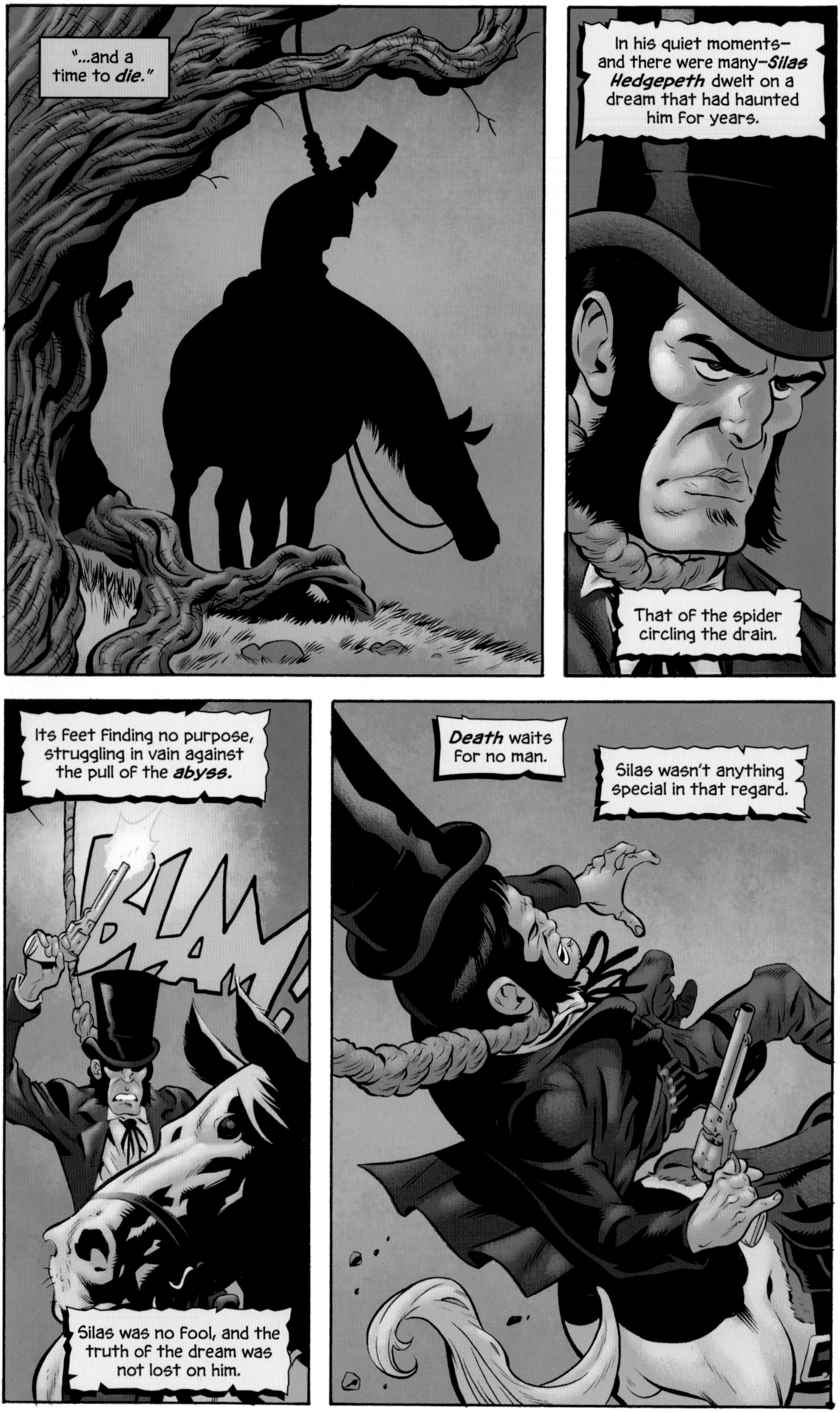
"...and a time to *die.*"
In his quiet moments— and there were many—*Silas Hedgepeth* dwelt on a dream that had haunted him for years.
That of the spider circling the drain.
Its feet finding no purpose, struggling in vain against the pull of the *abyss.*
BLAM
Silas was no fool, and the truth of the dream was not lost on him.
Death waits for no man.
Silas wasn't anything special in that regard.

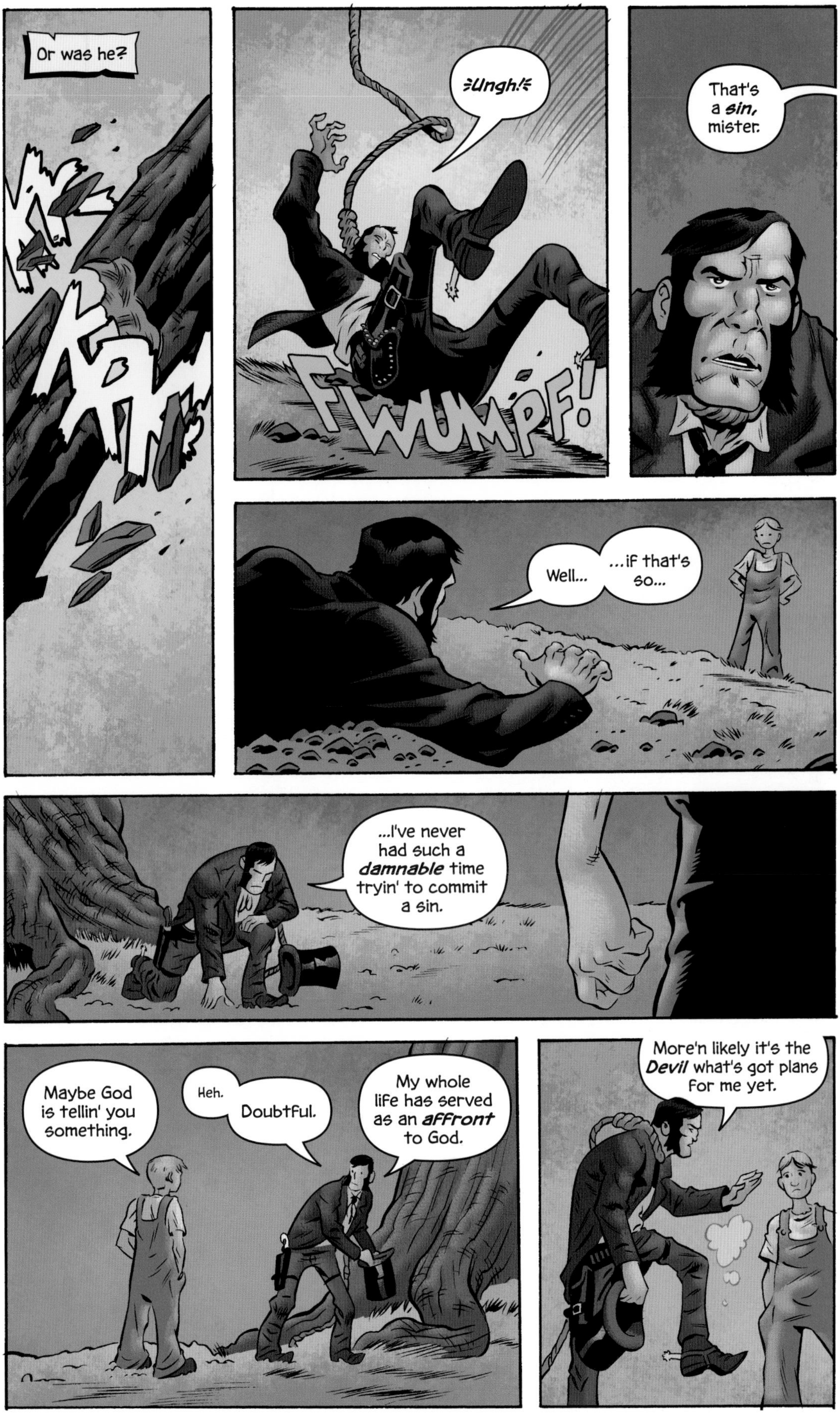
Or was he?
Ungh!
FWUMPF!
That's a *sin,* mister.
Well...
...if that's so...
...I've never had such a *damnable* time tryin' to commit a sin.
Maybe God is tellin' you something.
Heh.
Doubtful.
My whole life has served as an *affront* to God.
More'n likely it's the *Devil* what's got plans for me yet.

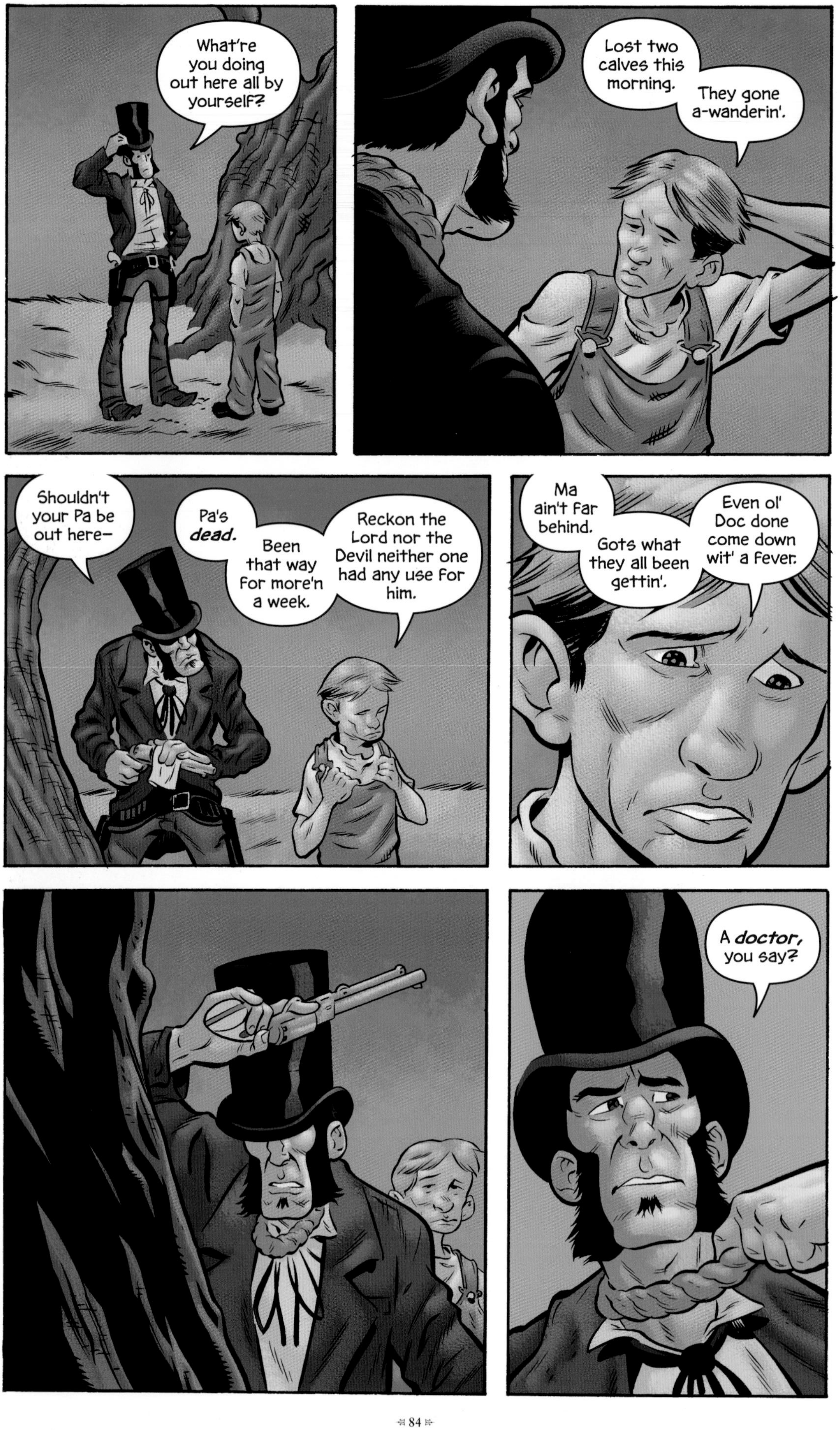
What're you doing out here all by yourself?
Lost two calves this morning.
They gone a-wanderin'.
Shouldn't your Pa be out here—
Pa's *dead.*
Been that way for more'n a week.
Reckon the Lord nor the Devil neither one had any use for him.
Ma ain't far behind.
Gots what they all been gettin'.
Even ol' Doc done come down wit' a fever.
A *doctor,* you say?

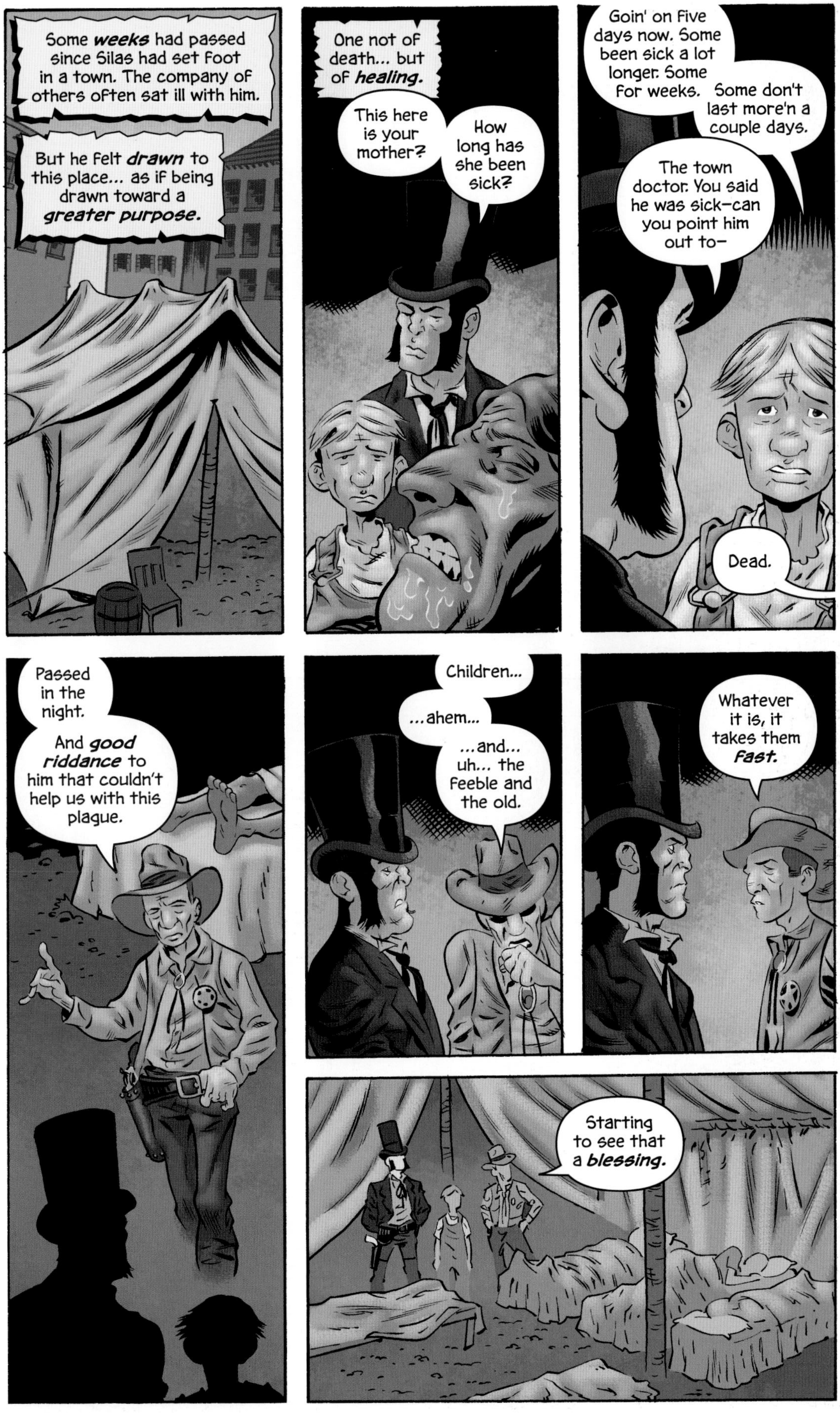
Some *weeks* had passed since Silas had set foot in a town. The company of others often sat ill with him.
But he felt *drawn* to this place... as if being drawn toward a *greater purpose.*
One not of death... but of *healing.*
This here is your mother?
How long has she been sick?
Goin' on five days now. Some been sick a lot longer. Some for weeks.
Some don't last more'n a couple days.
The town doctor. You said he was sick—can you point him out to—
Dead.
Passed in the night.
And *good riddance* to him that couldn't help us with this plague.
Children...
...ahem...
...and... uh... the feeble and the old.
Whatever it is, it takes them *fast.*
Starting to see that a *blessing.*

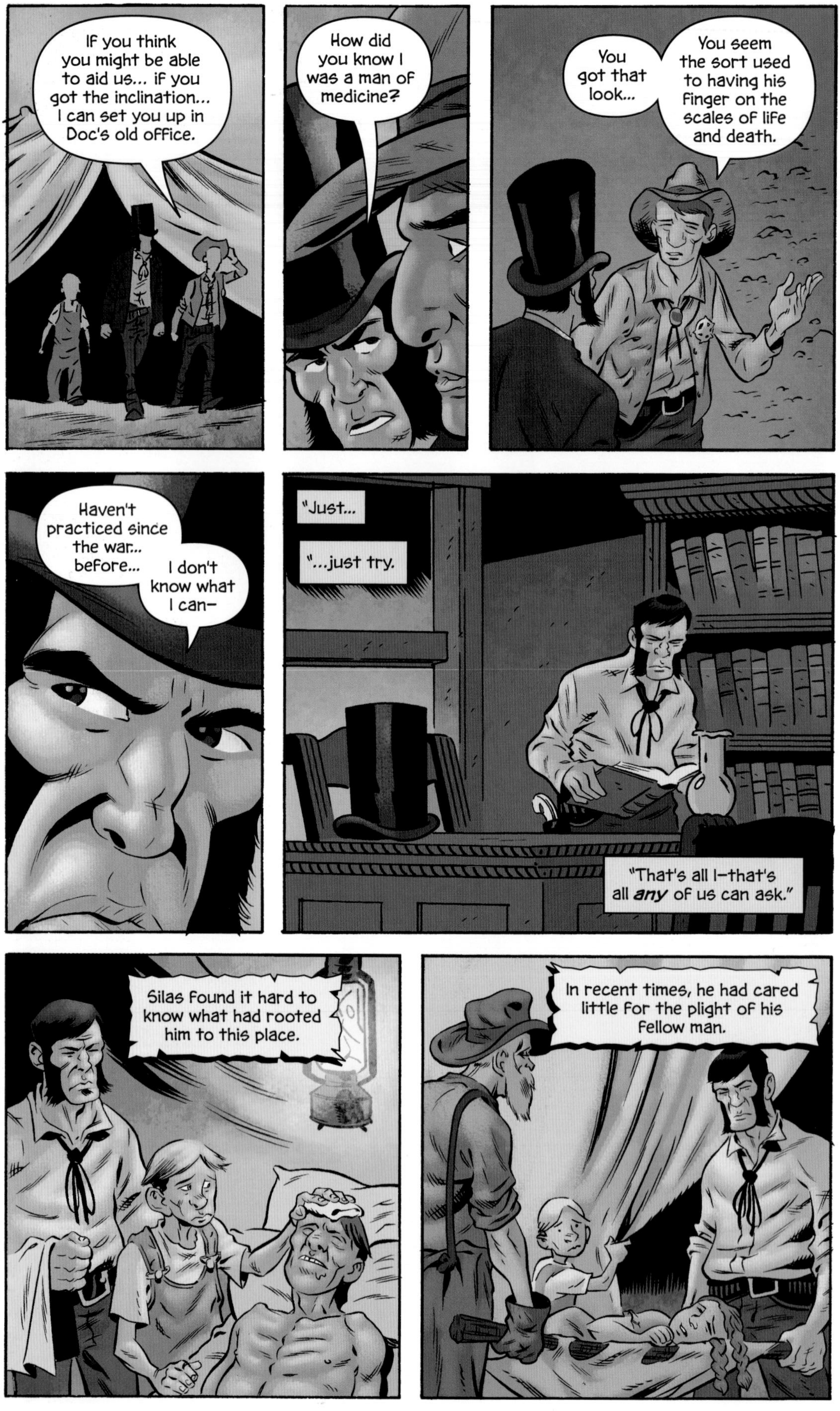
If you think you might be able to aid us... if you got the inclination... I can set you up in Doc's old office.
How did you know I was a man of medicine?
You got that look...
You seem the sort used to having his finger on the scales of life and death.
Haven't practiced since the war... before...
I don't know what I can–
"Just...
"...just try.
"That's all I–that's all *any* of us can ask."
Silas found it hard to know what had rooted him to this place.
In recent times, he had cared little for the plight of his fellow man.

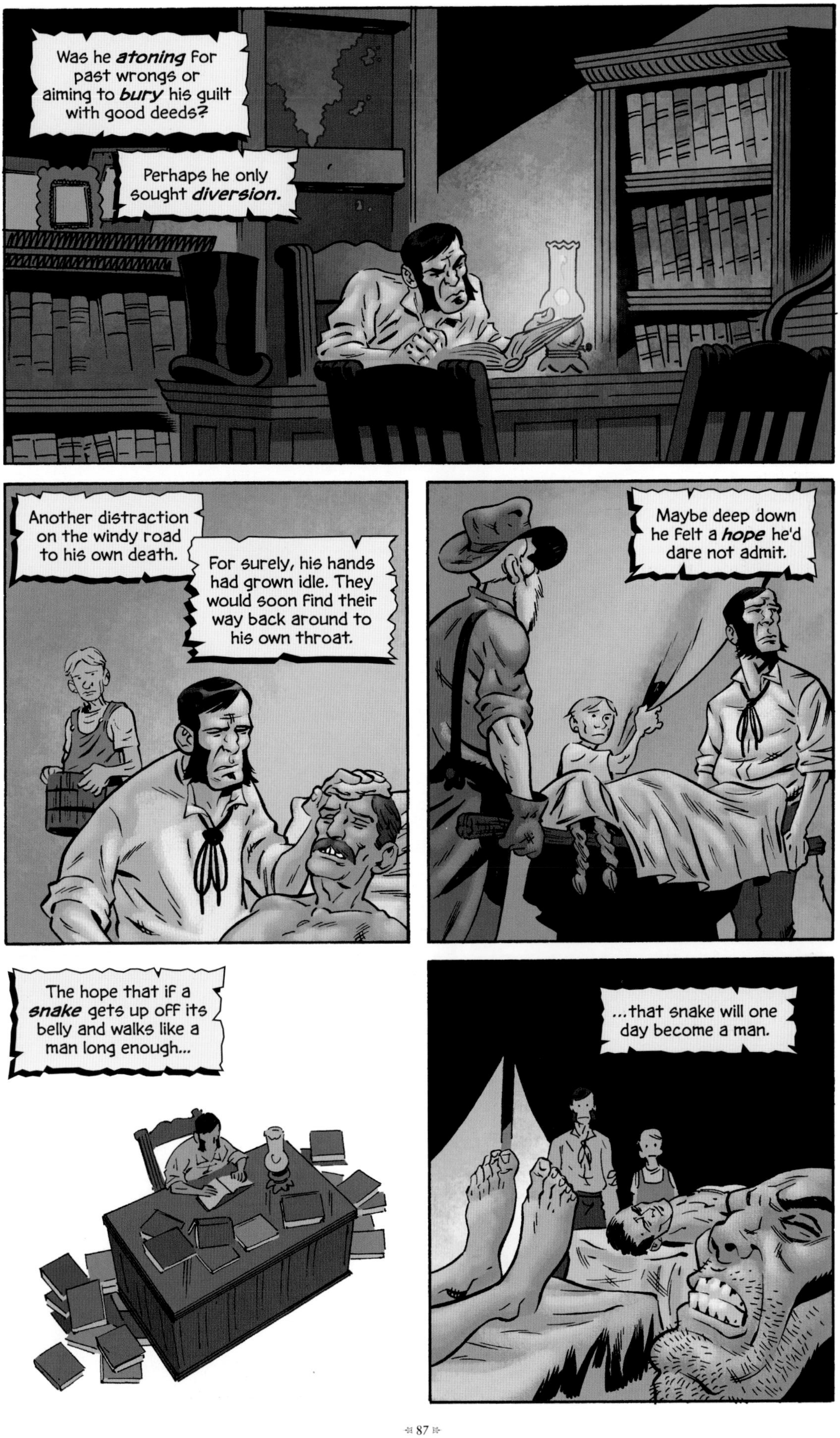
Was he *atoning* for past wrongs or aiming to *bury* his guilt with good deeds?
Perhaps he only sought *diversion.*
Another distraction on the windy road to his own death.
For surely, his hands had grown idle. They would soon find their way back around to his own throat.
Maybe deep down he felt a *hope* he'd dare not admit.
The hope that if a *snake* gets up off its belly and walks like a man long enough...
...that snake will one day become a man.

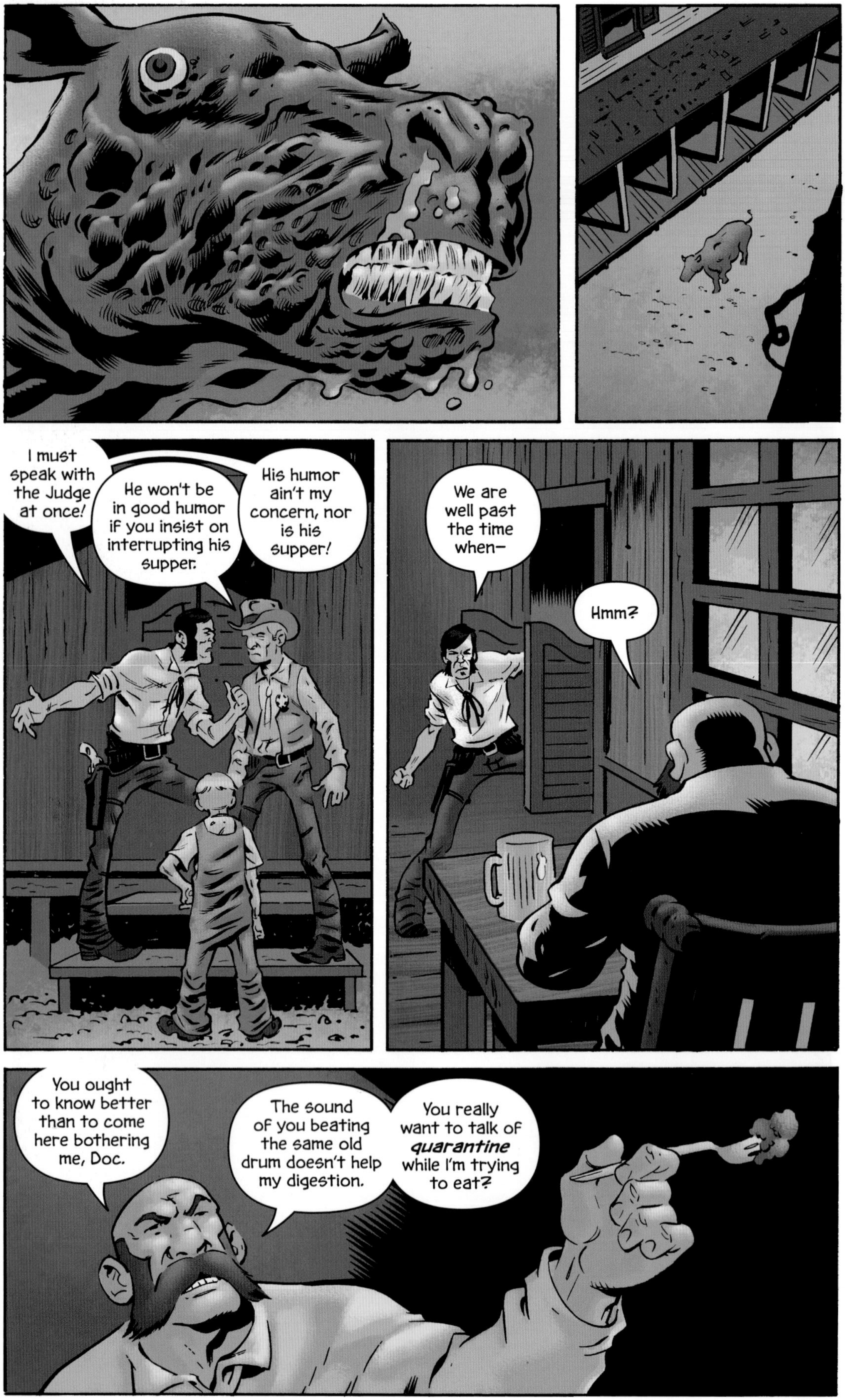
I must speak with the Judge at once!
He won't be in good humor if you insist on interrupting his supper.
His humor ain't my concern, nor is his supper!
We are well past the time when–
Hmm?
You ought to know better than to come here bothering me, Doc.
The sound of you beating the same old drum doesn't help my digestion.
You really want to talk of *quarantine* while I'm trying to eat?

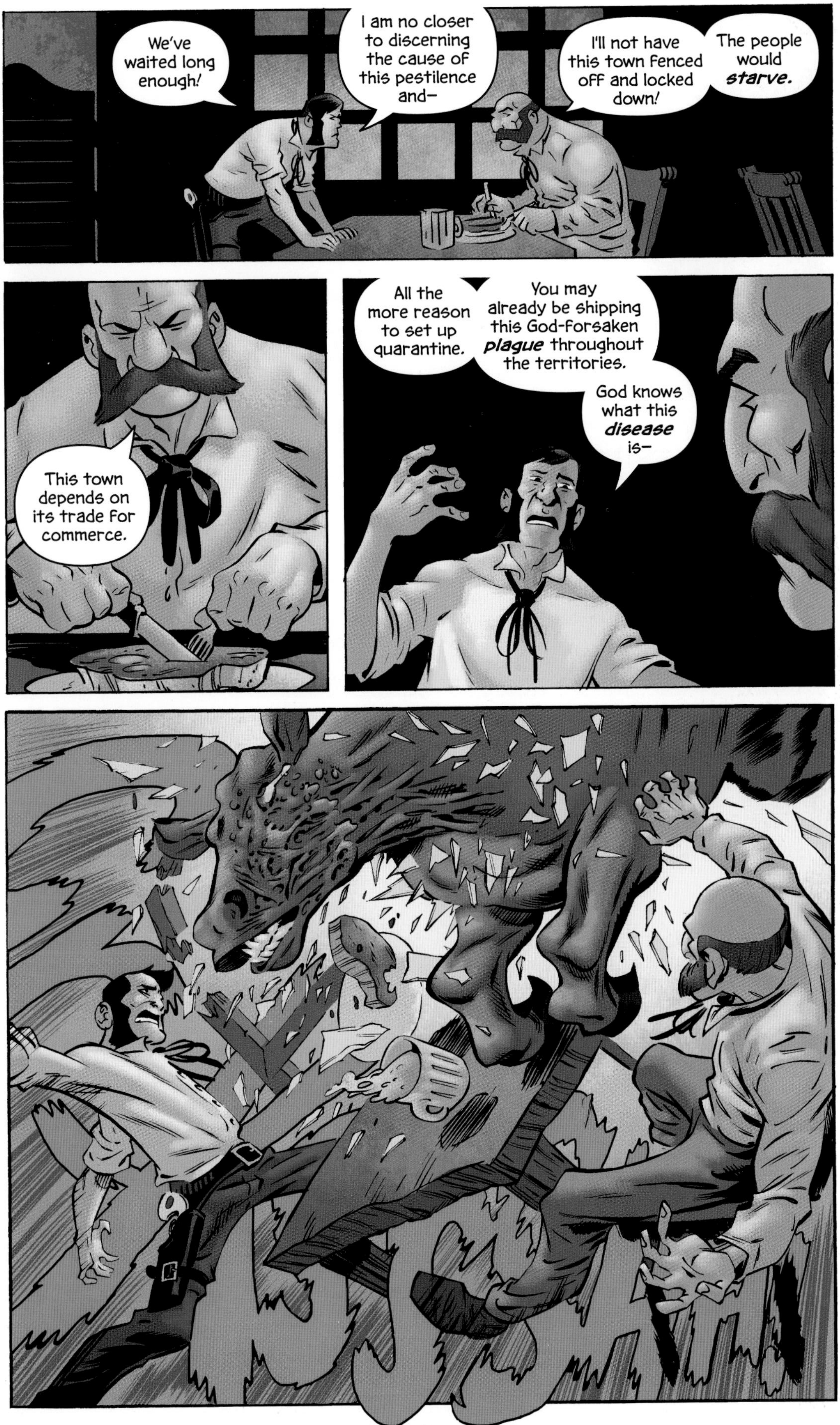
We've waited long enough!
I am no closer to discerning the cause of this pestilence and–
I'll not have this town fenced off and locked down!
The people would *starve.*
This town depends on its trade for commerce.
All the more reason to set up quarantine.
You may already be shipping this God-forsaken *plague* throughout the territories.
God knows what this *disease* is–

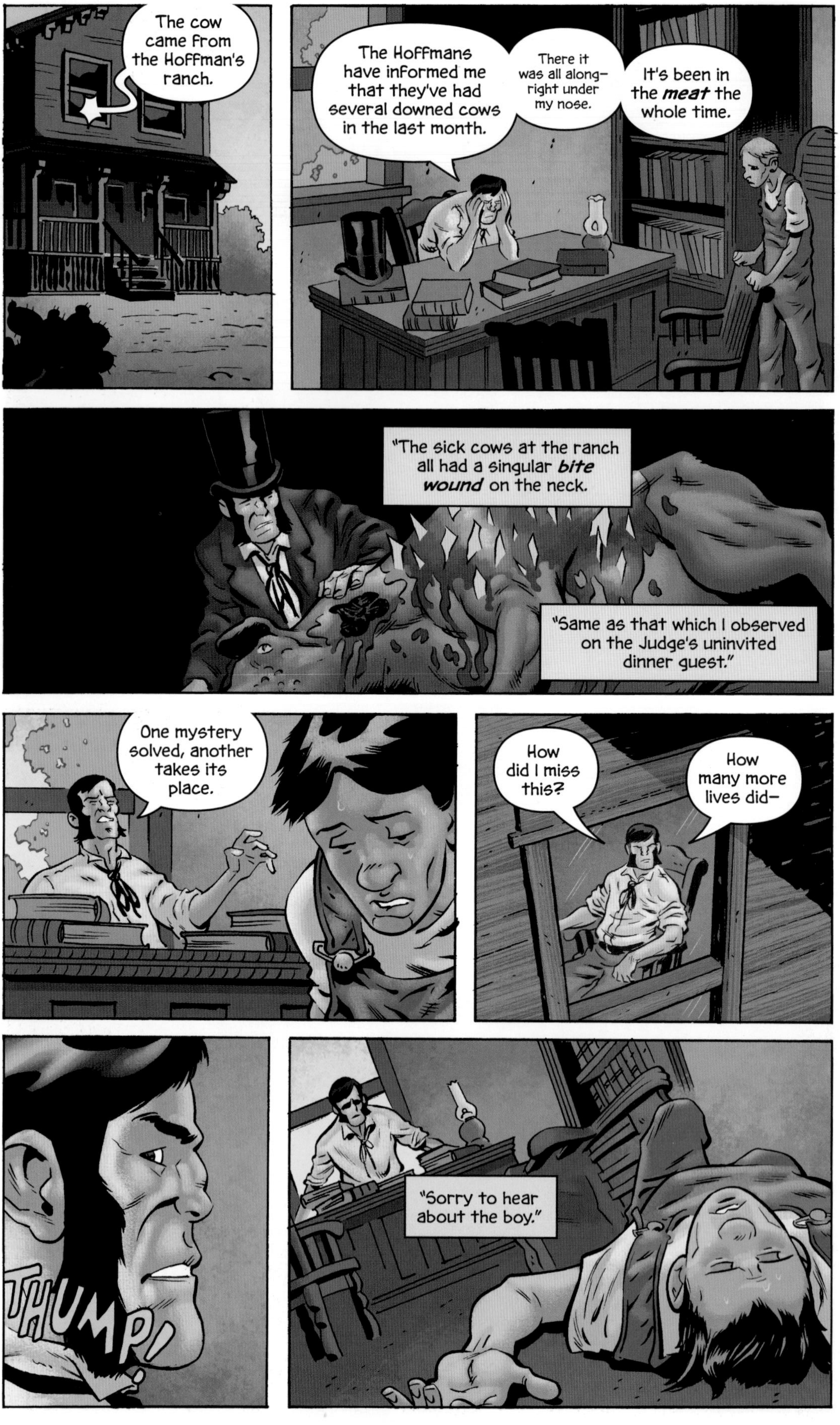
The cow came from the Hoffman's ranch.
The Hoffmans have informed me that they've had several downed cows in the last month.
There it was all along— right under my nose.
It's been in the *meat* the whole time.
"The sick cows at the ranch all had a singular ***bite wound*** on the neck.
"Same as that which I observed on the Judge's uninvited dinner guest."
One mystery solved, another takes its place.
How did I miss this?
How many more lives did—
THUMP!
"Sorry to hear about the boy."

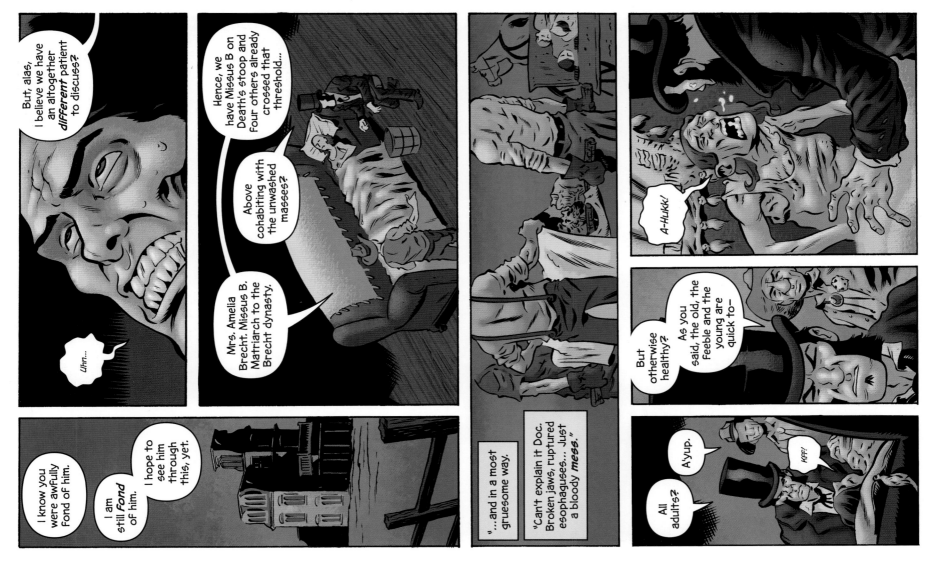

But, alas, I believe we have an altogether *different* patient to discuss?

Uhm...

Hence, we have Missus B on Death's stoop and four others already crossed that threshold...

Above cohabiting with the unwashed masses?

Mrs. Amelia Brecht. Missus B. Matriarch to the Brecht dynasty.

I know you were awfully fond of him.

I am still *fond* of him.

I hope to see him through this, yet.

"...and in a most gruesome way.

"Can't explain it Doc. Broken jaws, ruptured esophaguses... Just a bloody *mess.*"

A-HUKK!

But otherwise healthy?

As you said, the old, the feeble and the young are quick to—

All adults?

A'yup.

KFF!

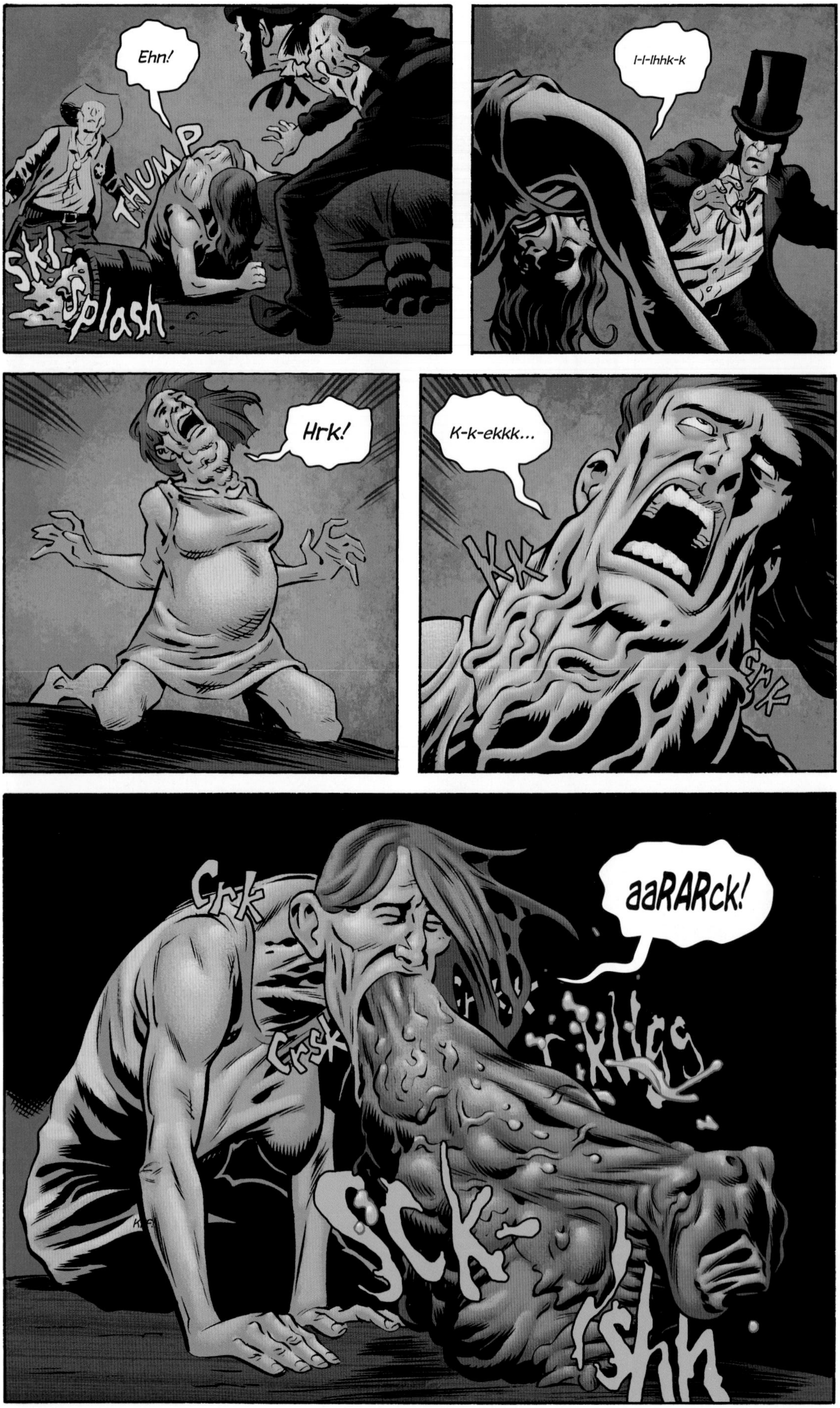
Ehn!
THUMP
SKI-splash
I-I-Ihhk-k
Hrk!
K-k-ekkk...
Kk
Crk
Crk
Crsk
aaRARck!
SCK-shh

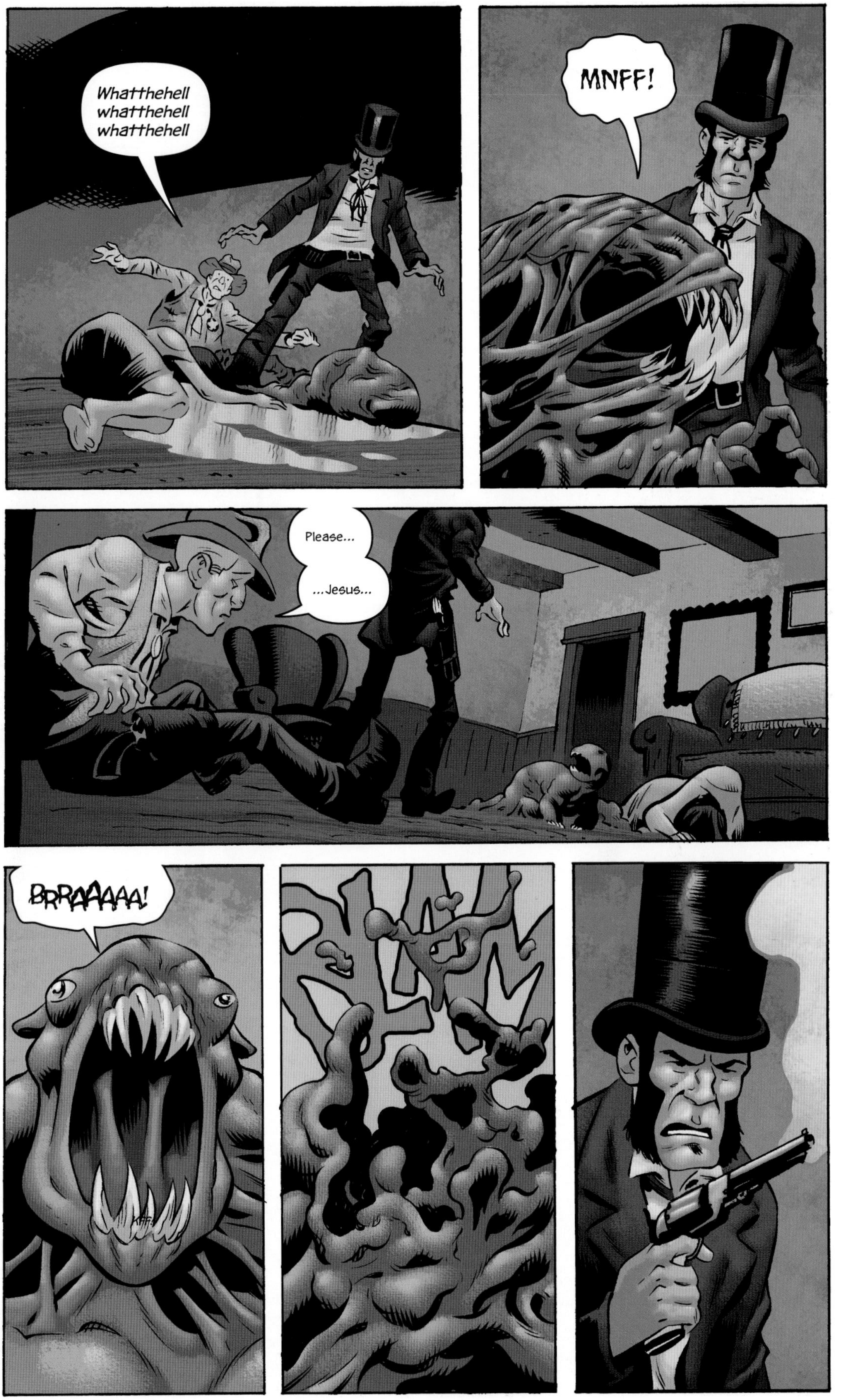
Whatthehell
whatthehell
whatthehell
MNFF!
Please...
...Jesus...
BRRAAAAA!

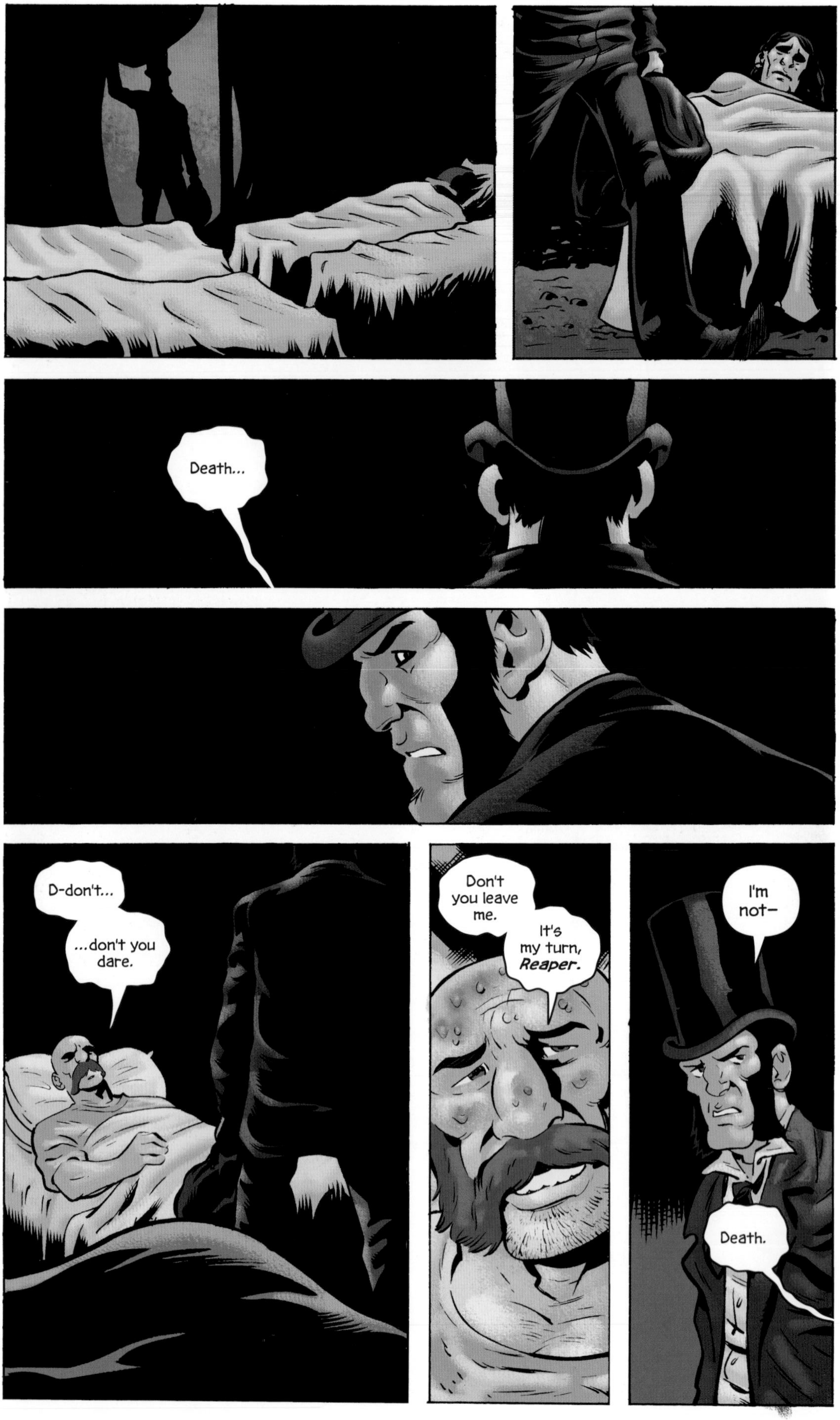
Death...
D-don't...
...don't you dare.
Don't you leave me.
It's my turn, ***Reaper.***
I'm not–
Death.

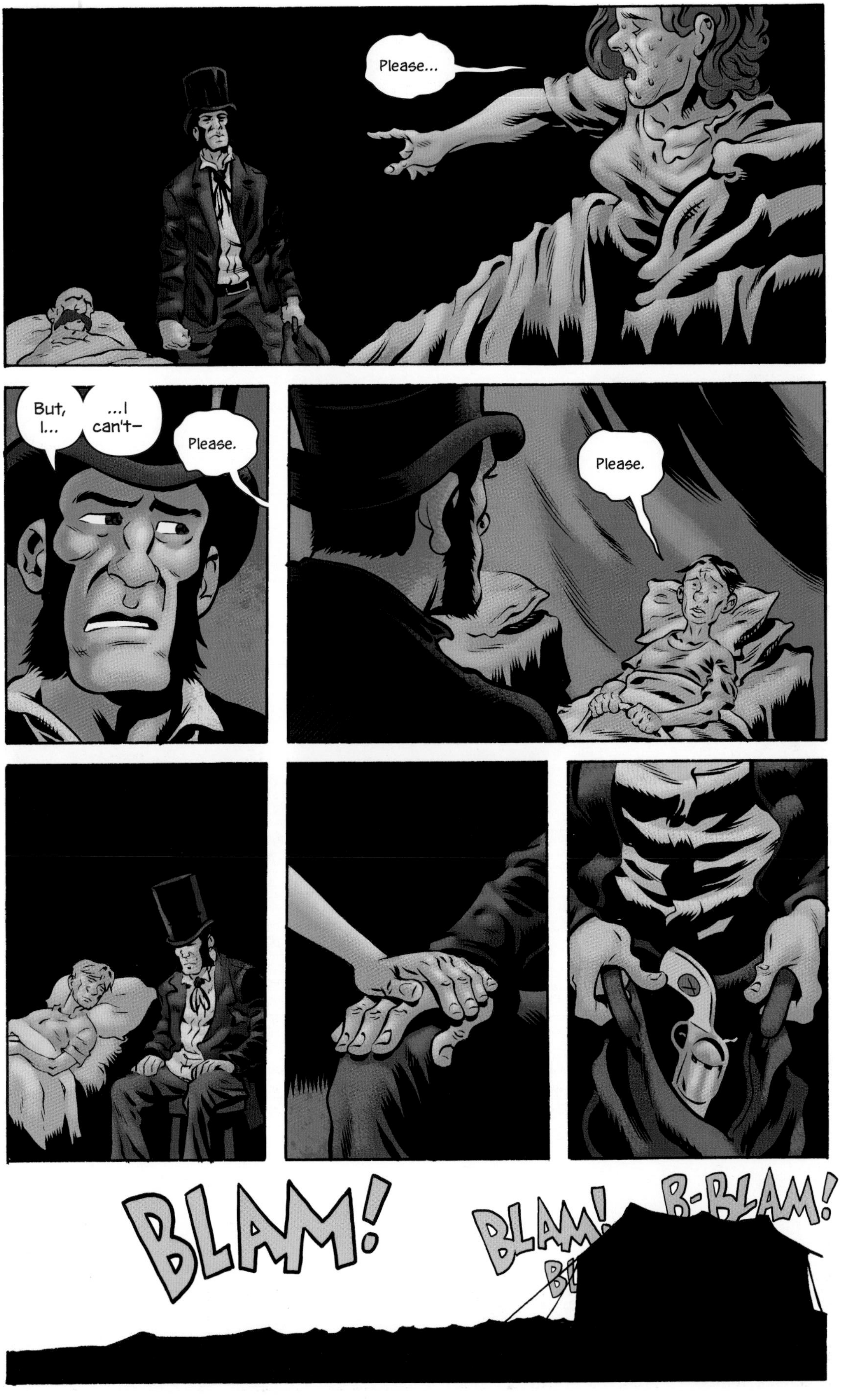
Please...
But, I...
...I can't-
Please.
Please.
BLAM!
BLAM!
B-BLAM!

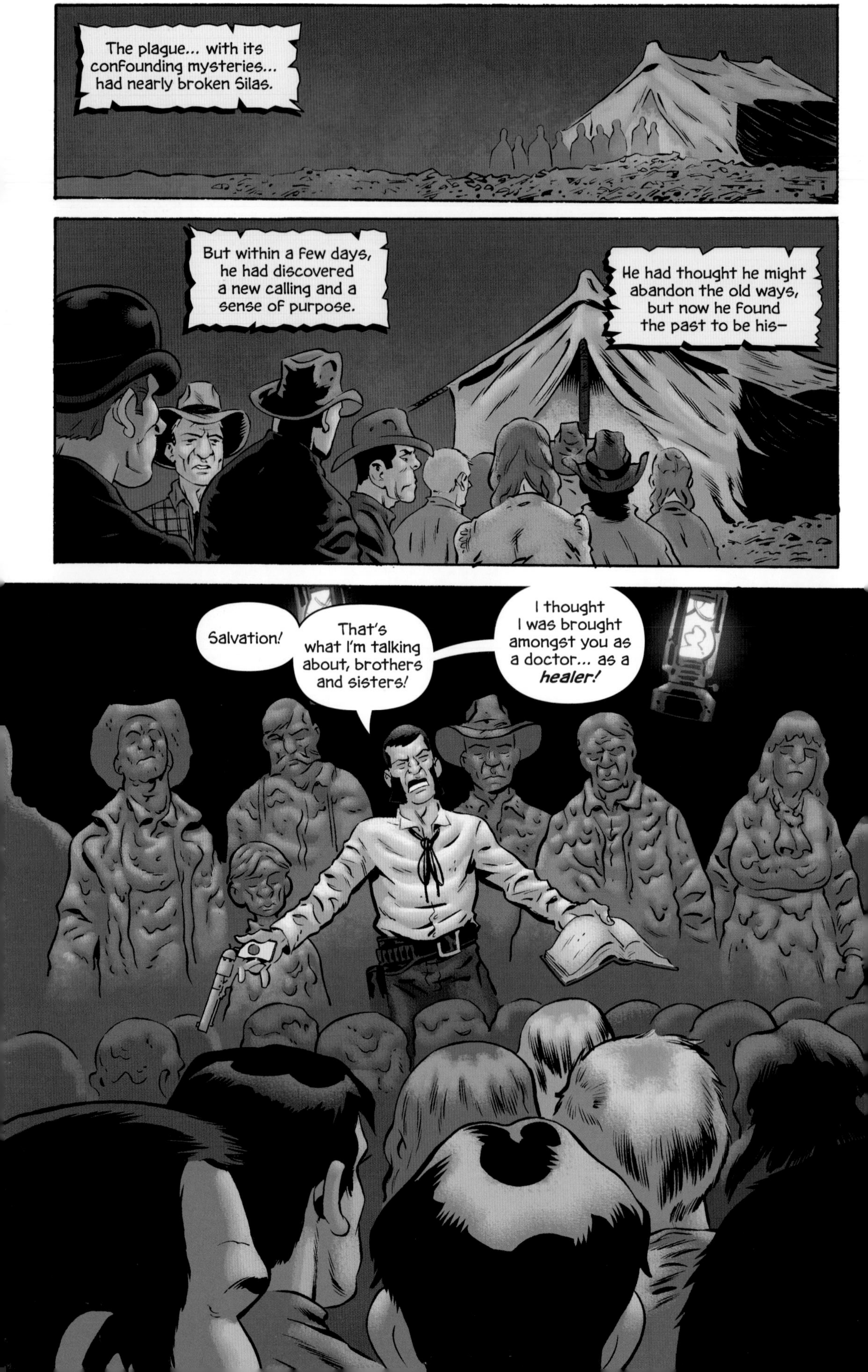
The plague... with its confounding mysteries... had nearly broken Silas.
But within a few days, he had discovered a new calling and a sense of purpose.
He had thought he might abandon the old ways, but now he found the past to be his—
I thought I was brought amongst you as a doctor... as a *healer!*
Salvation!
That's what I'm talking about, brothers and sisters!

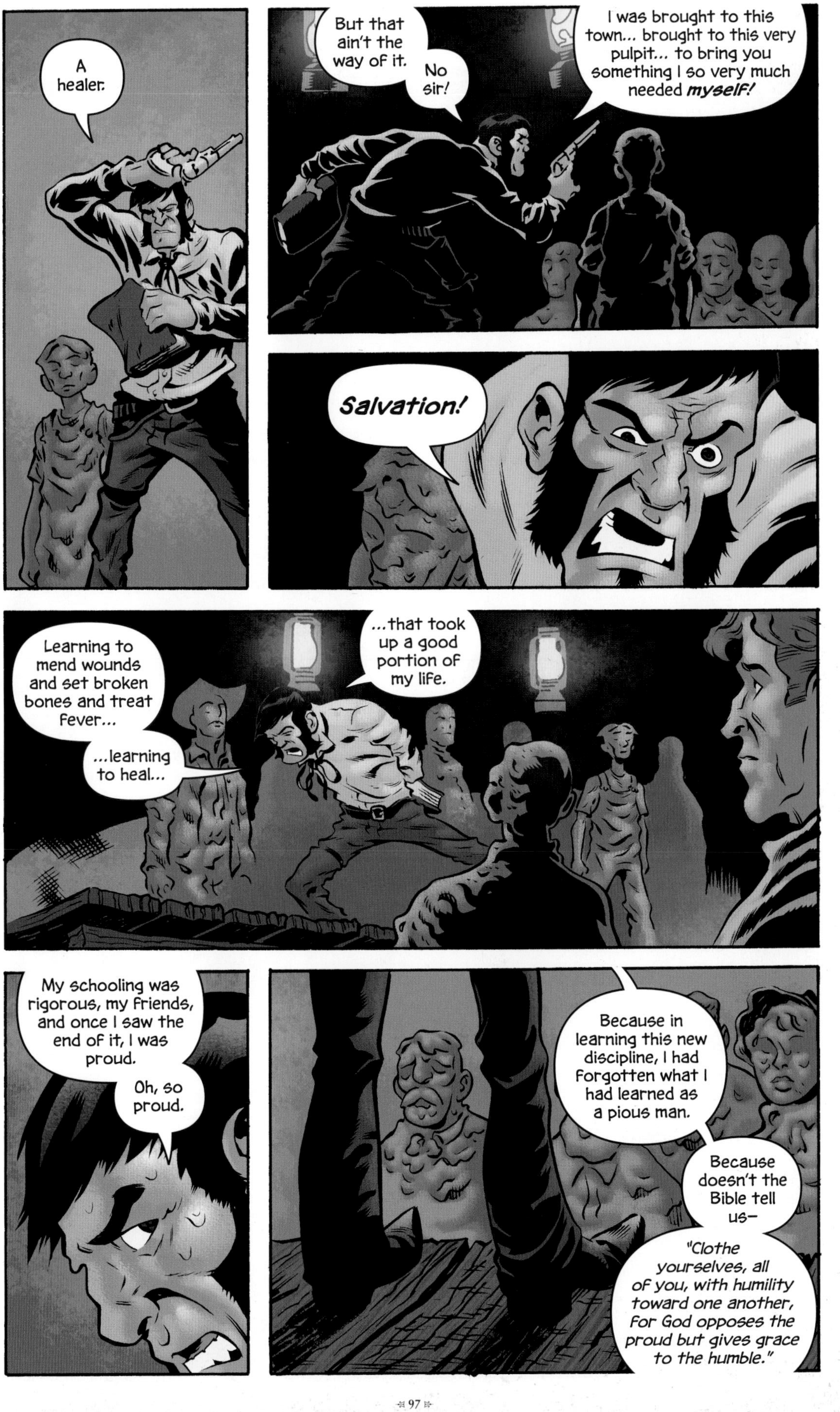
A healer.
But that ain't the way of it.
No sir!
I was brought to this town... brought to this very pulpit... to bring you something I so very much needed *myself!*
Salvation!
Learning to mend wounds and set broken bones and treat fever...
...learning to heal...
...that took up a good portion of my life.
My schooling was rigorous, my friends, and once I saw the end of it, I was proud.
Oh, so proud.
Because in learning this new discipline, I had forgotten what I had learned as a pious man.
Because doesn't the Bible tell us—
"Clothe yourselves, all of you, with humility toward one another, for God opposes the proud but gives grace to the humble."

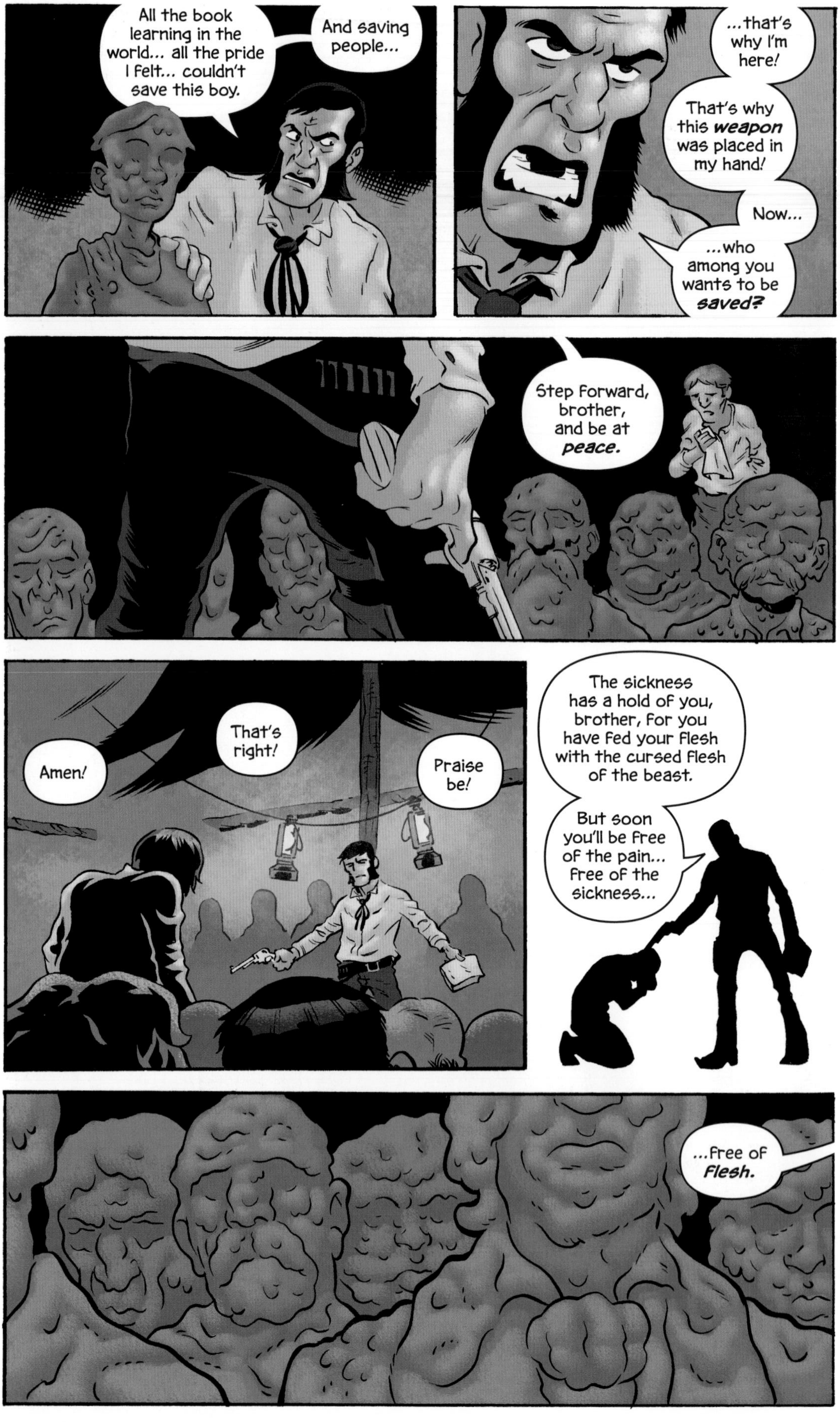
All the book learning in the world... all the pride I felt... couldn't save this boy.
And saving people...
...that's why I'm here!
That's why this ***weapon*** was placed in my hand!
Now...
...who among you wants to be ***saved?***
Step forward, brother, and be at ***peace.***
Amen!
That's right!
Praise be!
The sickness has a hold of you, brother, for you have fed your flesh with the cursed flesh of the beast.
But soon you'll be free of the pain... free of the sickness...
...free of ***flesh.***

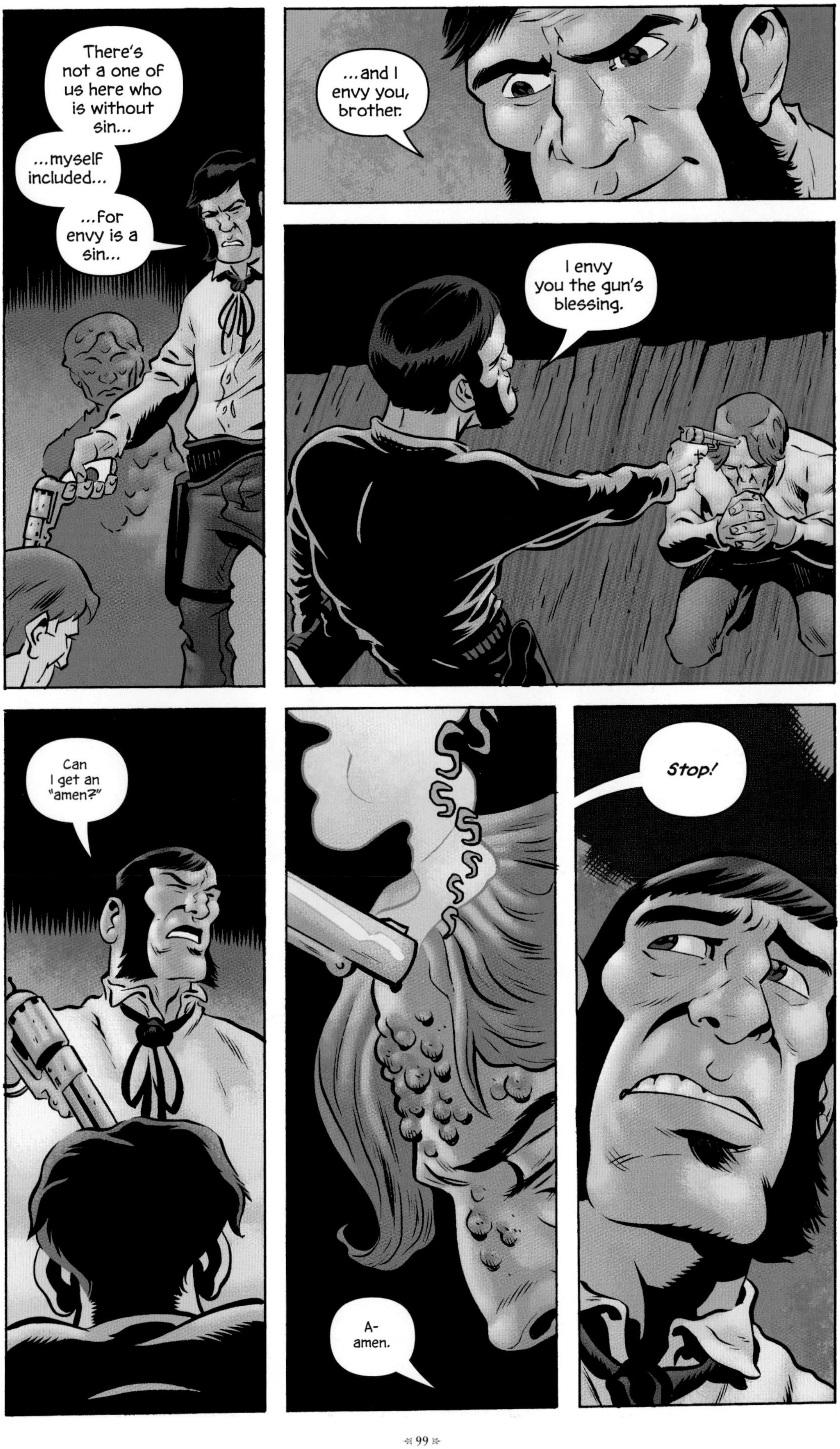

There's not a one of us here who is without sin...
...myself included...
...for envy is a sin...
...and I envy you, brother.
I envy you the gun's blessing.
Can I get an "amen?"
A-amen.
Stop!

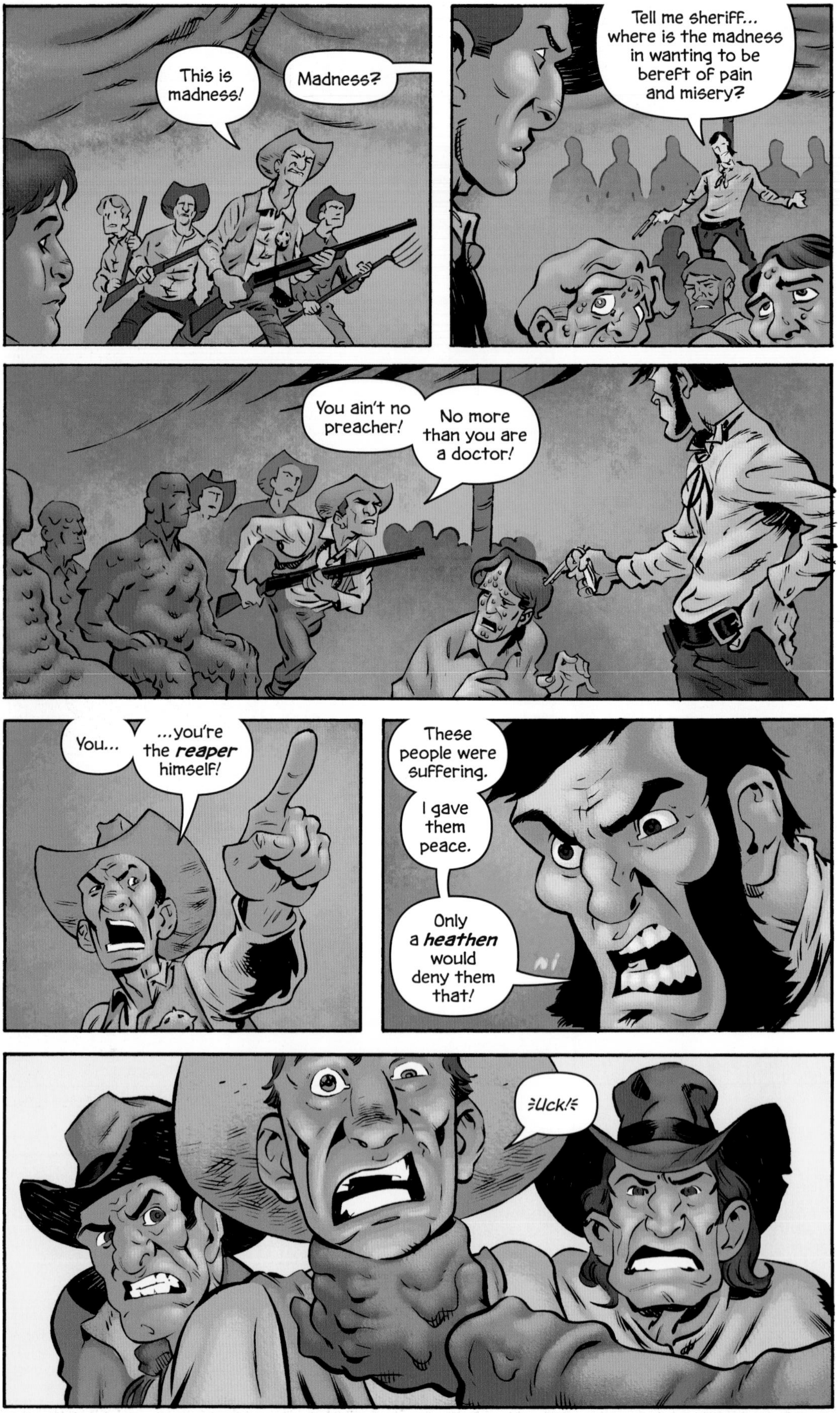
This is madness!
Madness?
Tell me sheriff... where is the madness in wanting to be bereft of pain and misery?
You ain't no preacher!
No more than you are a doctor!
You...
...you're the ***reaper*** himself!
These people were suffering.
I gave them peace.
Only a ***heathen*** would deny them that!
Uck!

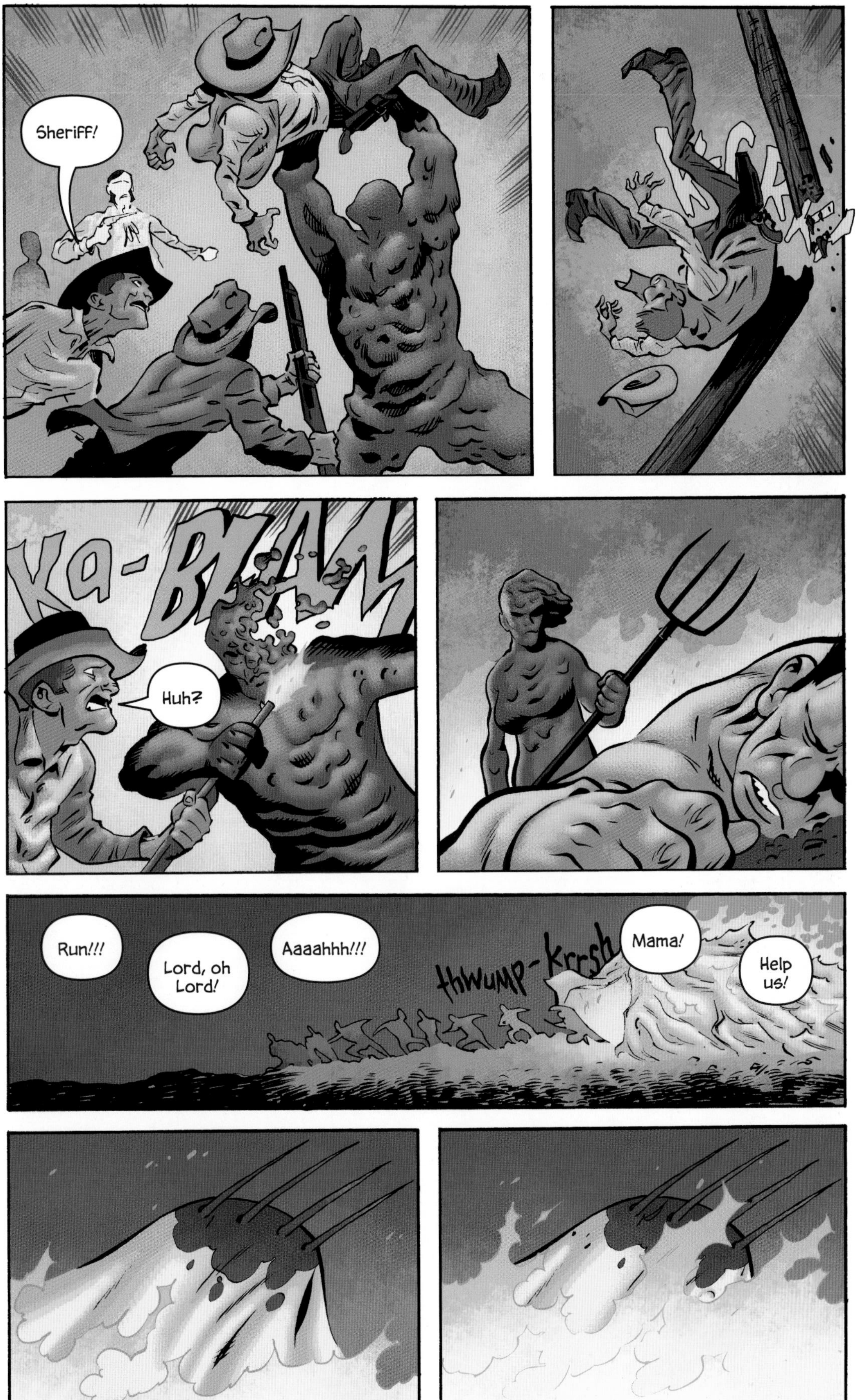
Sheriff!
Ka-BLAM
Huh?
Run!!!
Lord, oh Lord!
Aaaahhh!!!
thwump-krrsh
Mama!
Help us!

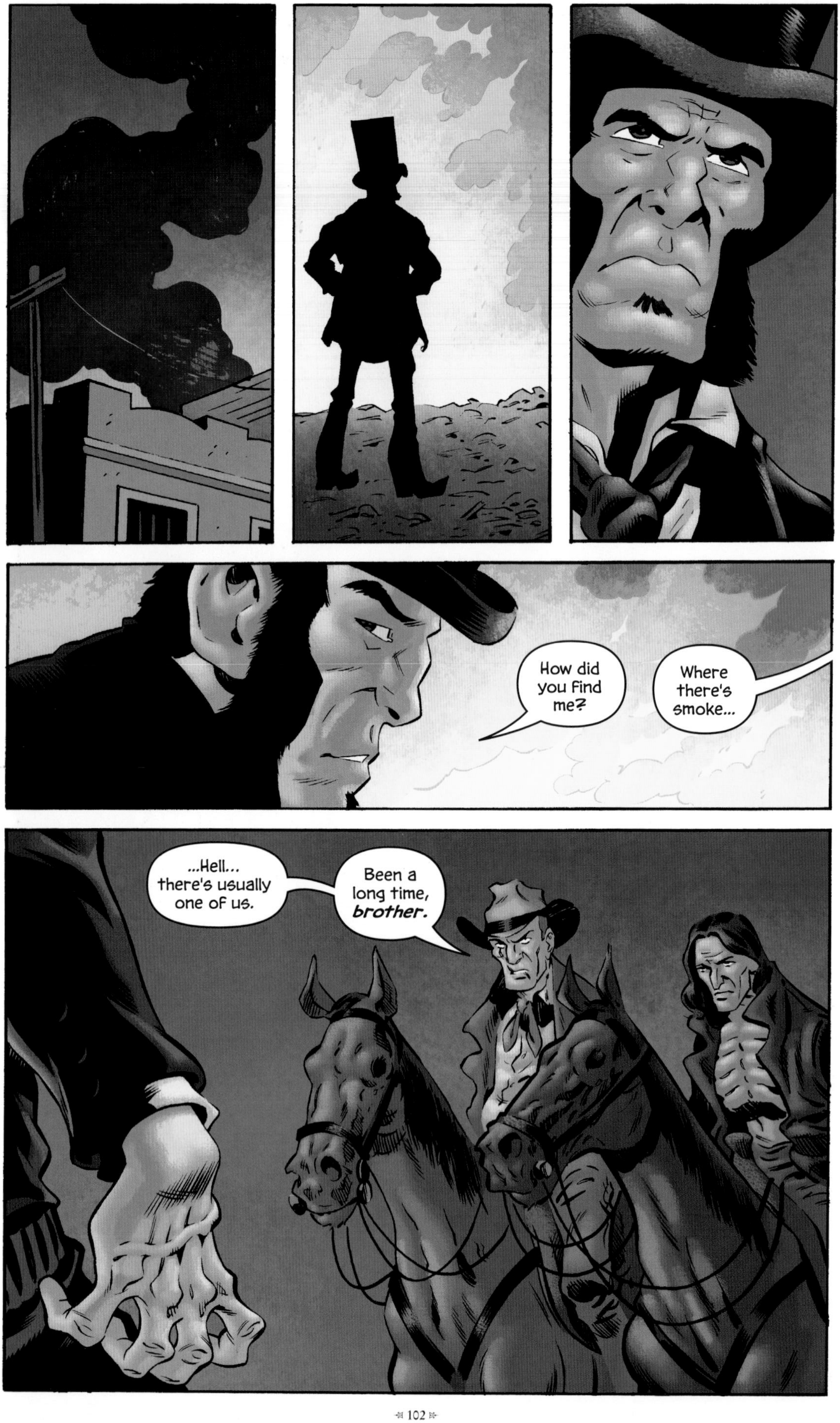
How did you find me?
Where there's smoke...
Been a long time, *brother*.
...Hell... there's usually one of us.

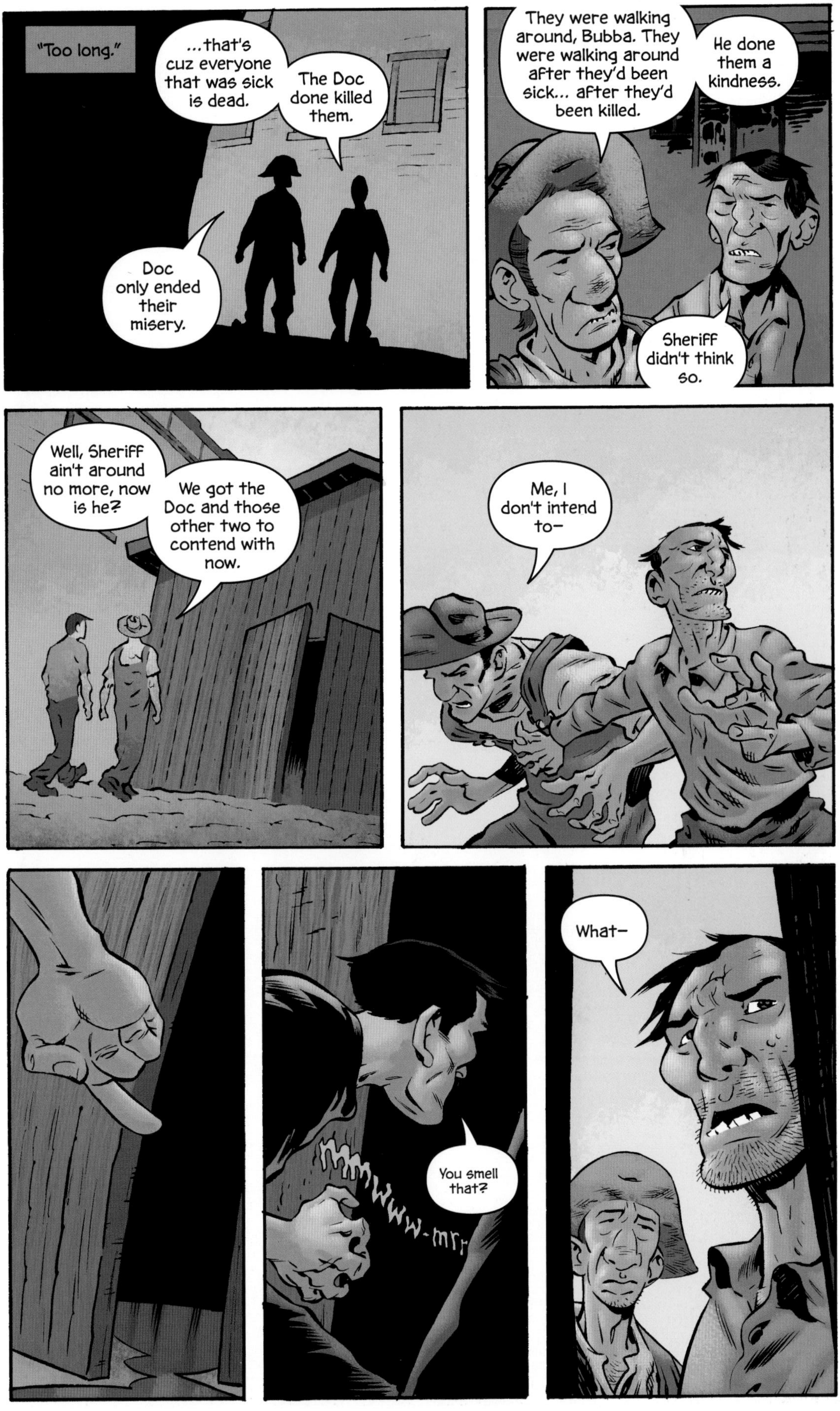

"Too long."
...that's cuz everyone that was sick is dead.
The Doc done killed them.
Doc only ended their misery.
They were walking around, Bubba. They were walking around after they'd been sick... after they'd been killed.
He done them a kindness.
Sheriff didn't think so.
Well, Sheriff ain't around no more, now is he?
We got the Doc and those other two to contend with now.
Me, I don't intend to–
mmwww-mrr
You smell that?
What–

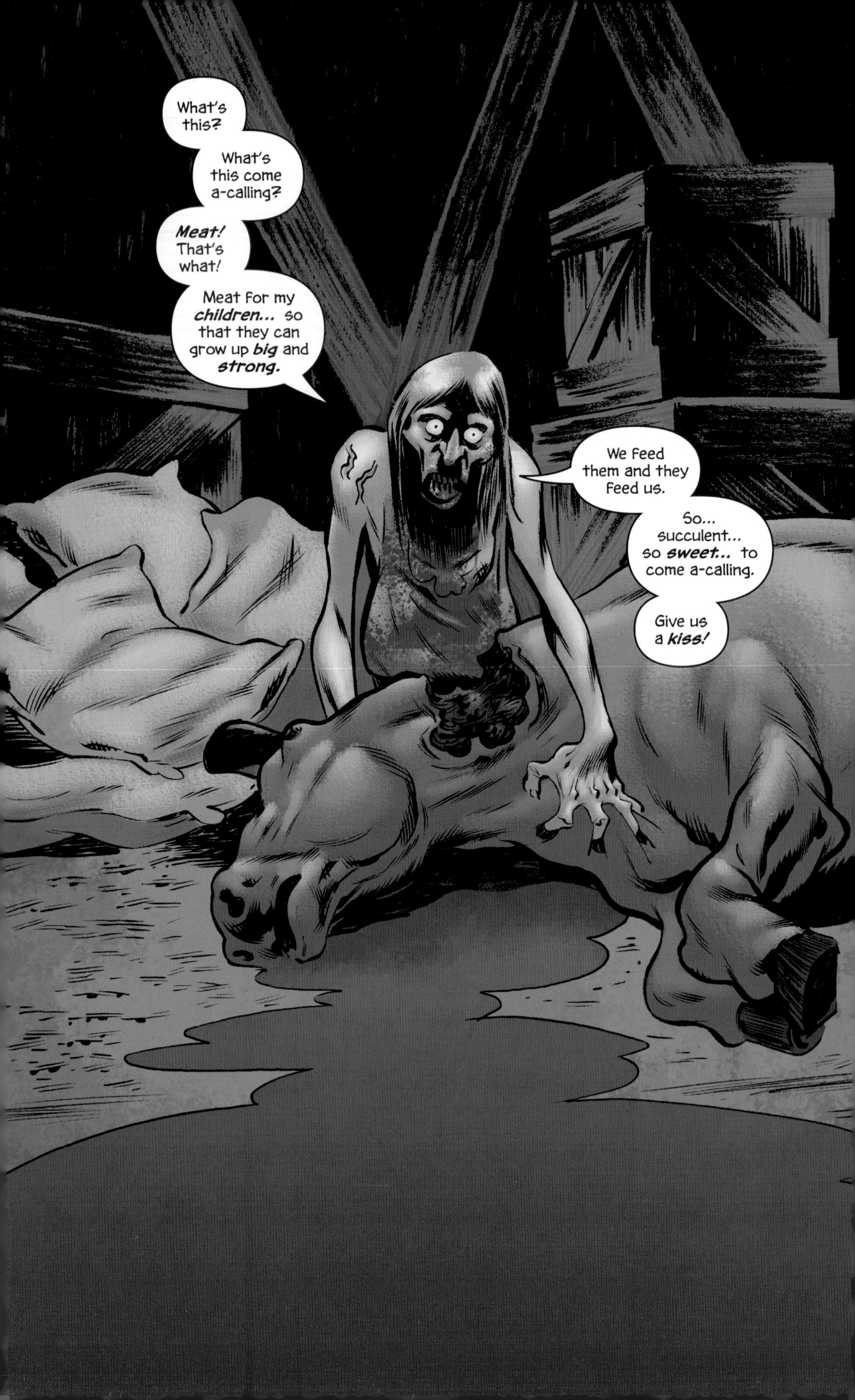
What's this?
What's this come a-calling?
Meat! That's what!
Meat for my *children...* so that they can grow up *big* and *strong.*
We feed them and they feed us.
So... succulent... so *sweet...* to come a-calling.
Give us a *kiss!*

CHAPTER FIVE

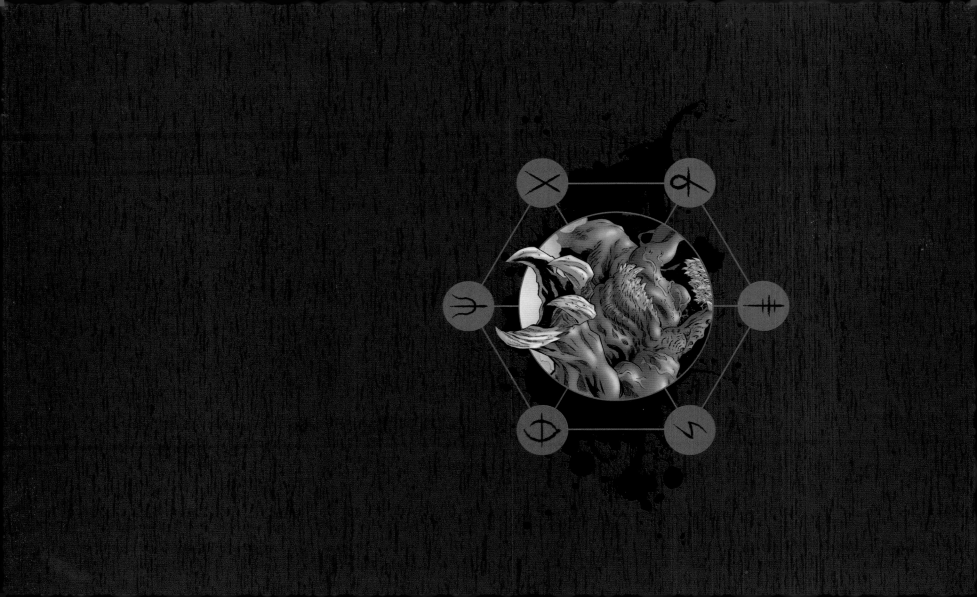

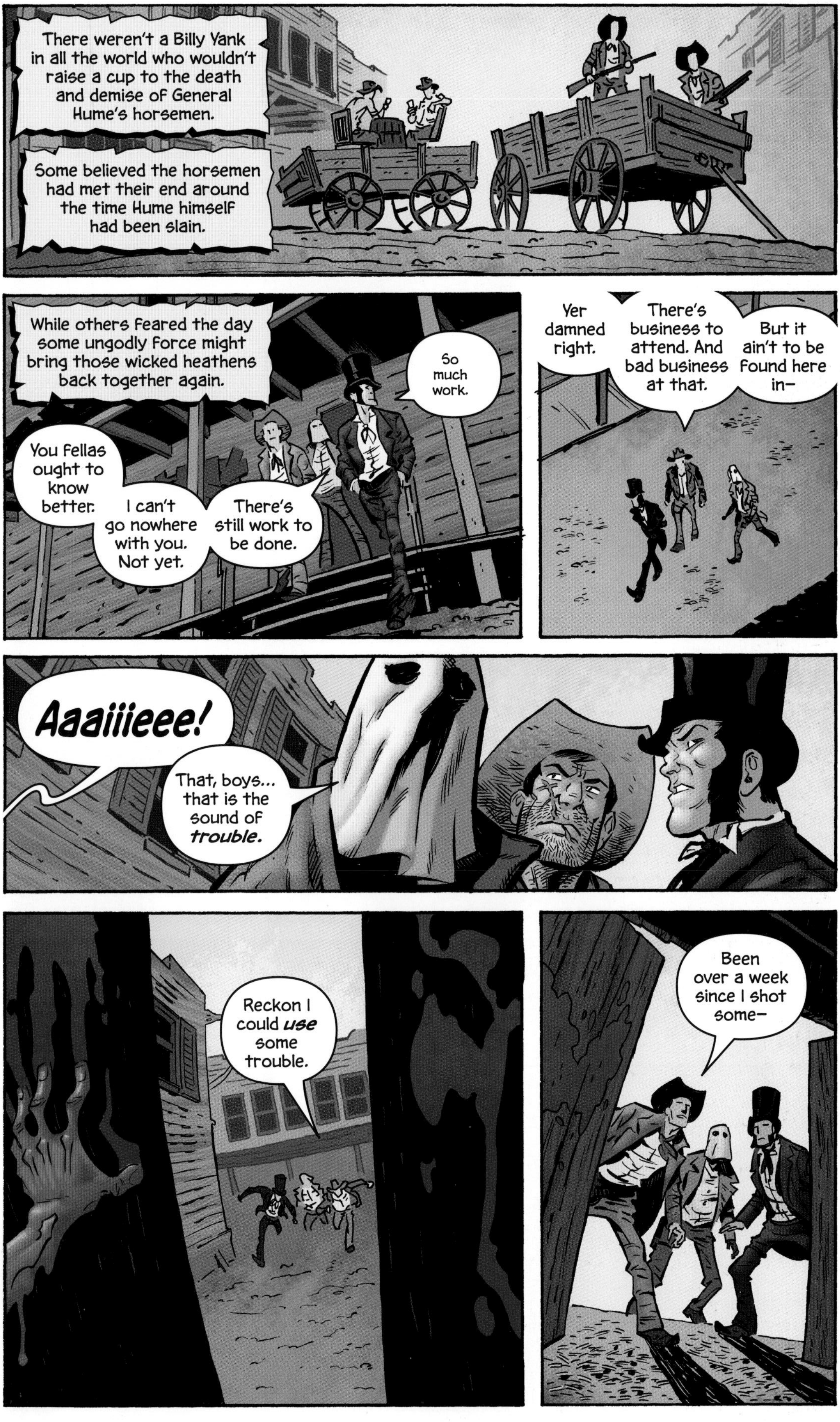

There weren't a Billy Yank in all the world who wouldn't raise a cup to the death and demise of General Hume's horsemen.
Some believed the horsemen had met their end around the time Hume himself had been slain.
While others feared the day some ungodly force might bring those wicked heathens back together again.
So much work.
You fellas ought to know better.
I can't go nowhere with you. Not yet.
There's still work to be done.
Yer damned right.
There's business to attend. And bad business at that.
But it ain't to be found here in—
Aaaiiieee!
That, boys... that is the sound of *trouble.*
Reckon I could *use* some trouble.
Been over a week since I shot some—

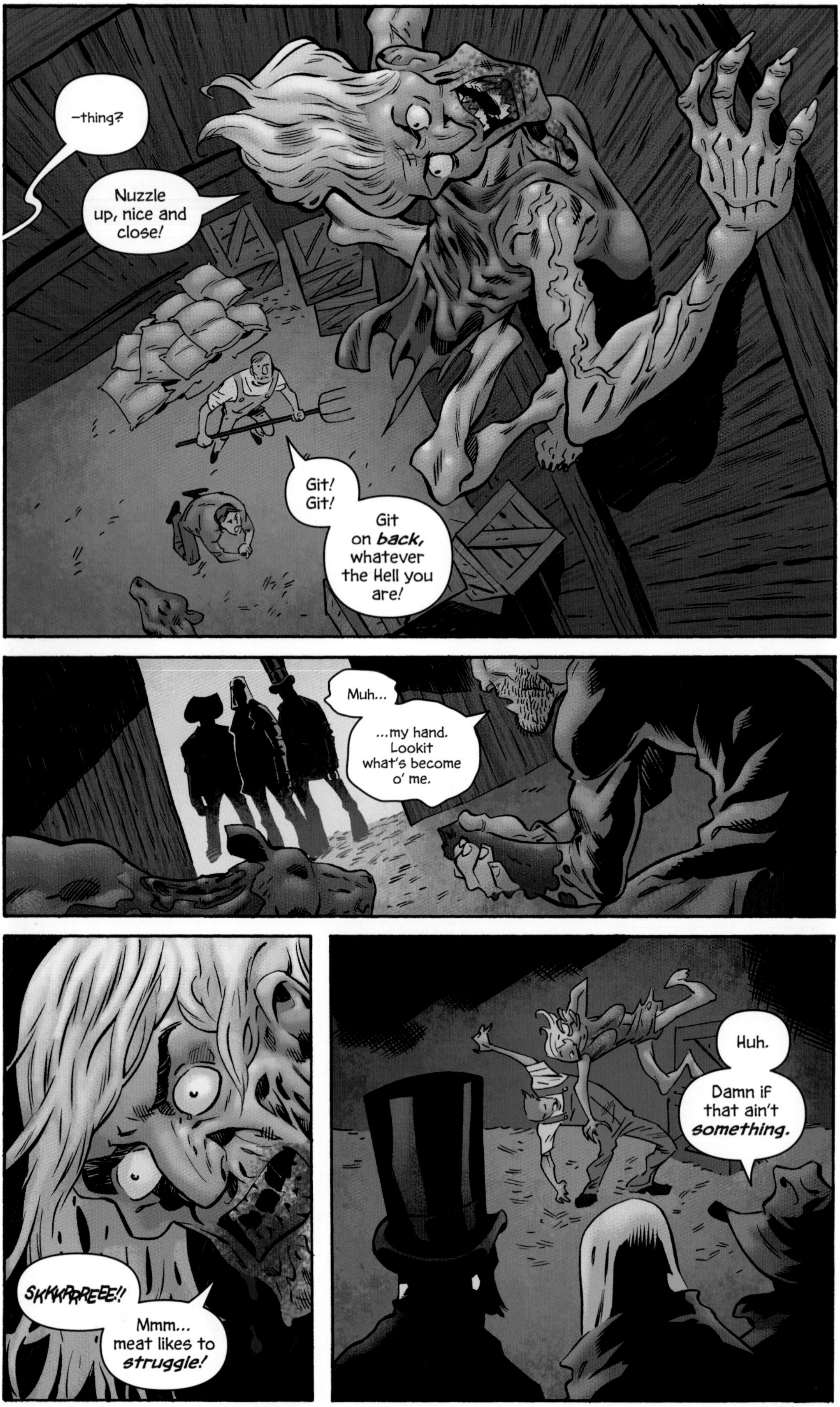
—thing?
Nuzzle up, nice and close!
Git! Git!
Git on **back,** whatever the Hell you are!
Muh...
...my hand. Lookit what's become o' me.
SKKKRRREEE!!
Mmm... meat likes to *struggle!*
Huh.
Damn if that ain't *something.*

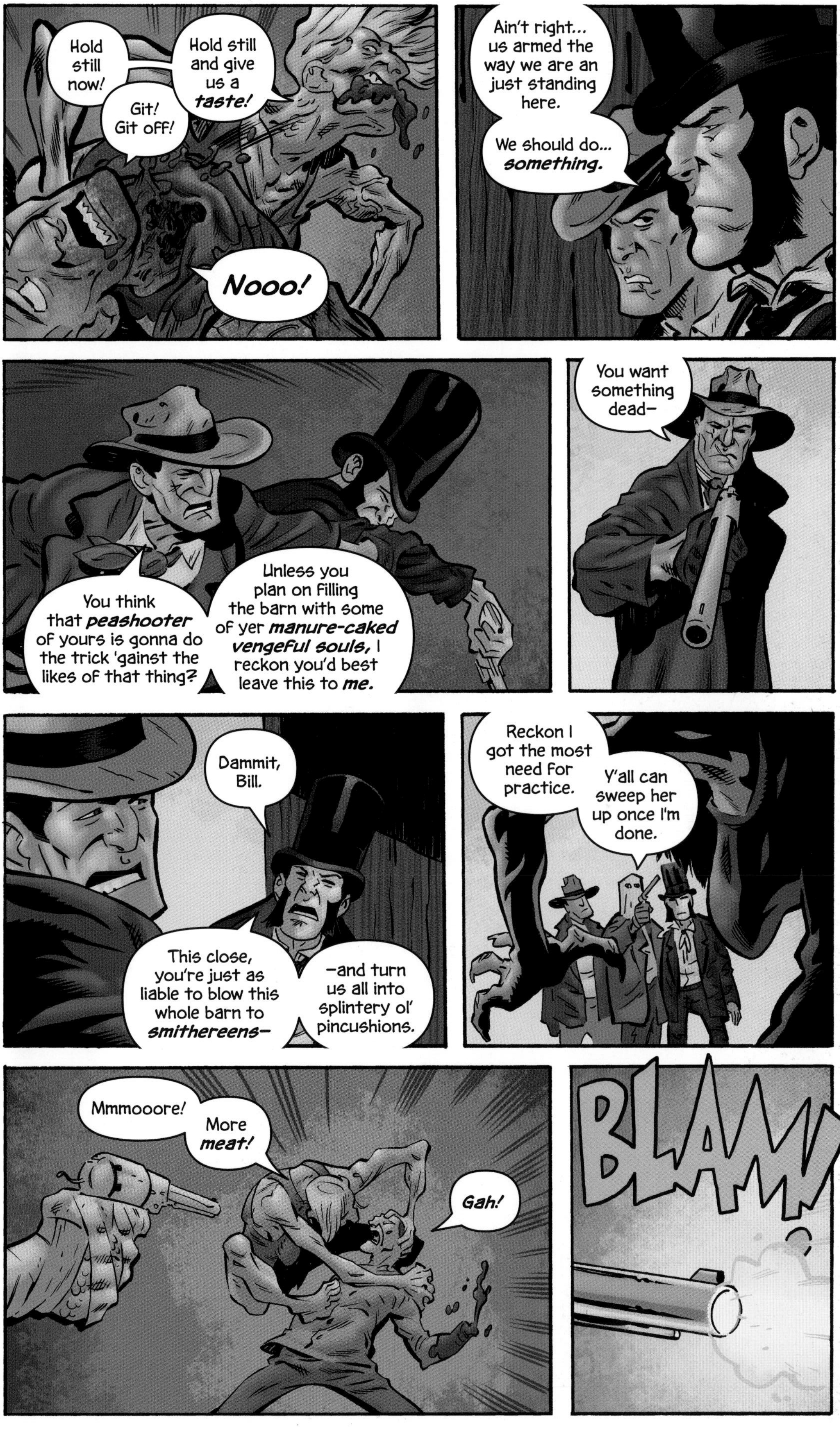

Hold still now!
Hold still and give us a *taste!*
Git! Git off!
Nooo!
Ain't right... us armed the way we are an just standing here.
We should do... ***something.***
You think that ***peashooter*** of yours is gonna do the trick 'gainst the likes of that thing?
Unless you plan on filling the barn with some of yer ***manure-caked vengeful souls,*** I reckon you'd best leave this to ***me.***
You want something dead—
Dammit, Bill.
This close, you're just as liable to blow this whole barn to ***smithereens—***
—and turn us all into splintery ol' pincushions.
Reckon I got the most need for practice.
Y'all can sweep her up once I'm done.
Mmmooore!
More ***meat!***
Gah!
BLAM

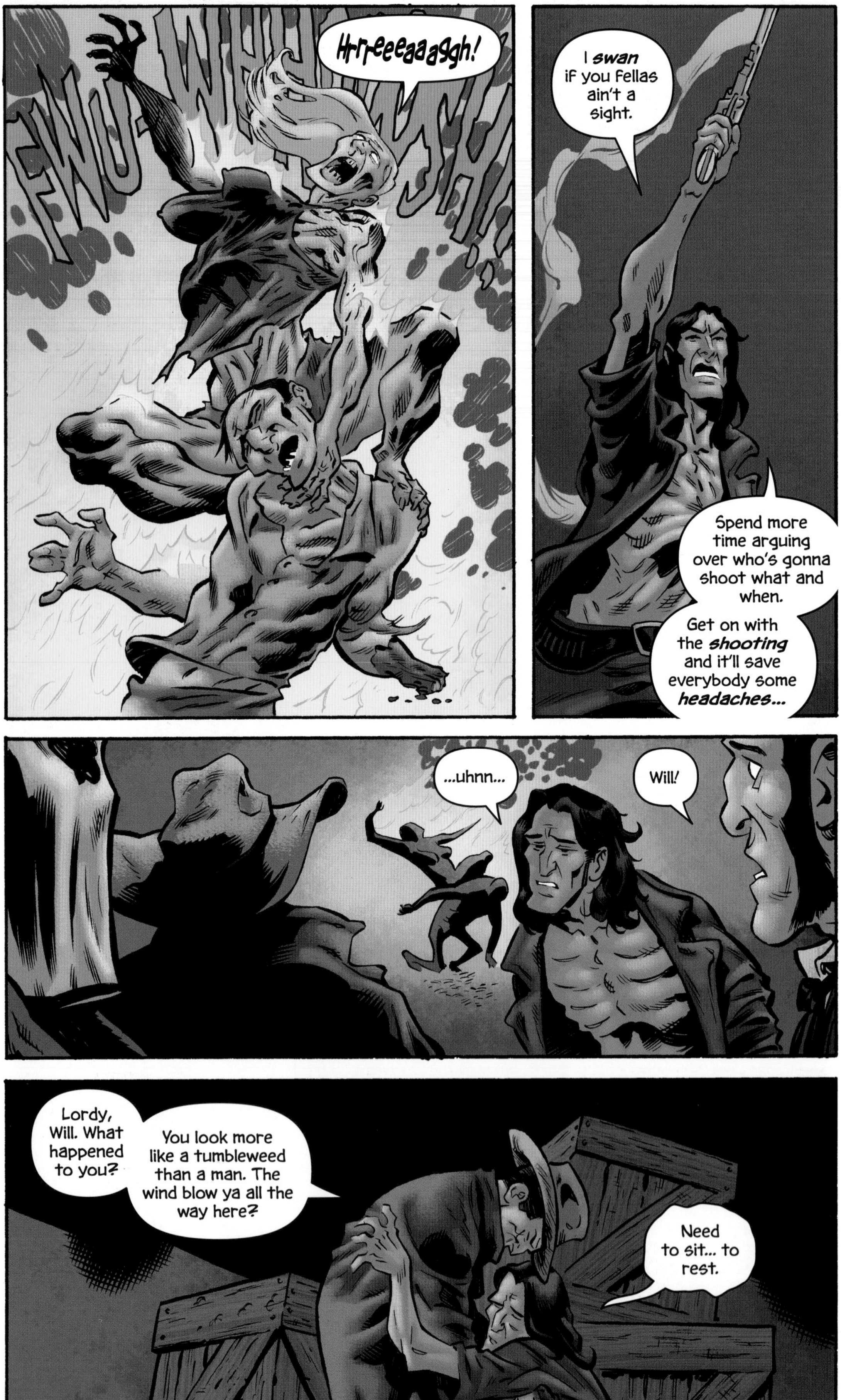
FWU-WHOOSH!!
Hrrreeeaaagh!
I *swan* if you fellas ain't a sight.
Spend more time arguing over who's gonna shoot what and when.
Get on with the *shooting* and it'll save everybody some *headaches...*
...uhnn...
Will!
Lordy, Will. What happened to you?
You look more like a tumbleweed than a man. The wind blow ya all the way here?
Need to sit... to rest.

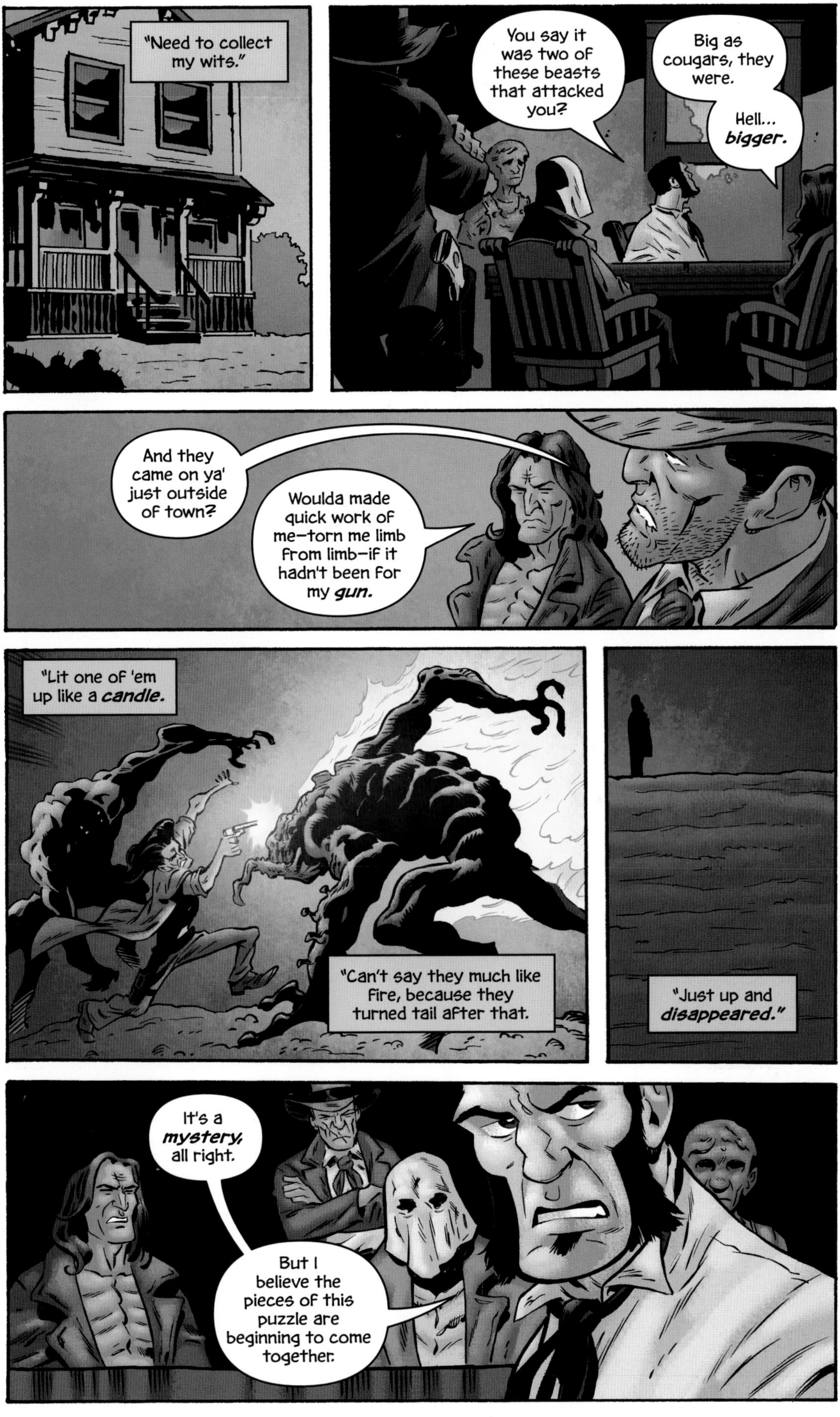
"Need to collect my wits."
You say it was two of these beasts that attacked you?
Big as cougars, they were.
Hell... **bigger.**
And they came on ya' just outside of town?
Woulda made quick work of me—torn me limb from limb—if it hadn't been for my **gun.**
"Lit one of 'em up like a **candle.**
"Can't say they much like fire, because they turned tail after that.
"Just up and **disappeared.**"
It's a **mystery,** all right.
But I believe the pieces of this puzzle are beginning to come together.

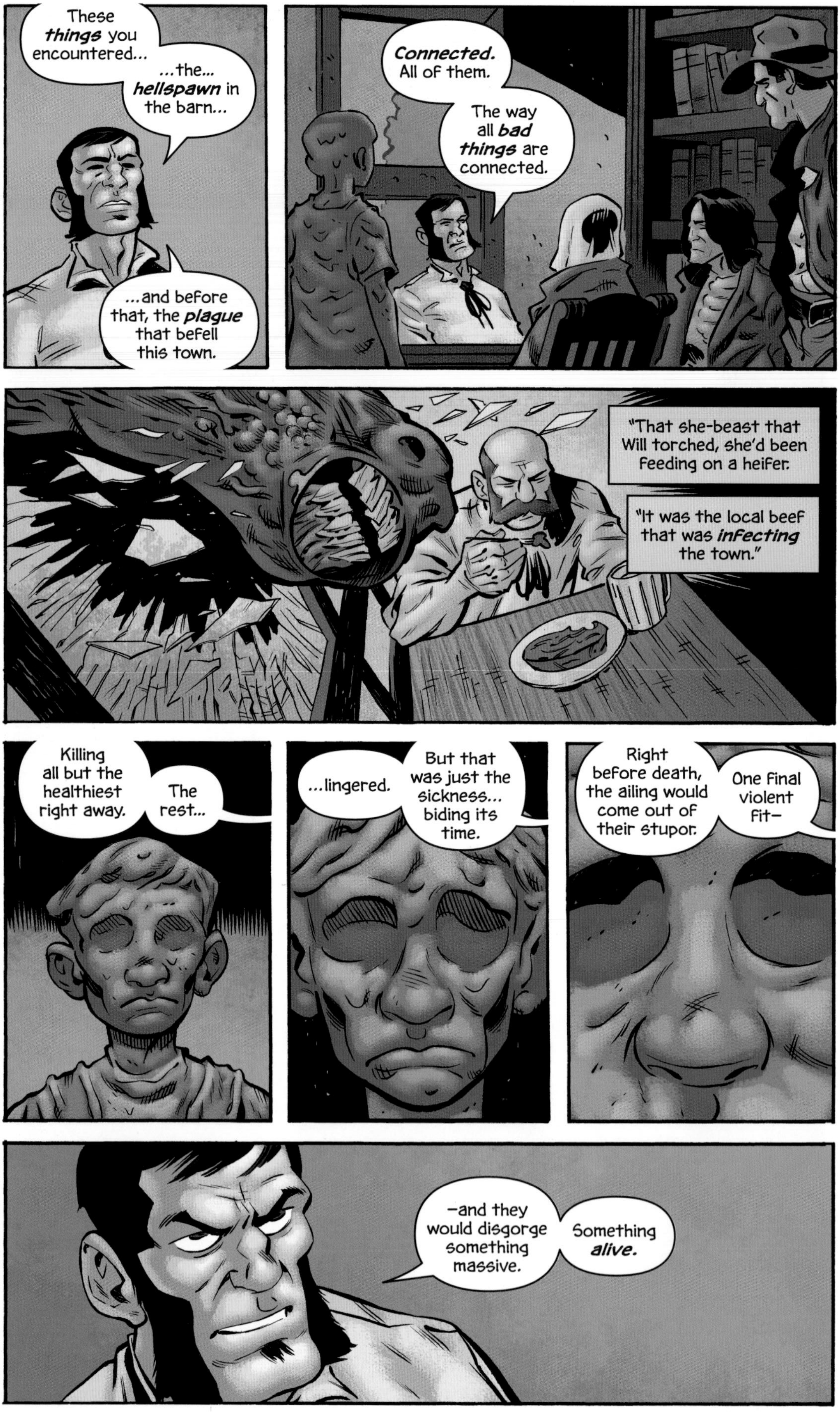
These *things* you encountered...
...the... *hellspawn* in the barn...
...and before that, the *plague* that befell this town.
Connected. All of them.
The way all *bad things* are connected.
"That she-beast that Will torched, she'd been feeding on a heifer.
"It was the local beef that was *infecting* the town."
Killing all but the healthiest right away.
The rest...
...lingered.
But that was just the sickness... biding its time.
Right before death, the ailing would come out of their stupor.
One final violent fit–
–and they would disgorge something massive.
Something *alive.*

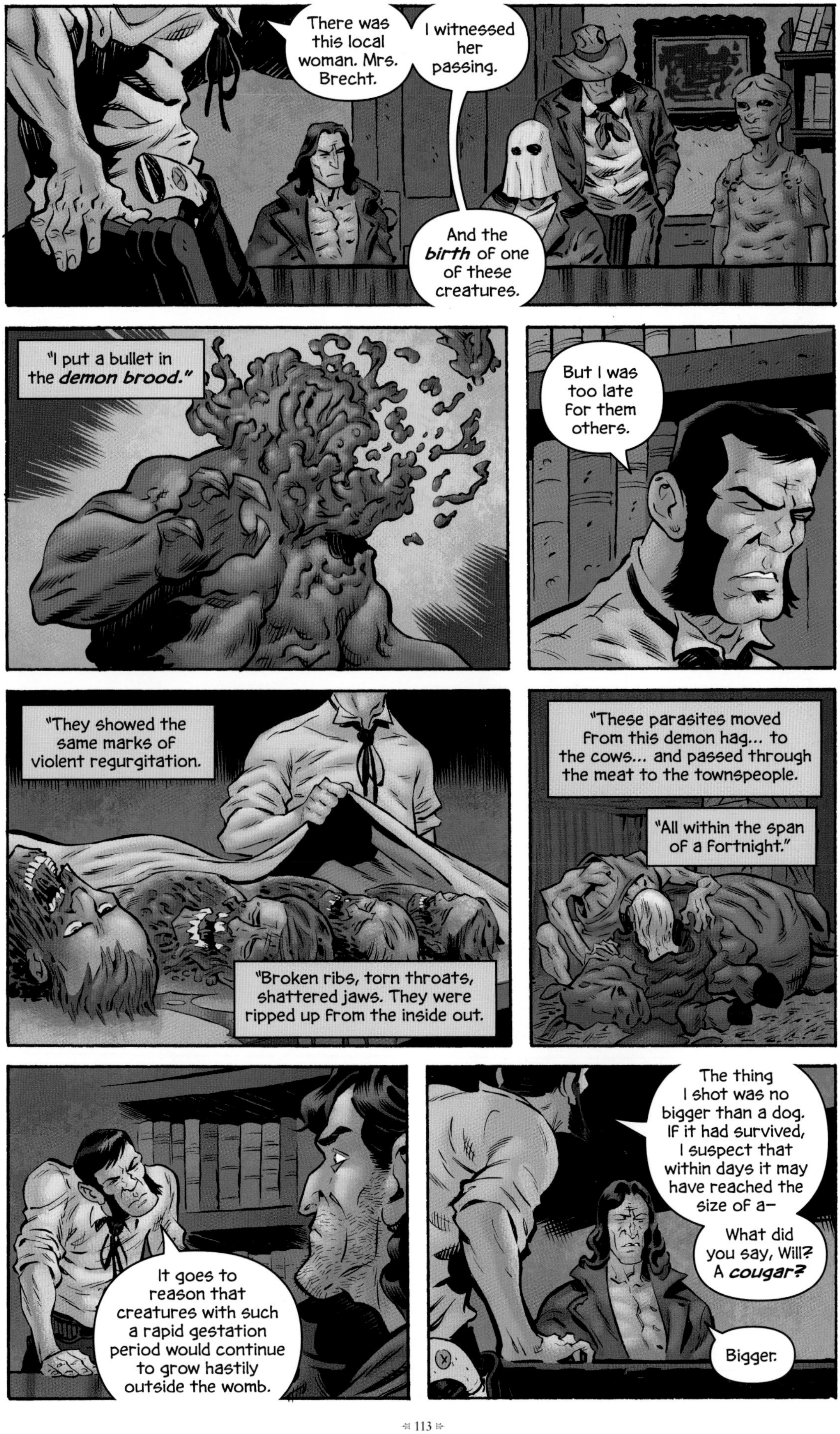
There was this local woman. Mrs. Brecht.
I witnessed her passing.
And the *birth* of one of these creatures.
"I put a bullet in the *demon brood.*"
But I was too late for them others.
"They showed the same marks of violent regurgitation.
"Broken ribs, torn throats, shattered jaws. They were ripped up from the inside out.
"These parasites moved from this demon hag... to the cows... and passed through the meat to the townspeople.
"All within the span of a fortnight."
It goes to reason that creatures with such a rapid gestation period would continue to grow hastily outside the womb.
The thing I shot was no bigger than a dog. If it had survived, I suspect that within days it may have reached the size of a—
What did you say, Will? A *cougar?*
Bigger.

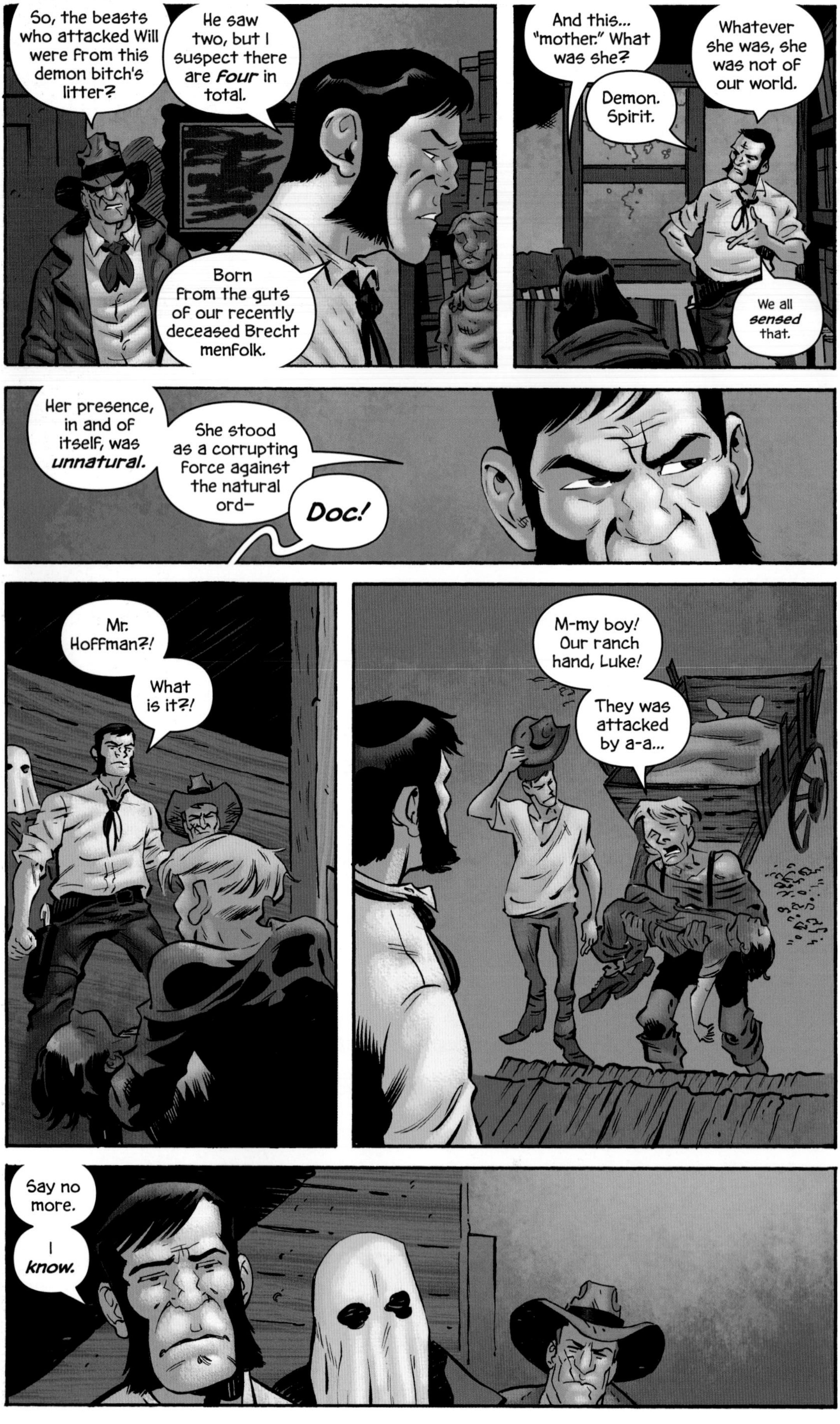
So, the beasts who attacked Will were from this demon bitch's litter?
He saw two, but I suspect there are *four* in total.
Born from the guts of our recently deceased Brecht menfolk.
And this... "mother." What was she?
Demon. Spirit.
Whatever she was, she was not of our world.
We all *sensed* that.
Her presence, in and of itself, was ***unnatural.***
She stood as a corrupting force against the natural ord–
Doc!
Mr. Hoffman?!
What is it?!
M-my boy! Our ranch hand, Luke!
They was attacked by a-a...
Say no more.
I ***know.***

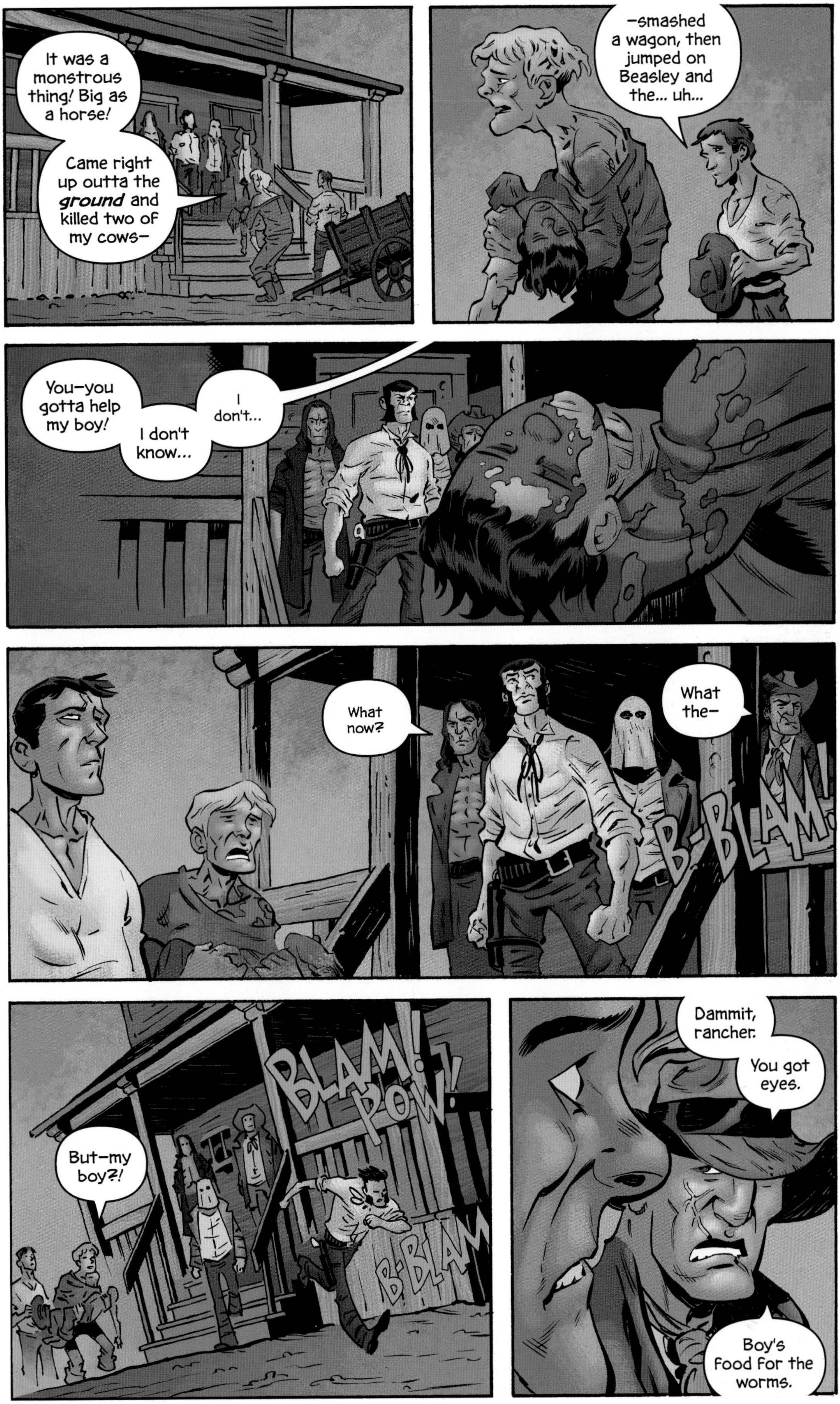
It was a monstrous thing! Big as a horse!
Came right up outta the ground and killed two of my cows—
—smashed a wagon, then jumped on Beasley and the... uh...
You—you gotta help my boy!
I don't know...
I don't...
What now?
What the—
B-BLAM!
BLAM! POW!
B-BLAM
But—my boy?!
Dammit, rancher.
You got eyes.
Boy's food for the worms.

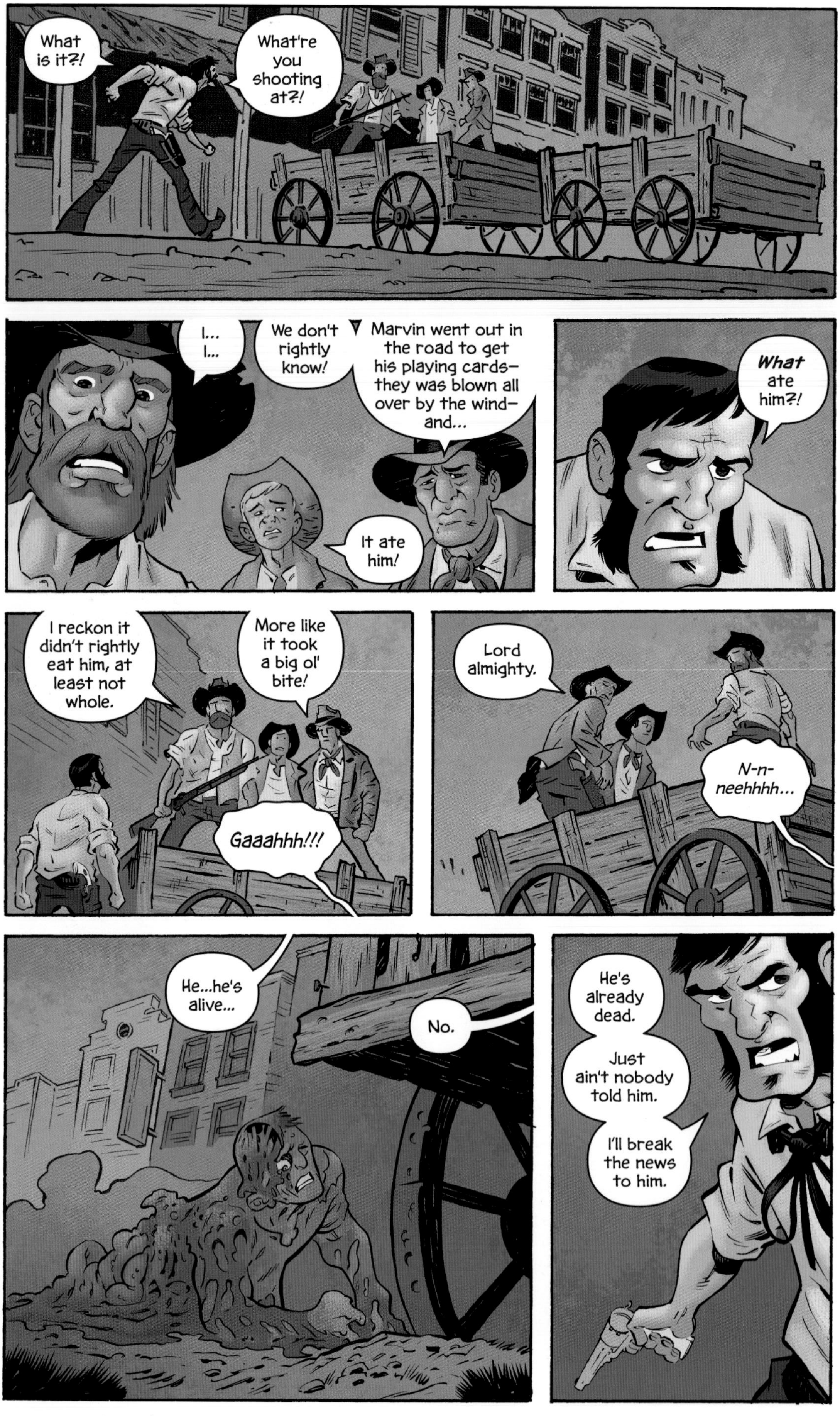
What is it?!
What're you shooting at?!
I... I...
We don't rightly know!
Marvin went out in the road to get his playing cards—they was blown all over by the wind—and...
It ate him!
What ate him?!
I reckon it didn't rightly eat him, at least not whole.
More like it took a big ol' bite!
Gaaahhh!!!
Lord almighty.
N-n-neehhhh...
He...he's alive...
No.
He's already dead.
Just ain't nobody told him.
I'll break the news to him.

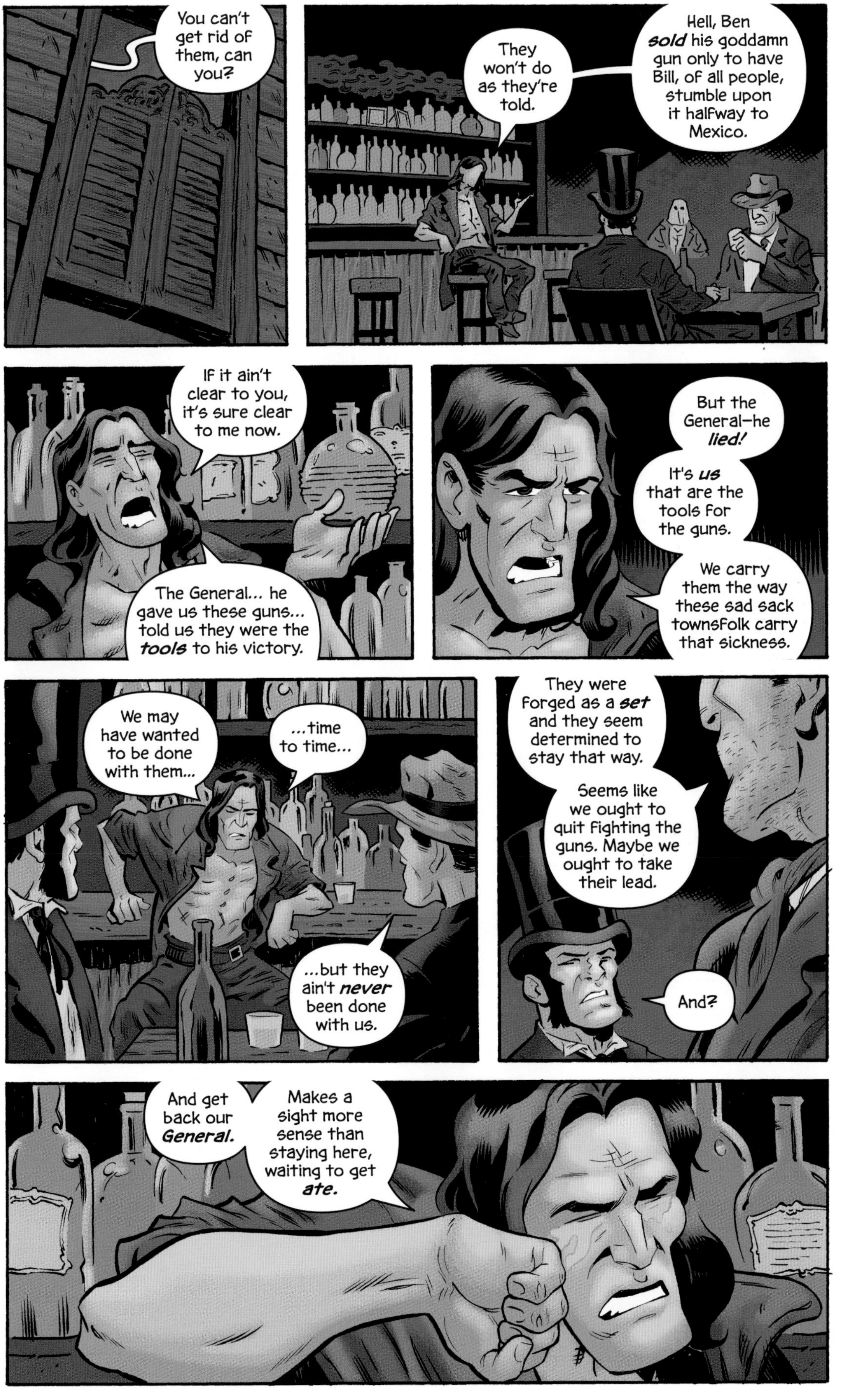
You can't get rid of them, can you?
Hell, Ben ***sold*** his goddamn gun only to have Bill, of all people, stumble upon it halfway to Mexico.
They won't do as they're told.
If it ain't clear to you, it's sure clear to me now.
The General... he gave us these guns... told us they were the ***tools*** to his victory.
But the General—he ***lied!***
It's ***us*** that are the tools for the guns.
We carry them the way these sad sack townsfolk carry that sickness.
We may have wanted to be done with them...
...time to time...
...but they ain't ***never*** been done with us.
They were forged as a ***set*** and they seem determined to stay that way.
Seems like we ought to quit fighting the guns. Maybe we ought to take their lead.
And?
Makes a sight more sense than staying here, waiting to get ***ate.***
And get back our ***General.***

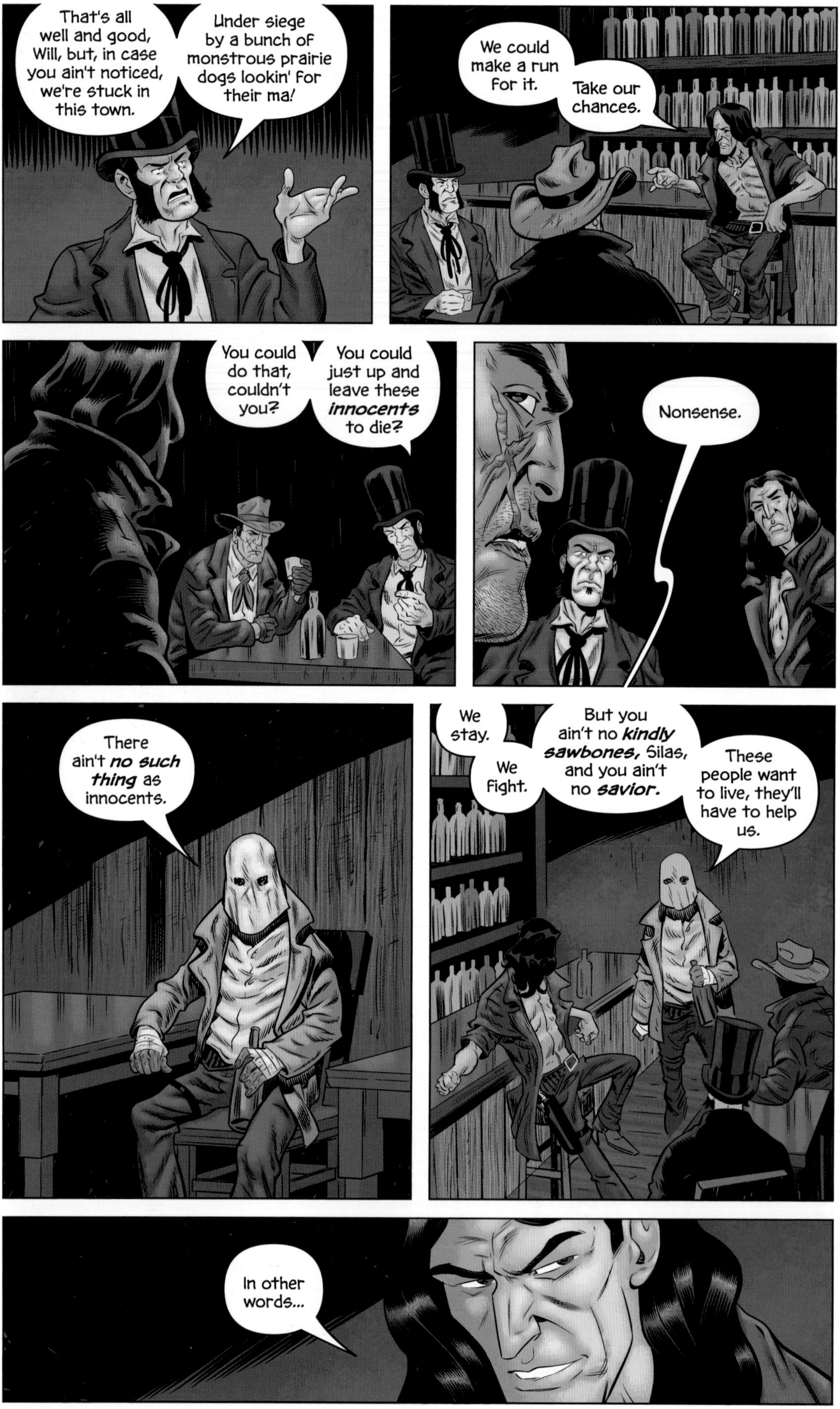
That's all well and good, Will, but, in case you ain't noticed, we're stuck in this town.
Under siege by a bunch of monstrous prairie dogs lookin' for their ma!
We could make a run for it.
Take our chances.
You could do that, couldn't you?
You could just up and leave these *innocents* to die?
Nonsense.
There ain't ***no such thing*** as innocents.
We stay.
We fight.
But you ain't no ***kindly sawbones,*** Silas, and you ain't no ***savior.***
These people want to live, they'll have to help us.
In other words...

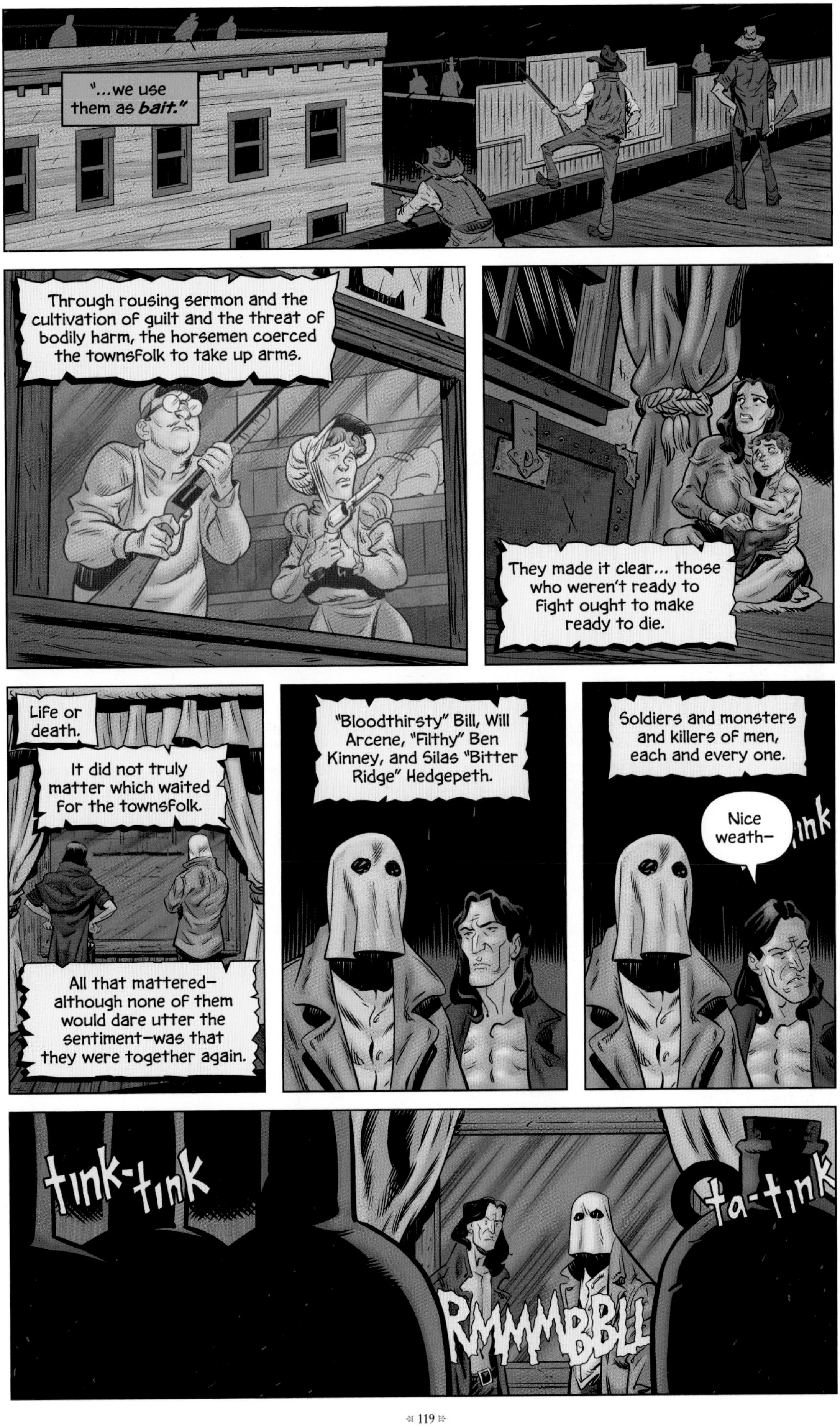
"...we use them as *bait.*"
Through rousing sermon and the cultivation of guilt and the threat of bodily harm, the horsemen coerced the townsfolk to take up arms.
They made it clear... those who weren't ready to fight ought to make ready to die.
Life or death.
It did not truly matter which waited for the townsfolk.
All that mattered—although none of them would dare utter the sentiment—was that they were together again.
"Bloodthirsty" Bill, Will Arcene, "Filthy" Ben Kinney, and Silas "Bitter Ridge" Hedgepeth.
Soldiers and monsters and killers of men, each and every one.
Nice weath—
tink-tink
ta-tink
RMMMBBLL

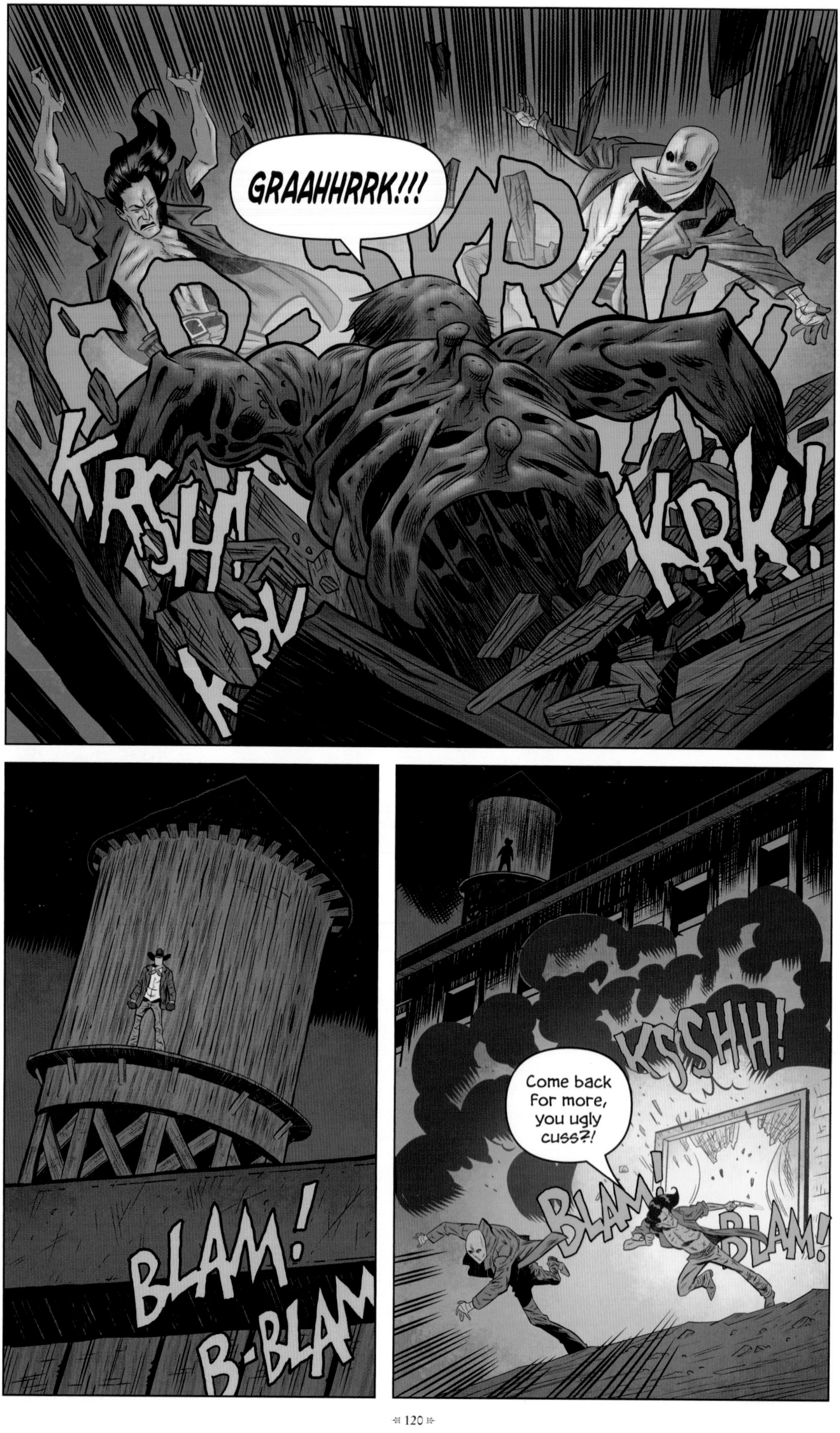
GRAAHHRRK!!!
KRSH!
KRK!
BLAM!
B-BLAM
KSSHH!
Come back for more, you ugly cuss?!
BLAM!
BLAM!

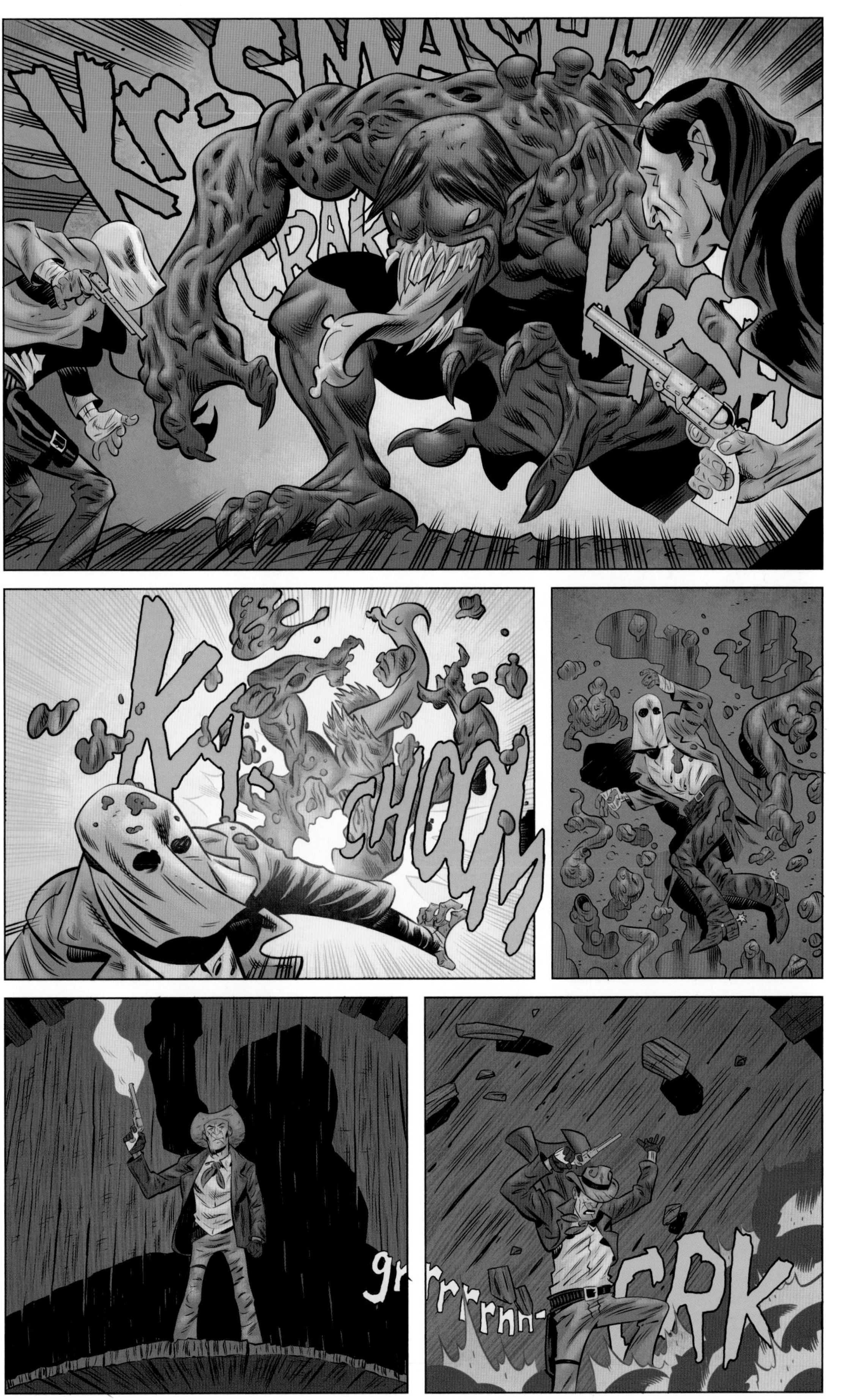
CRAK
KA-CHOOM
grrrrrnn-
CRK

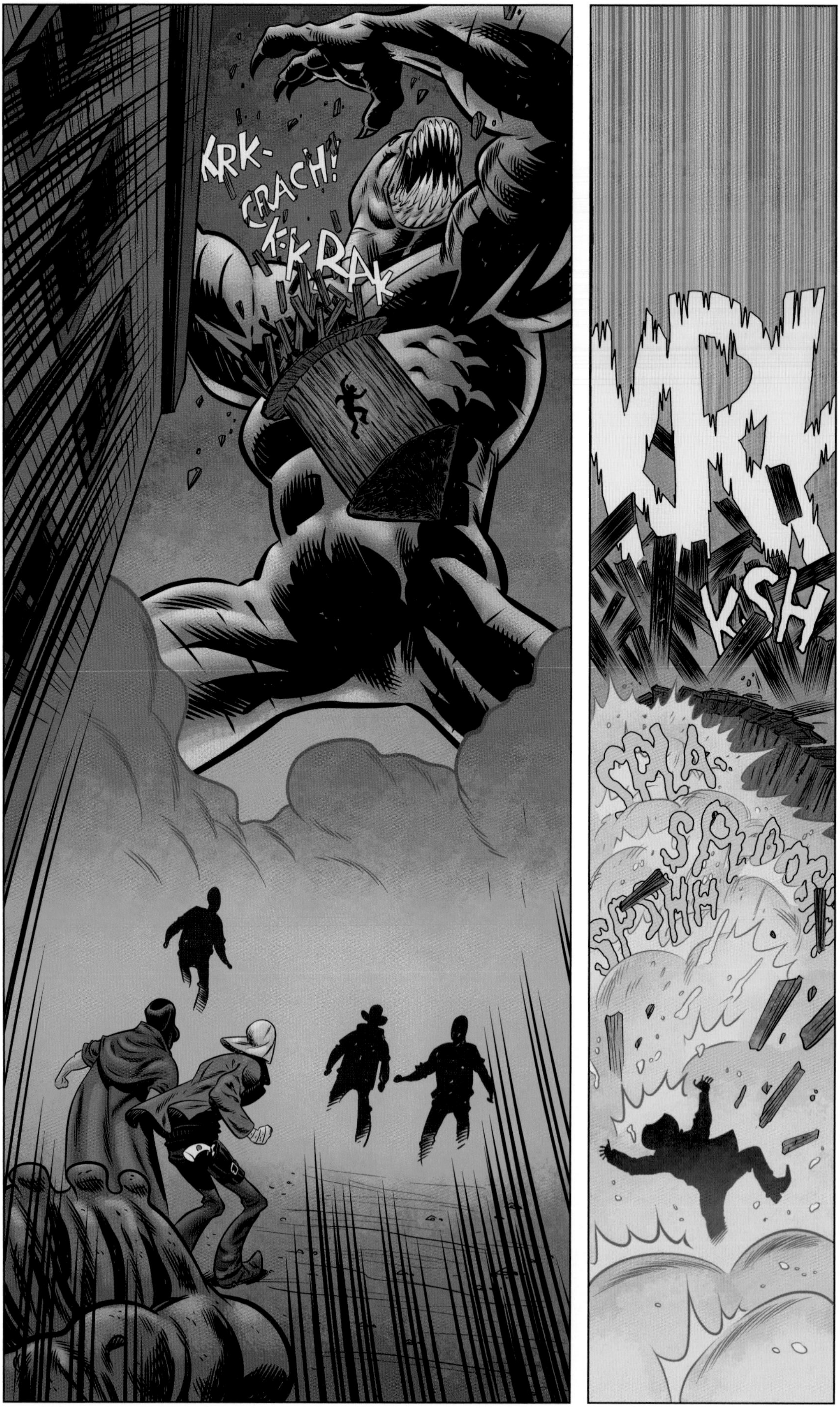
KRK-
CRACH!
K-K-KRAK
KSH
SPLA-
SPLOOSH!
SPSHH

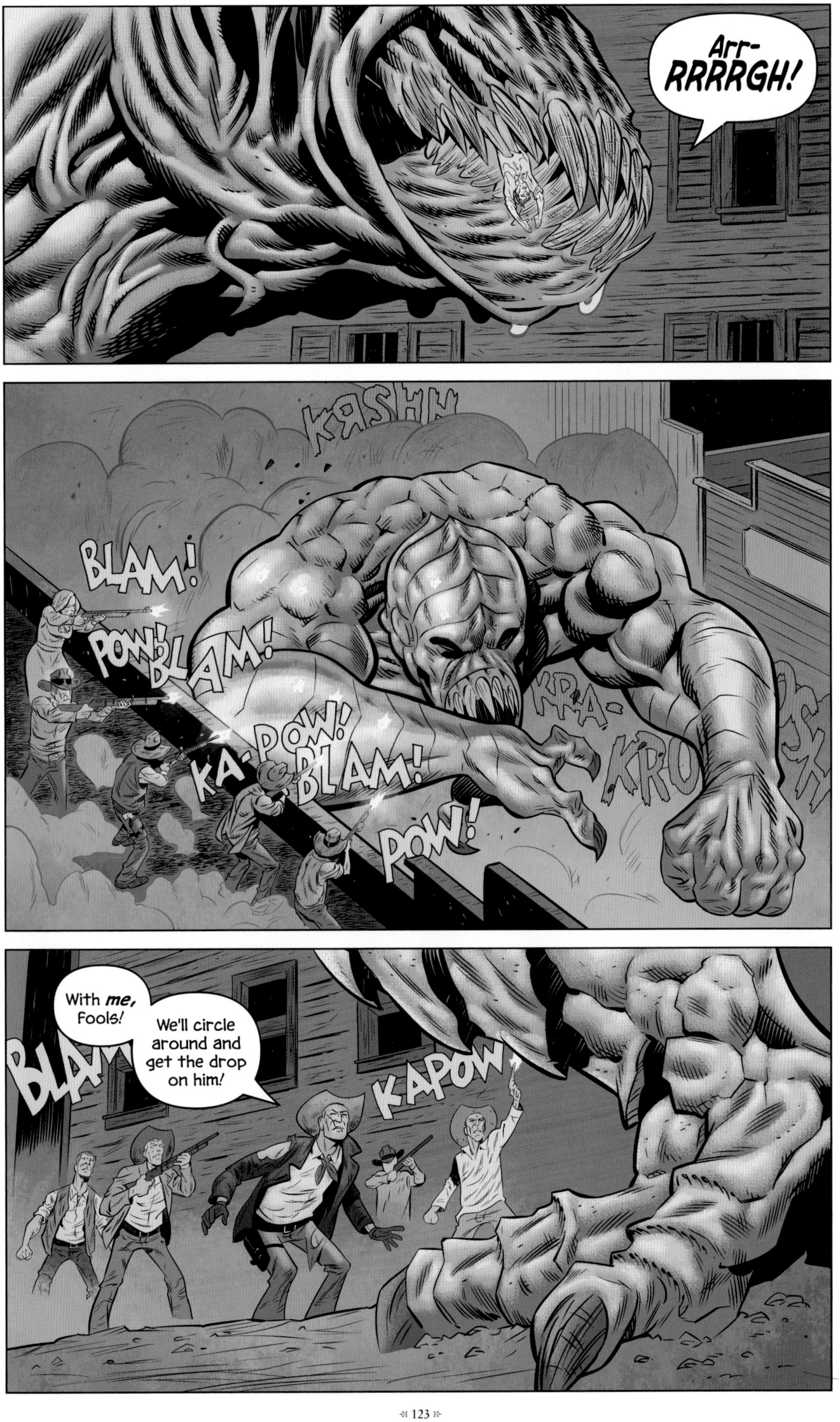
Arr-
RRRRGH!
KRASHH
BLAM!
POW! BLAM!
KA-POW! BLAM!
POW!
KRA-
KRO
With *me*, Fools!
We'll circle around and get the drop on him!
KAPOW

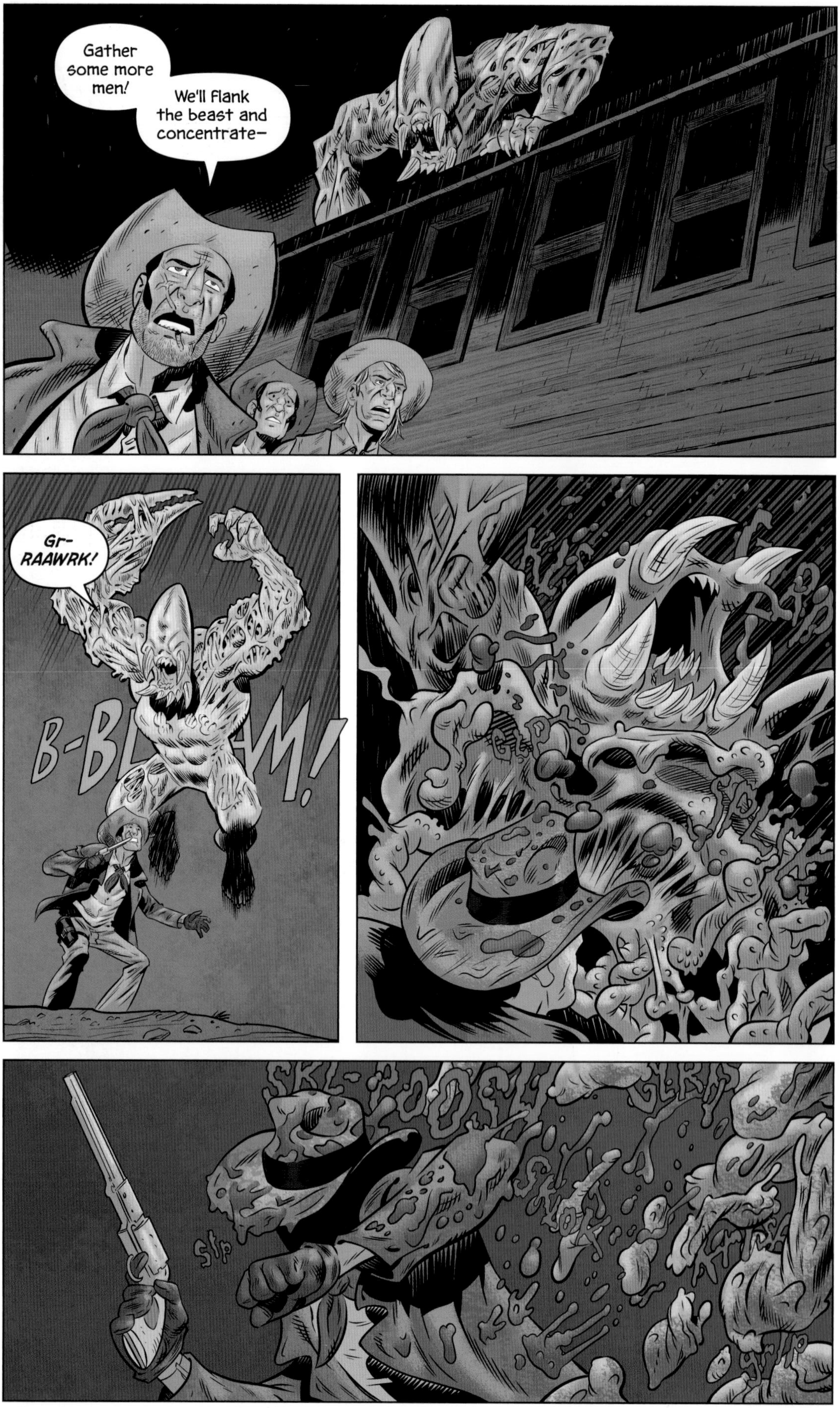
Gather some more men!
We'll flank the beast and concentrate—
Gr-RAAWRK!
B-BLAM!
slip

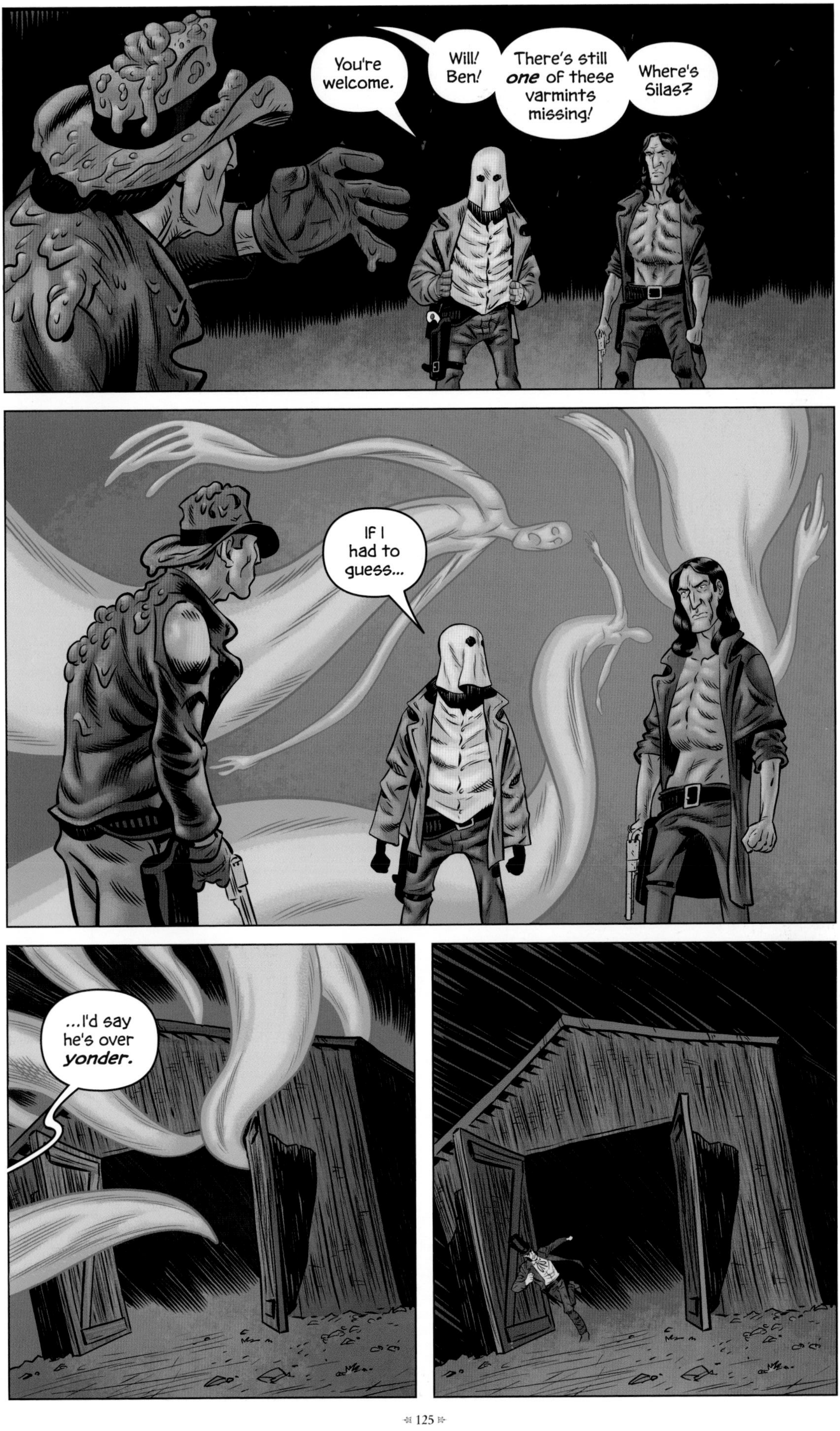
You're welcome.
Will! Ben!
There's still *one* of these varmints missing!
Where's Silas?
If I had to guess...
...I'd say he's over *yonder.*

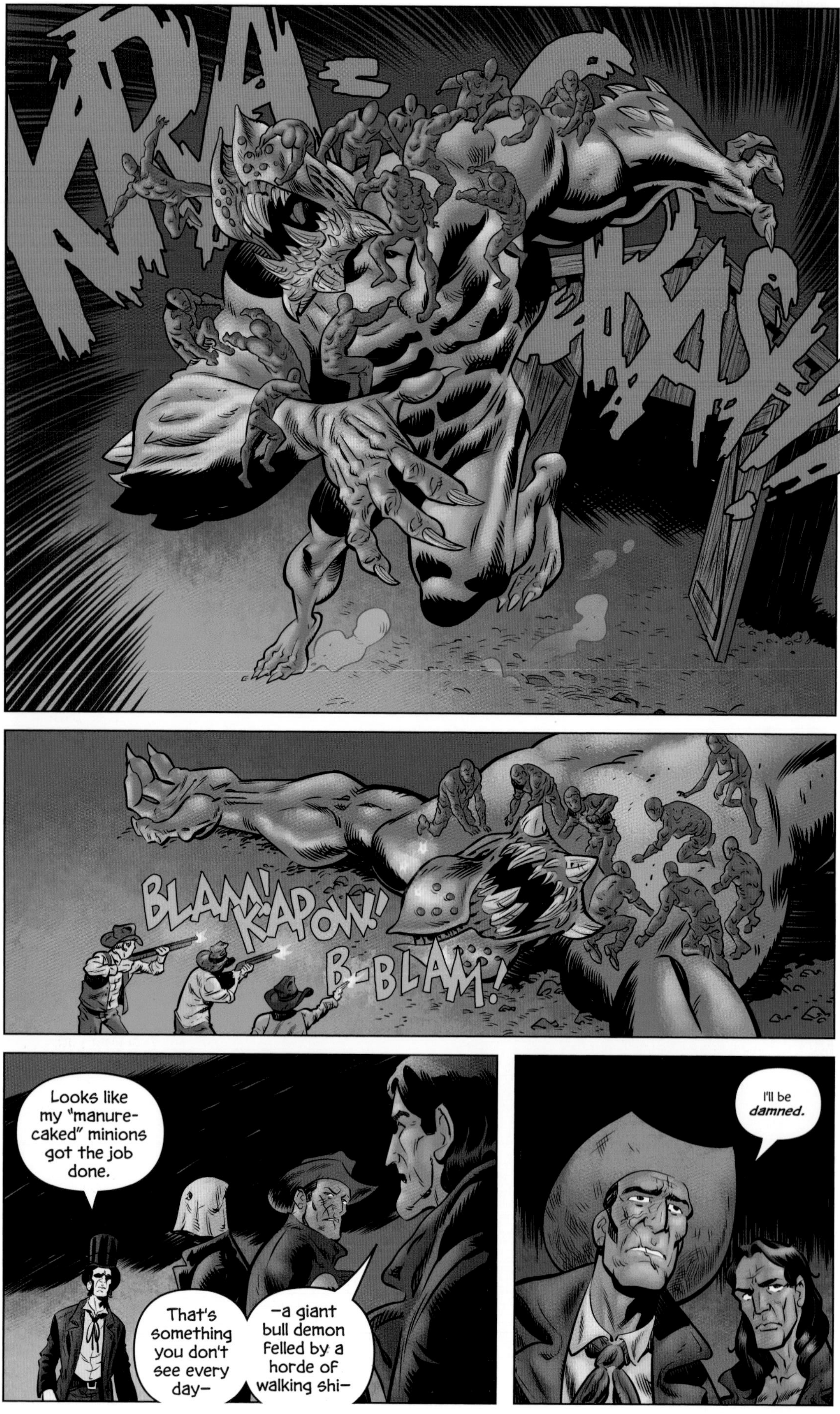
BLAM! K-APOW!
B-BLAM!
Looks like my "manure-caked" minions got the job done.
That's something you don't see every day—
—a giant bull demon felled by a horde of walking shi—
I'll be *damned.*

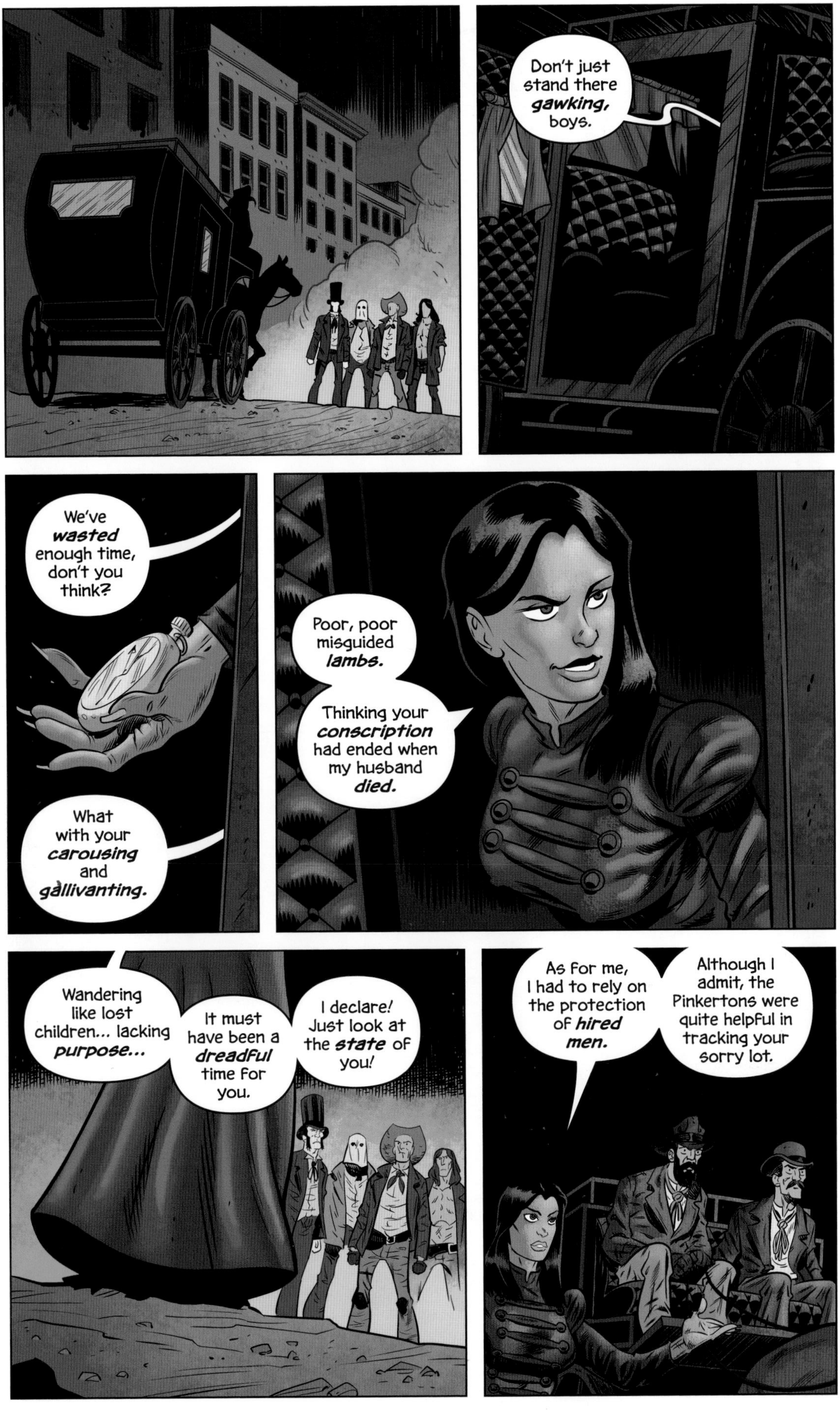
Don't just stand there ***gawking,*** boys.
We've ***wasted*** enough time, don't you think?
What with your ***carousing*** and ***gallivanting.***
Poor, poor misguided ***lambs.***
Thinking your ***conscription*** had ended when my husband ***died.***
Wandering like lost children... lacking ***purpose...***
It must have been a ***dreadful*** time for you.
I declare! Just look at the ***state*** of you!
As for me, I had to rely on the protection of ***hired men.***
Although I admit, the Pinkertons were quite helpful in tracking your sorry lot.

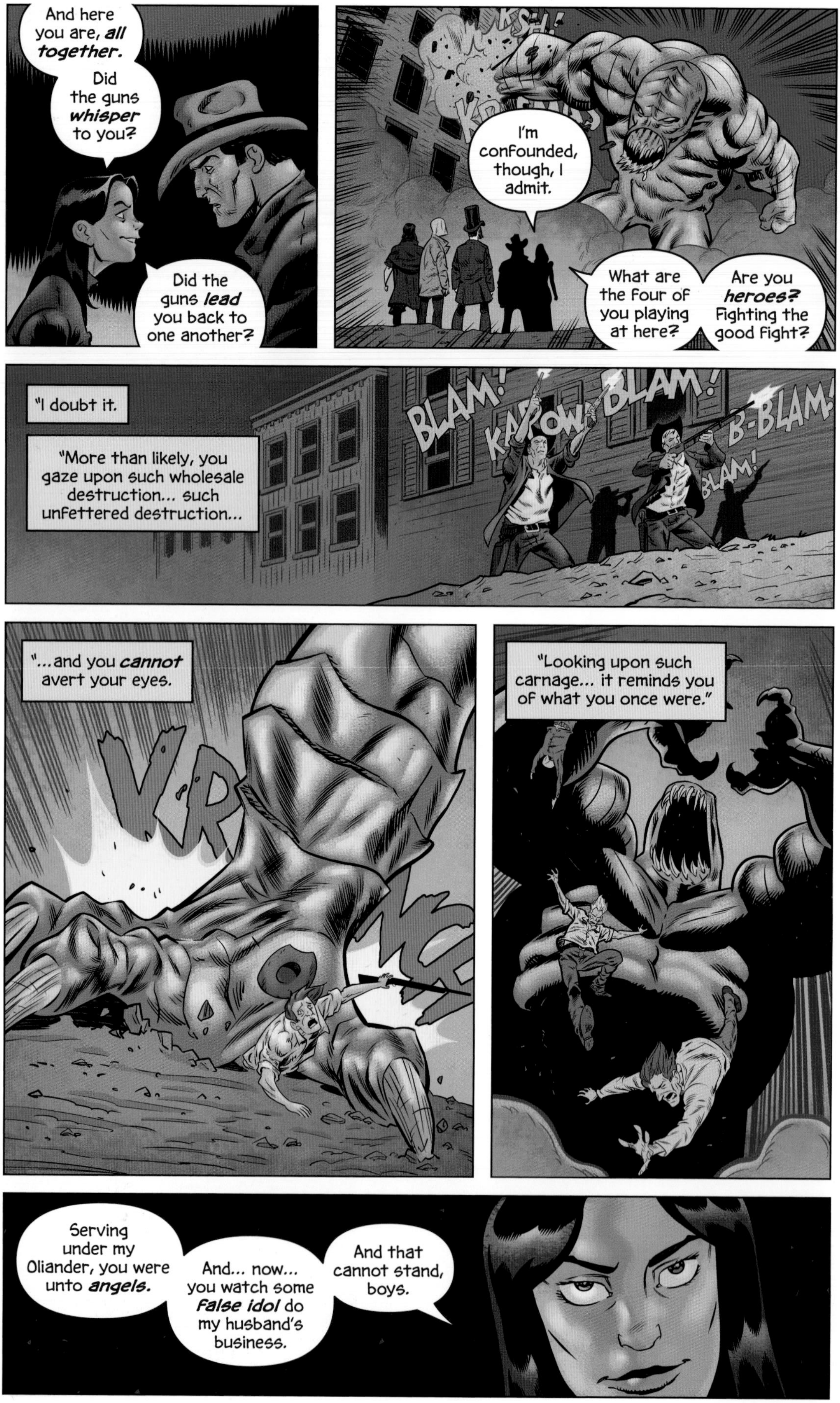

And here you are, *all together.*
Did the guns *whisper* to you?
Did the guns *lead* you back to one another?
I'm confounded, though, I admit.
What are the Four of you playing at here?
Are you *heroes?* Fighting the good fight?
"I doubt it.
"More than likely, you gaze upon such wholesale destruction... such unfettered destruction...
BLAM!
KAPOW!
BLAM!
B-BLAM!
BLAM!
"...and you *cannot* avert your eyes.
"Looking upon such carnage... it reminds you of what you once were."
Serving under my Oliander, you were unto *angels.*
And... now... you watch some *false idol* do my husband's business.
And that cannot stand, boys.

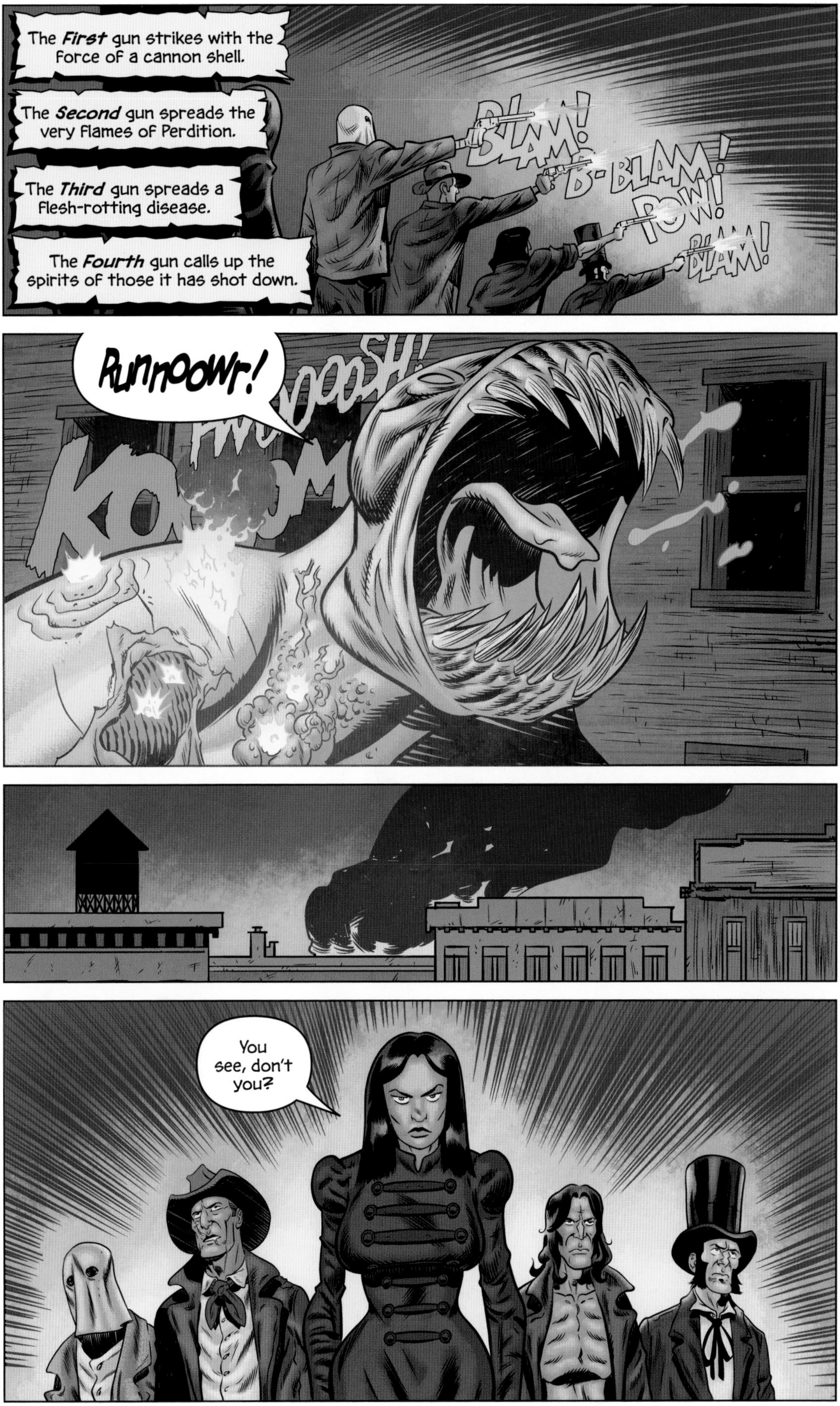
The *First* gun strikes with the force of a cannon shell.
The *Second* gun spreads the very flames of Perdition.
The *Third* gun spreads a flesh-rotting disease.
The *Fourth* gun calls up the spirits of those it has shot down.
BLAM!
BLAM!
B-BLAM!
POW!
BLAM!
Runnoowr!
You see, don't you?

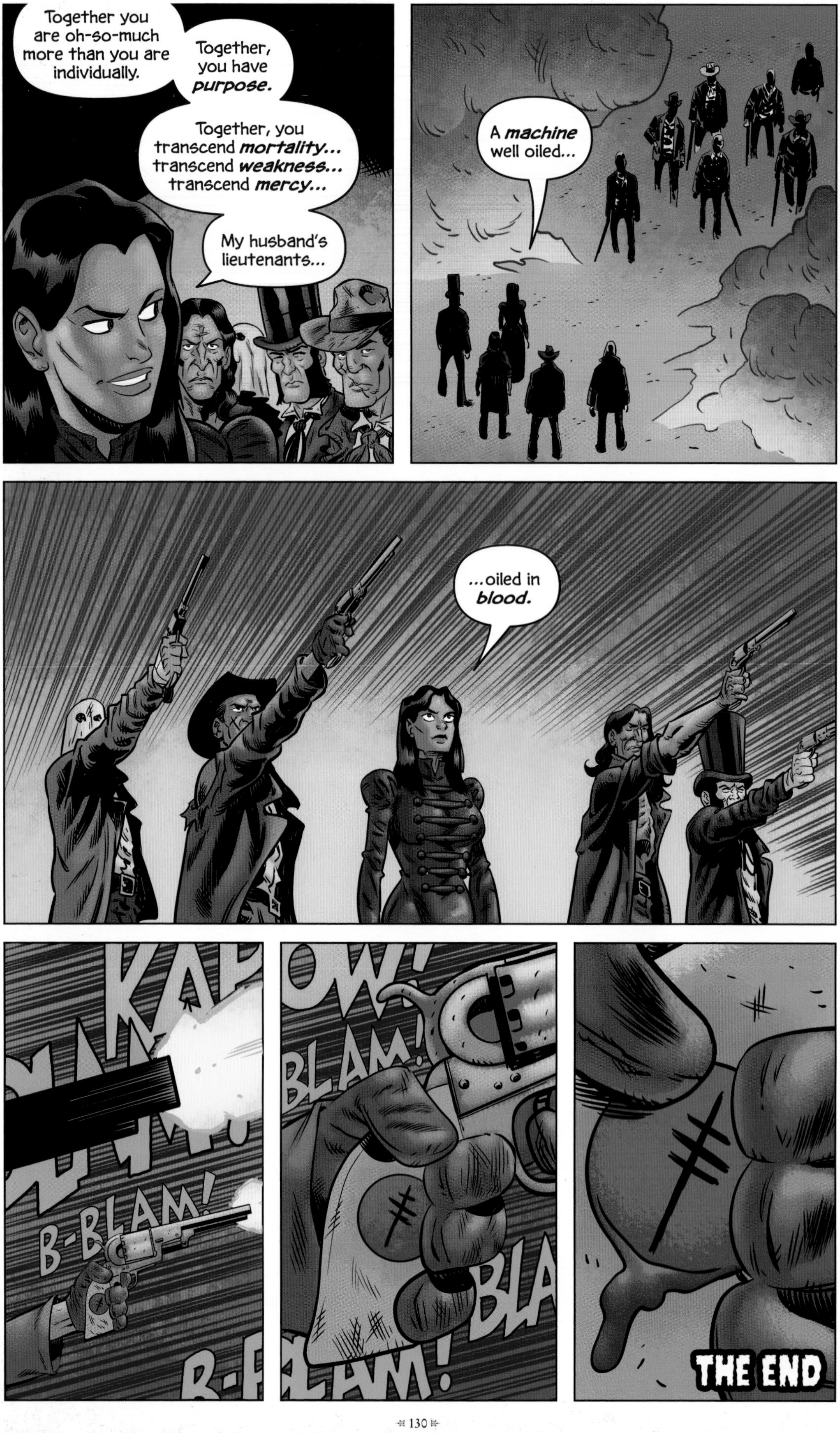
Together you are oh-so-much more than you are individually.
Together, you have *purpose.*
Together, you transcend *mortality...* transcend *weakness...* transcend *mercy...*
My husband's lieutenants...
A *machine* well oiled...
...oiled in *blood.*
KAPOW!
BLAM!
B-BLAM!
BLA
B-BLAM!
THE END

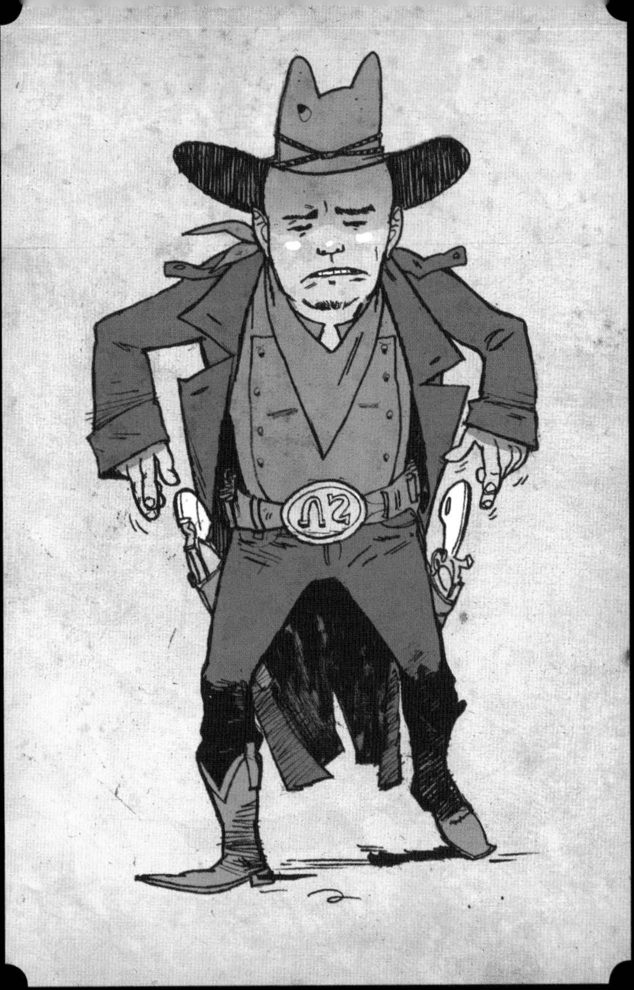

Author portrait illustrations by Jason Latour. jasonlatour.com

Cullen Bunn is the writer of comic books such *The Sixth Gun*, *The Damned*, *Helheim*, and *The Tooth* for Oni Press. He has also written titles including *Fearless Defenders*, *Venom*, *Deadpool Killustrated*, and *Wolverine* for Marvel Comics.

In addition, he is the author of the middle reader horror novel, *Crooked Hills*, and the collection of short fiction, *Creeping Stones and Other Stories*.

His prose work has appeared in numerous magazines and anthologies. Somewhere along the way, he founded Undaunted Press and edited the critically acclaimed horror zine *Whispers From the Shattered Forum*.

Cullen claims to have worked as an Alien Autopsy Specialist, Rodeo Clown, Pro Wrestling Manager, and Sasquatch Wrangler. He has fought for his life against mountain lions and performed on stage as the World's Youngest Hypnotist. Buy him a drink sometime, and he'll tell you all about it.

cullenbunn.com / @cullenbunn.

Author portrait illustrations by Jason Latour. jasonlatour.com

Brian Hurtt got his start in comics pencilling the second arc of Greg Rucka's *Queen & Country*. This was followed by art duties on several projects including *Queen & Country: Declassified*, *Three Strikes*, and Steve Gerber's critically acclaimed series *Hard Time*.

In 2006, Brian teamed with Cullen Bunn to create the Prohibition-era monster-noir sensation *The Damned*. The two found that their unique tastes and storytelling sensibilities were well-suited to one another and were eager to continue that relationship.

The Sixth Gun is their sophomore endeavor together and the next in what looks to be many years of creative collaboration.

Brian lives and works in St. Louis, Missouri.

briburtt.com / @briburtt

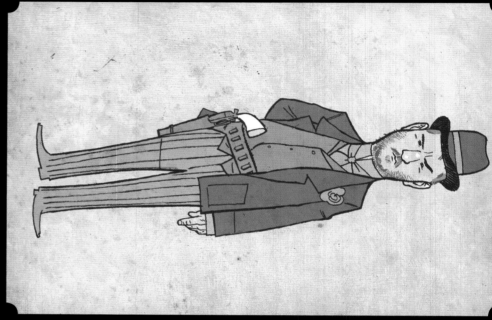

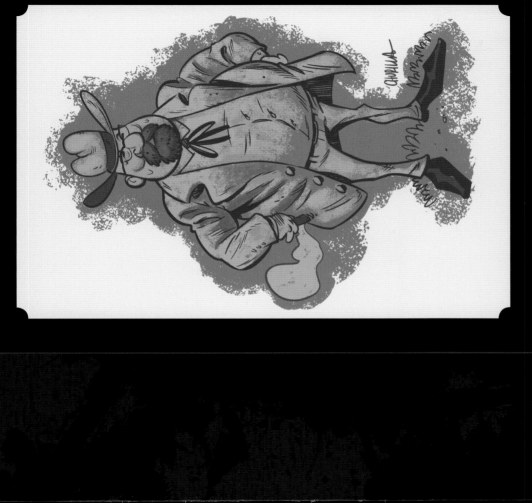

Illustration by Brian Churilla.

Brian Churilla is a comic book writer, artist and colorist who lives in Portland, Oregon with his wife, son and daughter. He is the creator of the critically-acclaimed comic book *The Secret History of D.B. Cooper*. His work has been published by a variety of companies including Marvel Comics, Dark Horse Comics, Boom! Studios, Archaia and Image Comics. Currently, he's preparing a new ongoing series with writer Cullen Bunn for Oni Press.

Bill Crabtree's career as a colorist began in 2003 with the launch of Image Comic's *Incredible* and *Firebreather*. His work on *Invincible* was Harvey Awards nominated, and he went on to color the first 50 issues of what would become a flagship Image Comics title. He continues to color *Firebreather*, which was recently made into a feature film on Cartoon Network, *Godland*, and *Jack Staff*.

Perhaps the highlight of his comics career, his role as colorist on *The Sixth Gun* began with issue 6, and has since been described as "like Christmas morning, but with guns."

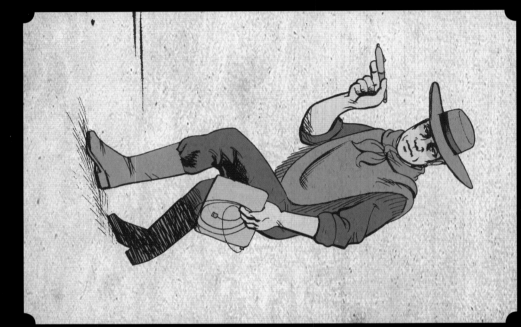

Illustration by Bill Crabtree.